D1526553

SACRIFICES AND OFFERINGS IN ANCIENT ISRAEL

HARVARD SEMITIC MUSEUM

HARVARD SEMITIC MONOGRAPHS

edited by
Frank Moore Cross

Number 41
SACRIFICES AND OFFERINGS IN ANCIENT ISRAEL
Studies in their Social and Political Importance
by
Gary A. Anderson

Gary A. Anderson

SACRIFICES AND OFFERINGS IN ANCIENT ISRAEL
Studies in their Social and Political Importance

Scholars Press
Atlanta, Georgia

SACRIFICES AND OFFERINGS IN ANCIENT ISRAEL

Gary A. Anderson

© 1987
The President and Fellows of Harvard College

Library of Congress Cataloging in Publication Data

Anderson, Gary, A. 1955–
  Sacrifices and offerings in ancient Israel.

  (Harvard Semitic monographs ; no. 41)
  Spine title: Sacrifices & offerings in ancient Israel.
  Includes bibliographical references and index.
  1. Sacrifice—Biblical teaching. 2. Bible. O.T.—
Criticism, intrepretation, etc. I. Title. II. Title:
Sacrifices & offerings in ancient Israel. III. Series.
BS1199.S2A53 1987   241.6'7   87-20498
ISBN 1-55540-169-4

Printed in the United States of America
on acid-free paper

For Lisa Detlefs

PREFACE

The present book is a partial revision of a doctoral dissertation which was submitted to the Department of Near Eastern Languages and Civilizations at Harvard University in 1985. The dissertation was directed by Frank Moore Cross Jr. Additional readers included William Moran and Paul Hanson. To each of these individuals, I am exceedingly grateful. They spent many hours going over the manuscript and helped me improve it in innumerable ways. I should also thank other readers who assisted me with sections of the work. These include John Huehnegard, Douglas Gropp, Gordon Hamilton and Benjamin Ray. Finally I would like to thank Jacob Milgrom and Baruch Levine for their desire to read this manuscript in its final form. It is only with the greatest hesitation that I risked disagreeing with either of these individuals. The influence of their past research on the present work will be evident in almost every chapter.

The present work is by no means a synthetic treatment of any one aspect of Israel's sacrificial system. When the thesis was begun, it was hoped that a comprehensive social history of this system might be written. This proved to be far too ambitious. Instead, this thesis explores several different themes within Israel's cultic life from a variety of periods. The studies were chosen on the grounds that they provided a framework to analyze some important social dimensions of ancient Israelite cultic life.

Gary Alan Anderson

University of Virginia
Charlottesville, Virginia
June, 1987

TABLE OF CONTENTS

ABBREVIATIONS

AB	Anchor Bible
AfO	*Archiv für Orientforschung*
AHw	W. von Soden, *Akkadisches Handwörterbuch*
ANEP	J. B. Pritchard (ed.), *Ancient Near Eastern Pictures* (2nd ed.)
ANET	J. B. Pritchard (ed.), *Ancient Near Eastern Texts* (3rd ed.)
ARM	*Archives Royales de Mari*
AS	*Assyriological Studies*
ASOR	The American Schools of Oriental Research
ATD	Das Alte Testament Deutsch
BASOR	*Bulletin of the American Schools of Oriental Research*
Bib	*Biblica*
BZAW	Beihefte zur *ZAW*
CAD	*The Assyrian Dictionary of the Oriental Institute of the University of Chicago*
CAH	*Cambridge Ancient History* (rev. ed.)
CBQ	*Catholic Biblical Quarterly*
CIS	*Corpus Inscriptionum Semiticarum*
CMHE	F. M. Cross, *Canaanite Myth and Hebrew Epic*
CTA	A. Herdner, *Corpus des tablettes en cunéiformes alphabétiques découvertes à Ras-Shamra de 1929 à 1939.*
EA	J. A. Knudtzon (ed.), *Die El-Amarna Tafeln*
EI	*Eretz Israel*
EJ	*Encyclopedia Judaica*
ESE	M. Lidzbarski, *Ephemeris für semitische Epigraphik*
GKC	E. Kautzsch (ed.), *Gesenius' Hebrew Grammar*
HAT	Handbuch zum Alten Testament
HSM	Harvard Semitic Monographs
HSS	Harvard Semitic Series
HTR	*Harvard Theological Review*

ICC	International Critical Commentary
IDB	G. A. Buttrick (ed.), *Interpreter's Dictionary of the Bible*
IDBS	*Interpreter's Dictionary of the Bible, Supplementary Volume*
IEJ	*Israel Exploration Journal*
JAOS	*Journal of the American Oriental Society*
JBL	*Journal of Biblical Literature*
JCS	*Journal of Cuneiform Studies*
JESHO	*Journal of the Economic and Social History of the Orient*
JNES	*Journal of Near Eastern Studies*
JSS	*Journal of Semitic Studies*
KAI	H. Donner and W. Röllig, *Kanaanäische und aramäische Inschriften*
KTU	*Keilalphabetischen Texte aus Ugarit*
LXX	The Greek translation of the Hebrew Bible (Septuagint)
LXX^b	Codex Vaticanus
LXX^l	The Lucianic Recension of the Septuagint
MA	Middle Assyrian Period
MB	Middle Babylonian Period
MT	Massoretic Text
MVAG	*Mitteilungen der vorderasiatisch-ägyptischen Gesellschaft*
NA	Neo-Assyrian Period
NB	Neo-Babylonian Period
OA	*Oriens antiquus*
OB	Old Babylonian Period
OLZ	*Orientalistische Literaturzeitung*
Or	*Orientalia*
OTL	Old Testament Library
PRU	*Le Palais royal d'Ugarit*
RA	*Revue d'assyriologie*
RAI	Rencontre d'assyriologique international
RS	*Ras-Shamra*
SB	*Standard Babylonian*
SVT	Supplement to Vetus Testamentum
UF	*Ugarit-Forschungen*

UT	C. H. Gordon, *Ugaritic Textbook*
VT	*Vetus Testamentum*
WZKM	*Wiener Zeitschrift für Kunde des Morgenlandes*
YGC	W. F. Albright, *Yahweh and the Gods of Canaan*
YOS	*Yale Oriental Series*
ZAW	*Zeitschrift für die alttestamentliche Wissenschaft*

CHAPTER ONE

Introduction

A. The Distinctive Nature of the Israelite Cult

The most important social and political institution in tribal Israel was the cult of the league's patron deity.[1] The cultic gatherings of the Israelites were the primary fashioners of social and religious unity. The league shrine functioned as the meeting place for the muster of the militia and it was to this shrine that the victorious warriors returned with the spoils of battle.[2] Unlike the city-state which had enforceable, centralized programs of military conscription and taxation, the tribal league's constitution was much more tenuous. The league had to depend on tribal participation in the cult of the league shrines for both its muster and its collection of offerings.[3] Indeed, it is difficult to speak of an entity "Israel" in the tribal period outside of the gathered body of clan members around the shrines of their patron, YHWH.[4]

It is most likely for this reason that the religion of a tribal confederation is typologically distinct from that of the city-state. As Cross has noted: "In Phoenician and Aramean city states there are city gods, triads of city gods, and patron gods of the king who often differ from the chief city gods, but in both documentary evidence and in the onomastica, we find multiple state deities

---

[1]This study is concerned exclusively with the pan-tribal YHWHistic cult. Although Israel's religion will be spoken of only in terms of this public manifestation the writer acknowledges the varied types of religious expression which were to be found in the private cults of individual families or extended clan groups. The public cult of YHWH was not the only form of religious expression in ancient Israel, but it is one of the few to which modern scholarship has access.

[2]On the role of the cult in early Israelite wars see Von Rad, *Der heilege Krieg im alten Israel* (Zürich: Zwingli Verlag, 1951). One should also note the reaction of M. Weippert, "Heiliger Krieg' in Israel und Assyrien: Kritische Anmerkungen zu Gerhard von Rads Konzept des 'Heiligen Krieges im alten Israel," *ZAW* 84 (1972), pp. 460-93.

[3]Note the strong injunctions of the Covenant Code (Ex 23:14-17): all the men of Israel were required to participate in the pilgrim festivals and not to come empty-handed! Both of these injunctions were lost in the later priestly recensions of this list (Lev 23 and Num 28-29).

[4]This position was classically stated by M. Noth in his *Das System der zwölf Stämme Israels* (Stuttgart: Kohlhammer, 1930). See also G. Von Rad, *Theology of the Old Testament*, vol. 1, (New York: Harper and Row, 1962), pp. 17ff for a concurring view. Noth's perspective is, of course, firmly grounded in his theory of an early Israelite amphictyony. This theory has been subject to a number of criticisms in recent years. Especially problematic is his thesis that there was a central shrine for all of Israel. Yet Gottwald, one of Noth's strongest critics, agrees with Noth's basic premise—the cult is the center of early Israelite life (*The Tribes of Yahweh* (Maryknoll: Orbis, 1979), pp. 63-125 and 252-59).

and personal deities."5 It is different in the tribe. There the tribal members bind themselves to one particular god, the patron of that tribe.

In the annals of Assurbanipal, an Arab tribal confederation is called *i'lu ša dAtarsamain*, "the league of Atarsamain." The significant item is the word *i'lu*, "league." The word *i'lu* is derived from *e'ēlu*, "to bind an agreement." Cross associates it with Old South Arabic *'hl*, Lihyanite *'l*, "people" or "cult association."6 The linguistic development of this root shows the close connection between covenant, cult association, and ethnic identity. The formula *i'lu ša DN* points to the importance of the tribal patron deity in describing the tribal constituency. As Cross observes, "Israel may be called the *'am YHWH*, Moab the *'am kěmōš* (Num 21:29), and the Arab league, *'hl 'aθtar*."7 This phenomenon carries over into the onomastica as well. In the onomastica of Israel, Ammon, Moab, and Edom, the dominate divine element is the name or epithet of the patron deity. In Israel this is YHWH or El, in Ammon, Moab, and Edom the deities are El (or the epithet Milcom), Chemosh (an epithet of *'Aθtar*), and Qos (perhaps an epithet of Hadad) respectively.

The concept of a tribal clan bound to a single patron deity presumes some type of covenant.8 For tribal groups, the language of kinship was the favored means of expressing the mutually assumed covenantal obligations. Ideally, each clan stood on equal footing with the others; the political

5F. Cross, "The Epic Traditions of Early Israel," p. 36, in R. Friedman ed.,*The Poet and the Historian* (HSS 26, Chico: Scholars Press, 1983).

6The root is also found in Hebrew *'ōhel*, "tent" and Akkadian *ālu*, "city." We should note that von Soden, *AHw* p. 189, does not associate *e'ēlu* with Hebrew *'ōhel* or Akkadian *ālu*.

7F. Cross, "The Epic Traditions," p. 36.

8This idea is somewhat controversial, and, it should be noted, is not crucial to our thesis. There are still a number of scholars who feel that the covenantal theology of Israel is a late development. See for example, L. Perlitt, *Bundestheologie im alten Testament*, (WMANT 36, Neukirchen-Vluyn: Neukirchener Verlag, 1969). Their arguments have some basis. The Hittite formulary does not neatly fit any of the early pre-deuteronomistic narratives. Joshua 24 is probably the first biblical text to clearly outline Israelite belief on a covenantal model. Though this text is pre-deuteronomic, it cannot be conclusively put in the early period. On the other hand though, one must reckon with the fact that the Sinai narratives are the most heavily redacted narratives in the Bible. A neat survival of an original covenant formulary in this corpus is impossible to expect. Even with these reservations, though, one must come up with some type of legal or religious formula which enabled a diverse group of independent tribal clans to participate regularly in the militia and pilgrim feasts of a tribal confederacy and share a distinctive onomastic pattern. *These were not natural developments!* To disallow the existence of a covenantal agreement in the early period would pose more problems than it would solve. For a similar position see J. Barr, "Some Semantic Notes on the Covenant," in *Beiträge zur Alttestamentlichen Theologie: Festschrift für Walther Zimmerli*, ed. H. Donner et al. (Göttingen: Vandenhoeck und Ruprecht, 1977), p. 37: "Yet with all the will in the world it is a little hard to believe that the covenant of Yahweh with Israel became significant only so late."

constitution, like the genealogy, was segmented.[9] The tenuous link between these loosely articulated clans was the cult of the patron deity. It is no surprise that the very first commandment found in the Sinai material (Ex. 20:3) is: "You shall have no other gods before me (*lōʾ yihyeh lĕkā ʾĕlōhîm ʾăḥērîm ʿal-pānāy*)." To abstain from participation in the league cult was to absolve the covenantal bonds of the tribal group. In the later language of the Deuteronomist this commandment was couched in even more explicit covenantal idiom. The rubric "to go after other gods" (*laleket ʾĕlōhîm ʾăḥērîm*), found everywhere in Deuteronomy, was borrowed directly from covenantal charters.[10]

But what of the actual cult of YHWH? There can be little doubt that it was very different from that of Canaan. The Deuteronomistic redaction of Israel's early history clearly sets Israelite religion apart from its Canaanite environment. But the distinction does not begin at this late period. Already, in earliest Israel, one of YHWH's cultic epithets shows the self conscious distinction Israel herself made. YHWH is called *ʾēl qannāʾ*, "a jealous God." But of what did this jealousy consist? Was Israel's actual cultic service distinct?

The most basic answer to this question—which presumes no value judgment concerning the ethical or religious value of the two cultic systems—is that the Israelite cult consisted of those sacrificial gifts and offerings which were donated to YHWH (*lĕ-YHWH*). *The distinctiveness of the Israelite cult is nothing other than the limitation of cultic activity to one particular patron deity.* This view makes no claim to the superiority of the Israelite cult. We could just as easily have said the distinctiveness of the Moabite cult is the limitation of public cult to its patron god, Chemosh. This provisional statement will guide the beginning of this study.

This definition might appear so general as to be without value. But such a statement is of primary importance for the beginning of any discussion of the Israelite cult. For one, this statement presupposes that the Israelite rites were not significantly different from Canaanite rites. As de Vaux has observed, the Bible itself makes this observation.[11] In the sacrificial rites mentioned in Elijah's confrontation with the prophets of Baal, the holocaust offering is

---

[9]On the political importance of segmented genealogies see R. Wilson, *Genealogy and History in the Biblical World* (New Haven: Yale University Press, 1977).

[10]See W. Moran, "The Ancient Near Eastern Background of the Love of God in Deuteronomy," *CBQ*, 25 (1963), p. 82, n. 35.

[11]R. de Vaux, *Studies in Old Testament Sacrifice* (Cardiff: University of Wales Press, 1964), p. 44. Also see I. Engnell, *A Rigid Scrutiny* (Nashville: Vanderbilt University Press, 1969), pp. 35-39.

prepared in exactly the same way between the two parties.[12] The story presumes that the outward form of the rite itself was undifferentiated. Also the story of Naaman's allegiance to YHWH presumes that it is not how the rite is executed, but to whom the sacrifice is offered which is significant. [13] Finally we would mention the evidence of the Punic cultic tariff texts whose sacrificial terminology parallels so closely that found in the Bible.[14] This terminological similarity is an indication of the basic continuity of cultic rites between Israel and Canaan. The next chapter will investigate more closely these similarities as well as some important differences.

B.   Canaanite Magic and Israelite Ethic?

Many scholars have not been satisfied with this sparse and unnuanced definition. More analytical and value-oriented differentiations have been proposed. By far the most common means of distinguishing the two cult spheres has been that of contrasting the Israelite ethical and covenantal religion with the magical rites of the Canaanite fertility cult. This view distinguishes the historical quality of YHWH's self-revelation from the pagan interests in natural religion and agrarian rites.[15] The agricultural festivals of Israel are suspect in this view. Their agrarian appearance is evidence of their pagan (Canaanite) background. These pagan agrarian rites become legitimate only when they are subordinated to the covenantal religion of Israel.[16] When the Israelite presents his produce to

---

[12]I Kg 18:23-24. One should note that the priestly behavior of the Canaanites is portrayed differently by the biblical writer though the actual preparation of the animal is the same.

[13]II Kg 5:17.

[14]This evidence was first used by R. Dussaud (Les origines cananéenes du sacrifice israélite (Paris: Leroux, 1921)) to argue against Wellhausen's assertion that Israelite sacrificial practice as described in the P code was exilic or later. When the Ugaritic material was first published, many of these same terms were found and, so given second millennium attestations. In light of this evidence, Dussaud revised his argument (2nd edition, 1941) and said Israel's earliest sacrifices paralleled that of Canaan. Some scholars (R.J. Thompson, Penitence and Sacrifice in Early Israel outside the Levitical Law (Leiden: Brill, 1963), pp. 30-33 and J. Gray, The Legacy of Canaan (SVT 5, Leiden: Brill, 1965), pp. 182-83, 195-204) deny the validity of such a claim on the basis of Israel's nomadic origins. The specious quality of such a counter-claim will be discussed below.

[15]The classic statement was made by J. Wellhausen in his Prolegomena to the History of Ancient Israel (Gloucester: Peter Smith, 1973), pp. 92-112.

[16]H.J. Kraus' remarks are typical here (Worship in Israel (Richmond: John Knox Press, 1965), p. 122): "The great achievement of the Old Testament is the inclusion of the whole sacrificial system within the saving events and the fact of the berit."

the priest in a religious festival, the magical fertility elements are expunged in the act of reciting the Credo.[17] History has usurped Nature.[18]

Mary Douglas has recently addressed the contrast biblical scholars draw between magical activity and ethical religion in her work *Purity and Danger*.[19] We mention her work because she perceives very clearly the intellectual foundations of such a view, which stem from anthropological methods that have long been dismissed. Biblical scholars borrowed these ideas when they were *au courant*, but many have not followed their development in the discipline from which they were taken.[20] The importance of this theory stems more from the vast quantity of publications which assume its veracity than from the sophistication of its methodological underpinnings. It was Frazer who advanced most eloquently the theory that primitive religion was based on magic.[21] Although Frazer claimed to be an admirer of Robertson Smith, their views on primitive religion could not have differed more. For Smith, primitive religion began with ritual activity out of which ethical values were formed.[22] Mythology or belief structures were secondary to ritual. Magic was a peripheral concern for Smith. He saw it as an aberration in the evolution of humanity, something which occurred only in times of social duress. Frazer took the opposite view. He began with the

---

[17]G. von Rad, in his *Old Testament Theology* vol. 1 (New York: Harper and Row, 1962), speaks of the Canaanite agrarian rites (pp. 19-35) and the role of the divine word and saving event (p. 262). The summary of the divine activity (Credo) transformed the material observances of the cult to the true worship of YHWH.

[18]This interpretive framework is often described as Hegelian because it assumes a logical progression from the realm of nature to history. This philosophical system was assumed by Wellhausen (and followed by Kraus, Von Rad and others) in the writing of his classic *Prolegomena to the History of Ancient Israel*. The dependence of Wellhausen on Hegelian ideas has long been assumed by many biblical scholars, though there are dissenting voices. See H.J. Kraus, *Worship in Israel* p. 6 and F.M. Cross, *CMHE* p. 82 for an analysis of Wellhausen's Hegelian presuppositions.

[19](New York: Praeger, 1966), pp. 7-28, 58-72.

[20]This is not an uncommon phenomenon in biblical studies. One could compare the development of Form Criticism. These methods were borrowed from Folklore and Classical studies of the late nineteenth century. They presumed, among other things, that the shorter the poetic unit the more archaic. Since then, modern studies of oral poetry have shown how unreliable a guide this is. Yet, many continue to operate under old assumptions. One could say the same about the recent use of anthropological methods in biblical studies. All scholars assume some sort of social model when writing about clans, tribes and city-states. Those who use these ancillary disciplines are said to be imposing models on the texts, but previous scholarship did the same thing. The only reason they are not perceived as such an imposition now is because of the vast amount of published material which presumes them.

[21]J.G. Frazer, *The Golden Bough: A Study in Magic and Religion* vols. 1-13 (London: Macmillan, 1980). This edition is a reprint. It was originally published in London in 1890 with the subtitle, "A Study in Comparative Religion." The subtitle was changed in the 3rd edition. The change illustrates the development of Frazer's thought and the manner in which he has been appropriated by scholarship.

[22]W. R. Smith, *Lectures on the Religion of the Semites* (Jerusalem: KTAV, 1969). The original work was published in London in 1889, and was the subject of numerous editions and translations during the course of Smith's life.

myth of the dying and rising god. From this myth, primitive society developed rituals as a magical aid in furthering the reproductive process.

Douglas characterizes Frazer as an evolutionist in the Hegelian sense. This is true, in part.[23] Like Hegel, Frazer believed that the ethical religion found in the biblical prophets—the highest form of religious thinking—was preceeded by a magical understanding of the world.[24] But Frazer's particular characterization of this intellectual evolution was not altogether comparable to Hegel. For Frazer the dominant intellectual issue was how humankind perceived causality in the natural world. Specifically, how did people account for change in the natural environment, and how could the natural environment be manipulated by human agents? The first attempts to manipulate the natural environment were magical. Frazer believed magical activity had two forms, homeopathic or imitative magic and contagious magic.[25] Through these activities primitive people thought they could alter certain physical properties of the natural world. When primitive peoples discovered that magical activity did not always yield the predictable results a new theory of causality had to arise. Thus, the beginnings of religion. Now the somewhat fickle and often arbitrary whims and desires of the gods could account for irregularity in the natural world. With the development of religious thinking, the control of nature was put in the hands of the gods instead of the artifice of the magician. Science is the apogee of this evolutionary sequence. With scientific thinking, humankind regained its desire to explain and control the natural environment through immutable laws. The arbitrary whims and desires of the gods no longer played a role in explaining causal relations in the natural world. Instead, empirical principles were developed which could explain and control the natural environment. As Frazer observes, there is greater similarity between science and magic than between religion and science. For both science and magic assert "that the succession of events is assumed to be perfectly regular and certain, being determined by immutable laws, the operation of which can be foreseen and calculated precisely; the elements of caprice, of chance and of accident are banished from the course of nature."[26] Religion, then, was not highly

---

[23]See Frazer's appendix on Hegel in the first volume of the third edition of *The Golden Bough*. He was not conscious of the Hegelian roots of his theory until they were pointed out to him after the publication of his work.

[24]Frazer, *The Golden Bough*, vol 1, pp. 50-51.

[25]Frazer, *The Golden Bough*, vol 1, pp. 11-47.

[26]Frazer, *The Golden Bough*, vol 1, p. 49.

esteemed in Frazer's system except when it expounded the values that he felt were found in the prophetic materials.

It is difficult, if not impossible, to find any modern anthropologist who respects Frazer's theoretical model.[27] He is extolled as an excellent composer of English prose and for the sheer massiveness of his folklore collection, but his theoretical and synthetic observations are dismissed if not scorned. He has been called an armchair anthropologist, one who spoke of primitive culture without ever leaving the world of the university. Douglas describes his contribution as a baneful one.[28]   Burkert has even criticized his insights from a classicist's perspective.[29] He claims that Frazer's allegorizing of all myth into stories about natural process had precedents already in late antiquity!

Yet, as Burkert cynically observed, even when Frazer's position is destroyed it will rise again.   In several areas of scholarly study, Frazer's presuppositions have had a lasting impact. In almost every biblical handbook one can read about the magical fertility rites of the Canaanites as opposed to the ethical values of Israel's cult.[30] In spite of the fact that we have little knowledge of the Canaanite cult, it has become an assumed scholarly position that it was inherently magical. The imposition of this rubric has affected not only biblical studies, but also studies of other ancient civilizations. Douglas noted that the well-respected classicist M. Finley used an ethical test to distinguish earlier elements of belief from later in his work *The World of Odysseus*.[31] Cassirer uses magical, non-ethical superstition as his criterion for historical primitiveness in his study of Zoroastrianism.[32]

Let us turn to a Ugaritic text many scholars have used as evidence of Canaan's fertility religion. The text has been read: "cook a kid in milk, a lamb in

---

[27]M. Douglas, *Purity and Danger* (New York: Praeger, 1966), pp. 13-28;   E. Evans-Pritchard, *A History of Anthropological Thought* (New York: Basic Books, 1981), pp. 132-152;   M. Harris, *The Rise of Anthropological Theory* (New York: Harper and Row, 1968), pp. 204-08;   E. Leach, "On the Founding Fathers," *Current Anthropology* 7 (1966), pp. 560-67;   E.J. Sharpe, *Comparative Religion* (New York: Scribners, 1975), pp. 87-94, and J.Z. Smith, "When the Bough Breaks," *History of Religions* 12 (1973), pp. 342-71.

[28]Douglas, *Purity and Danger*, p. 28.

[29]W. Burkert, *The Structure and History of Greek Mythology and Ritual* (Berkeley: University of California Press, 1979), pp. 35-36 and 99-122.

[30]On the priority of a primitive stage of magical thinking in Near Eastern lore see von Rad, *Theology of the Old Testament*, vol I, pp. 22-35. His summary statement is a classic expression of the ideas of late 19th century anthropology and folklore.

[31](New York: Penguin, 1979), pp. 136-41.

[32]E. Cassirer, *An Essay on Man* (Oxford: Oxford University Press, 1944), p. 100.

curd."[33] This harmless cultic directive becomes a symbol of fertility religion when
it is contrasted with the biblical injunction not to cook a kid in its mother's milk (Ex
23:19). No reason is given in the Bible for such a prohibition, but some biblical
scholars—under the influence of a Frazerian model—have been ready to supply
one. The Canaanite rite has been called a "milk-charm...performed...in order to
promote a flow of milk from the goats and cattle which was already failing in the
summer drought."[34] The *only source* for such an idea is the assumption that
Canaanite ritual is by definition magic, and Israelite resistance to it is derivable
from her ethical sensitivities.

This is not to deny the existence of magical elements in Canaanite
religion.   Rather, the concern is to point out how Frazer's typology of
development, from magic to religion, has been imposed on the ancient world. But
magic, in the eyes of modern social scientists, has become a very difficult term
not only to analyze but to define.[35]

Many discussions of magic in the anthropological literature trace their
scholarly lineage to Evans-Pritchard's work on Azande witchcraft and Nuer
religion.[36] Evans-Pritchard used the context of his ethnographic work among
these peoples as a means of disposing with some of Lévy-Bruhl's concepts about
primitive thought. Lévy-Bruhl, not unlike Frazer, believed that primitive people
inhabited a prelogical and mystical mental world unlike that of modern people.
Evans-Pritchard argued against this assessment. By means of a careful
ethnographic analysis he showed that primitive people lived in the same "world"
that modern people do for the most part. Like modern people most of their lives
were concerned with the "practical economic pursuits: gardening, hunting,
fishing, care of cattle, and the manufacture of weapons, utensils and ornaments,
and in their social contacts: the life of household, family and kin, relations with
friends and neighbours, with superiors and inferiors, dances and feasts, legal

---

[33]*CTA* 23.14. The irony of this reading is that it is erroneous. The word for kid,*gd*, is
better translated "coriander." In Ugaritic we would expect the spelling*gdy* for "kid." The corrected
translation renders unusable the supposed biblical parallel.

[34]J. Gray, *The Legacy of Canaan*, p. 97. Maimonides (*Moreh Nebukhim* III, 48) first
suggested that the rite must have been Canaanite. T. Gaster (*Thespis* (New York: Schuman, 1950),
p. 244) also concludes that the rite concerned fertility.

[35]Three volumes have appeared in the last fifteen years which address the issue of
the rationality of magical behavior. These are: B. Wilson ed. *Rationality* (Oxford: Basil Blackwell,
1970); R. Horton and Ruth Finnegan eds., *Modes of Thought* (London: Faber and Faber, 1973), and
M. Hollis and S. Lukes eds.,*Rationality and Relativism* (Oxford: Basil Blackwell, 1982).

[36]*Witchcraft, Oracles and Magic among the Azande* (Oxford: Clarendon Press, 1937)
and *Nuer Religion* (Oxford: Clarendon Press, 1956).

disputes, feuds and warfare."[37]   Mystical thinking was restricted to certain situations in social life.   Evans-Pritchard's comments are illuminating:

> I have often noticed Azande lean their spears up against, or hang baskets on, the shrines they build for the spirits of their ancestors in the centre of their homesteads, and as far as it is possible to judge from their behaviour they have no other interest in the shrine than as a convenient post or peg. At religious ceremonies their attitude is very different. Among the Ingassana of the Tabi Hills God is the sun and on occasions they pray to it but, as far as I could judge, in ordinary situations they looked upon the sun very much as I did as a convenient means of telling the time, as the cause of intense heat at midday, and so on. If one were not present at some religious ceremony on a special occasion, one would remain ignorant that the sun is God. Mystical thought is a function of particular situations.[38]

Evans-Pritchard suggests several reasons for why anthropologists believed primitive peoples think mystically. One would be the idiosyncratic fashion by which ethnographic records take shape.   European ethnographers were more likely to record the extraordinary experiences than the mundane.[39] It is also a fact that anthropologists were likely to devote most of their attention to those particular aspects of social life where mystical thinking is likely to appear, that is, in myth and ritual.   Once these particular and highly selective segments of primitive life become the staples of the ethnographic record the tendency arises to compare these selective segments with our everyday vocabulary.[40] If the everyday events of primitive life are properly noted, their thought appears no different from ours. Finally one must be careful to understand "mystical" statements of primitive peoples in the context of their symbolic system. For example, a favorite 19th century example of primitive irrationality was the statement by the Bororo of Central Brazil, "We are red macaws." This apparently mystical and irrational statement was examined by Crocker. On a careful reinvestigation he found out that "(1) only men say "We are red macaws"; (2) red macaws are owned as pets by Bororo women; (3) because of matrilineal descent and uxorilocal residence, men are in important ways dependent on women; (4) both men and macaws are thought to reach beyond the women's sphere through

[37]E. Evans-Pritchard, "Lévy-Bruhl's theory of primitive mentality," *Bulletin of the Faculty of the Arts* (Egyptian University, Cairo) II, 1 (1934), p. 9. A more recent opinion of Evans-Pritchard on Lévy-Bruhl can be found in his *Theories of Primitive Religion* (Oxford: Oxford University Press, 1965), pp. 78-99.

[38]"Lévy-Bruhl's Theory," p. 27.

[39]"Lévy-Bruhl's Theory," p. 8.

[40]On this misplaced comparison see M. Bloch, "The Past and the Present in the Present," *Man*, 12 (1977), pp. 278-92.

their contacts with spirits."[41]   Thus the statement, "We are red macaws," is hardly irrational or mystical, rather it is a symbol or metaphor of the masculine condition in Bororo culture. As Sperber notes, probably many such puzzling "irrational" statements in the ethnographic literature could be explained by such careful research.

But what of those special situations in the ritual life of a community which appear magical? How is the modern ethnographer to interpret these beliefs and rituals which seem, *prima facie*, irrational? Two schools of thought have arisen. On the one hand scholars like Horton argue that magical acts which attempt to bring rain, ward off disease and so forth are best understood as a primitive type of science.[42] They reflect attempts by pre-scientific peoples to construct a meaningful theory about causality in the world. Other anthropologists dislike this comparison of Horton's because it necessarily makes primitive thought inferior to modern thinking by compelling one to compare primitive religious thinking with modern scientific theory.[43] Some argue that this is Frazer's error rising again. As an alternative to Horton, these anthropologists argue that primitive magical rites must be understood on a symbolic level. To see these rites simply as instrumental activity arising from misplaced ideas about natural causality is to misread them. The 'symbolist school' argues the instrumental aspect of primitive ritual is of negligible importance in understanding the rite. What is of real importance is the symbolism involved in the rite. Those who hold this symbolic perspective view primitive myths and rituals as a form of artistic or theological expression rather than a form of scientific speculation. Thus a sensitive aesthetic judgment is required for interpretation.

A good example of this symbolic mode of interpretation can be found in Lienhardt's analysis of Dinka rain rituals.[44] As Lienhardt observes, the Dinka know when the rainy season is approaching and this point is important for the correct appreciation of their ceremony. These rain rituals are not simply an

[41]D. Sperber, "Apparently Irrational Beliefs," in *Rationality and Relativism*, pp. 152-53. For this analysis, Sperber is recounting the article by J.C. Crocker, "My Brother the Parrot," in J.D. Sapir and J.C. Crocker (eds.), *The Social Use of Metaphor: Essays on the Anthropology of Rhetoric* (Philadelphia: University of Pennsylvania, 1977) pp. 164-92.

[42]R. Horton, "African Traditional Thought and Western Science," *Africa* 37 (1967), pp. 50-71 and 155-87.

[43]For example see J. Beattie, *Other Cultures* (London: Cohen and West, 1964), pp. 202-40 and "On Understanding Ritual," in B. Wilson ed., *Rationality*, pp. 240-68; M. Douglas, *Purity and Danger*; E. Leach, *Political Systems of Highland Burma* (London: London School of Economics and Political Science, 1954); G. Lienhardt, *Divinity and Experience* (Oxford: Clarendon Press, 1961).

[44]For Lienhardt's views on symbolic action see his work, *Divinity and Experience*, pp. 252-297.

attempt to control the environment.   Rather, in these rituals, "their human symbolic action moves with the rhythm of the natural world around them, recreating that rhythm in moral terms and not merely attempting to *coerce* it to conformity with human desires."[45]   The religious impulse in the rite *does not* stem from an attempt to assist this natural order.   Rather, the moral life of the community itself is ordered around the fixed cycle of the seasonal rains.[46]

We are left at an apparent impasse.   How are we to interpret a ritual whose expressed purpose is to secure rain for a people?   Is the rite to be understood as an instrumental act practiced only for the expectation of material consequences, or is the rite primarily a symbolic activity concerned with moral and aesthetic values?   This impasse is not insoluble.   In commenting on this very problem several anthropologists have noted that the desire to distinguish between instrumental and symbolic meanings may be a peculiarity of the modern scholar. As Taylor observes: "It is a feature of our civilization that we have developed a practice of scientific research and its technological application from which the symbolic and expressive dimensions have been to a great extent purged."[47]   In pre-modern cultures the distinction between controlling the world and understanding it symbolically is not made.[48]   Thus when a primitive person both performs a rain ritual and waters his crop, chases birds away and provides natural fertilizers, he views this as all one technique.   Modern persons, on the other hand, would separate this activity into two types.   As Lukes observes, the Baseri nomads of South Persia, when they migrate each spring, are not only adapting to their environment but also participating in a social rite. [49]   Among the Kpelle:

> Rice growing is not an analyzed, isolated technical activity in the Kpelle way of life.   What Western cultures would compartmentalize into technical science, the Kpelle culture weaves into the whole fabric of existence.   The relevant question is not 'How do you grow rice?' but 'How do you live?'[50]

---

[45]G. Lienhardt, *Divinity and Experience,* p. 280.

[46]Horton's review of Lienhardt's work is quite critical (in *Africa* 32 (1962), p. 78).   He believes Lienhardt does not "call a spade a spade."   He observes, "though it seems clear from the material offered that the Dinka think certain actions symbolizing desired ends really do help in themselves to achieve those ends, the author seems at times to want to rationalize this magical element away."

[47]C. Taylor, "Rationality" in *Rationality and Relativism,* p. 94.

[48]See I. C. Jarvie and J. Agassi, "The Problem of the Rationality of Magic," in *Rationality,* pp. 172–93.

[49]S. Lukes, "Relativism in its Place," in *Rationality and Relativism,* p. 282.

[50]J. Gay and M. Cole, *The New Mathematics and an Old Culture* (New York: Holt, Reinhart and Winston, 1967) p. 21.   Our citation is from Lukes, "Relativism in its Place," p. 282.

A sophisticated understanding of primitive ritual is not easy to arrive at. We must put aside our modern sensibilities which seek to distinguish empirical from symbolic understandings of the environment. But we also must have a certain theological sensitivity for the role of symbolic activity within a particular world-view or belief system. As Evans-Pritchard observed, many ethnographers would be greatly aided by acquainting themselves with the subtleties of classical theological dogma and ritual so that the distinctions between sacrament and magic, belief and superstition can be appreciated.[51] Many of the same sorts of subtle dialectics which exist in Western theological traditions can be found elsewhere.

The student of ancient civilizations can learn a number of things from this discussion. Firstly, one should recall Evans-Pritchard's comment about the selectivity of many ethnographic reports. A comparable phenomenon exists in the studies of ancient Near Eastern documents. The propensity of modern scholars to describe the thought of ancient civilization through its mythological and ritual texts is a highly selective procedure. Yet, it is to these very texts that scholars turn in hope of discerning the ancient's views on the relationship between fertility and agriculture. These mythological texts obviously emphasize supernatural and sometimes "irrational" concerns. Yet mythic texts comprise only a small percentage of the information which is available for the study of ancient civilizations. The mythic view is hardly the perspective of everyday affairs. The greatest percentage of texts available in the ancient Near East are concerned with the practical side of agricultural life, when to plant, what to plant, who is to receive the harvest and so forth. These texts show us that ancient Near Eastern peoples had a very rational understanding, in the main, of agricultural affairs. Secondly one should be cognizant of the context of a ritual or symbolic statement. What often appears *prima facie* irrational often fits quite well into a larger symbolic frame. Finally one must be cognizant of the fact that modern culture devalues religious ritual and that this devaluation has affected the way scholars approach the study of ritual. As Douglas observes, this attitude is so pervasive that it is even common in Catholic circles.[52] Again we are reminded of Evans-

---

[51] *Theories of Primitive Religion*, pp. 16-17. Evans-Pritchard observes that many anthropologists in the past viewed religion from a very unsympathetic vantage point and often imported their prejudices into their ethnographies and analyses.

[52] *Natural Symbols* (New York: Pantheon Books, 1970), pp. 1-53. The result is that she, as an anthropologist, produces a work which is more sensitive toward religious ritual than many modern clerics and scholars of religion.

Pritchard's comments in regard to the study of primitive religion. One's appreciation and insight into the way myth and ritual operate in contemporary religions often parallels one's appreciation of their operation in primitive or archaic religions.

With these provisions in mind let us turn to another text which is often quoted as representative of magical Canaanite fertility rites. It is found in the Baal cycle, after Mot has swallowed the Divine Hero, Baal. As we join the text, Anat is effecting her revenge on Mot:

taʾḫud bina ʾili-mi môta	She seized El's son Mot
bi-ḫarbi tabaqqiʿunannu	with a sword she split him
bi-haθri tadriyunannu	with a sieve she winnowed him
bi-ʾišti tašrupunannu	with fire she burnt him
bi-riḫêma tiṭhanannu	with two millstones she ground him
bi-šadī tidraʿunannu	in the field she scattered him
(CTA 6.2.30-35)	

Does this text require us to believe that Canaanite fertility rites were primarily an instrumental activity oriented toward altering the physical environment? It is true that this text is related to the agricultural procedures of Canaan.[53] The narrative context is important too; the narrative is about to foretell the rising of Baal again and the consequent return of rain to the land. But can we extrapolate from this that the Canaanite peasant thought that he or she was somehow assisting this process through the sowing of grain? Is this action to be understood only in an instrumental fashion? What about the practical steps which were also taken to insure a productive crop yield; and what about the symbolic dimensions of such a rite? The legacy of Frazer would impel us to see this rite as irrational primitive magic which was one step below a higher form of intellectual life, ethical religion. Some modern biblical scholars have found this an attractive position because it allows them to set Israel's belief structure over and against that of her immediate environment for an apologetic goal. But the intellectual

---

[53]See Josephus (Antiquities, III, 250) regarding the preparation of grain for the new year and J. Gray, Legacy of Canaan, pp. 68-69 (esp. p. 68 note 3) for a good discussion of this. S. Loewenstamm ("The Ugaritic Fertility Myth—the Result of a Mistranslation," IEJ 12 (1962), pp. 87-88), U. Cassuto ("Baal and Mot in the Ugaritic Texts," IEJ 12 (1962), p. 79) and others have said it is not a fertility rite.

foundations of such an apologetic—though appropriate several generations back—are no longer adequate.[54]

This apologetic tendency on the part of modern biblical scholars has made several apects of biblical religion difficult to appreciate. One prominent example is the restoration programs of Haggai and Zechariah. If one assumes that the distinctive aspect of Israelite cultic life is its intent to eschew all vestiges of Canaanite fertility practice, then what does one do with a theological program which quite consciously and explicitly identifies Temple building with renewed vigor of the land? This restoration program has been somewhat of an embarrassment for biblical scholars who use Canaanite materials for apologetic reasons. In the last chapter of this study it will be argued that a sophisticated understanding of the *symbolic and instrumental* functions of fertility rituals in Canaanite religion will allow for a more sensitive appreciation of the restoration programs of Haggai and Zechariah.

C. Sacrifice as Food for the Gods?

Another approach to the problem of differentiating Israelite from Canaanite cultic structure is represented by the work of R. de Vaux.[55] As a Catholic, he is sensitive to a Protestant approach of opposing magic and ethics. [56] In contrast to a Protestant preoccupation with magical rites, de Vaux emphasizes

---

[54]See J. Roberts, "Myth *versus* History: Relaying the Comparative Foundations," *CBQ,* 38 (1976), pp. 1-13. We should note that the Scandanavian school does not do this. The remarks of Engnell (*A Rigid Scrutiny,* pp. 39-40) are quite contrary to the standard German view: "The argument that Israel took over the Canaanite cult and all its external furnishings, but not the ideas associated with this cult, cannot be successfully defended. This argument implies an abstraction which cannot be assumed in an era when cult and religion were to a great extent synonymous ideas. In opposition to this, it should be pointed out that the usual picture of Canaanite cultic religion needs to be radically revised. We are not to think of a sensuous and amoral cult which is supplanted by the elevated and pure faith of the Mosaic period. Behind its partly highly orgiastic cult, as is often the case in strongly emotional forms of religion, the Canaanite religion had room for profound and valuable ideas." Unfortunately, Engnell lapses into the Hegelian framework later in the same essay, "the general tendency is toward emancipation from the substratum of nature religion. . . .Out of this gradually changing cultic form, a new cult emerges which will prove revolutionary for all future time, even for the Christian age." He even adheres to the traditional Christian view of post-exilic biblical faith when he says that Ezra-Nehemiah "represent the beginning of Pharisaism. . . Here, legalism is triumphant" (p. 47).
[55]De Vaux, *Studies in Old Testament Sacrifice.*
[56]He is also cognizant of an implicitly anti-Catholic bias present in this framework. Another example of this is found in the work of L. Köhler (*Old Testament Theology* (London: Cutterworth Press, 1957)). It is his position that the sacrificial rites reflected the ethnic quality of Old Testament religion and that the cult was an "act of self-help, or even 'self-redemption' by men and women" (p. 181). Eichrodt (*Theology of the Old Testament*, vol 1(London: SCM Press, 1961), p. 168), represents a less extreme position when he says that the danger of paganism in Biblical times is just this, ritual action which has "*ex opere operato* efficacy."

the anthropomorphic conceptualization of the deity. Israelite sacrifice is unique because YHWH does not consume the food. In contrast to the primitive gods of its neighbors who regularly eat and are clothed, Israel's God was radically different. Her ethical development arose from a more exalted view of the deity. De Vaux's proof text comes from the much cited fiftieth Psalm:

> If I am hungry, will I not tell you?
> For the earth and what fills it are mine.
> Do I eat the flesh of bulls,
> the blood of goats do I drink?
> Sacrifice to God praise!
> Fulfill, to the Most High, your vows!
> (Ps 50:12-14)

To be sure, this Psalm explicitly says YHWH needs no food. But there remains an enormous amount of evidence which portrays Israelite sacrifice as food for YHWH. De Vaux, being a careful compiler, is very judicious in listing these data. Countless texts from every period describe YHWH's sacrifices as food. The altar itself is called the *šulḥān YHWH*, "the table of YHWH."[57] The sacrifices can be called *leḥem YHWH*, "YHWH's food."[58] The aroma of the burnt offerings is said to be *rēaḥ nîḥôaḥ lĕ-YHWH*, "a sweet savor to YHWH."[59] A common offering type consists of bread, oil and wine (Num 15:1-12; Ex 29:40), the common elements of a meal in the biblical period. Bread and wine are described as elements which gladden the hearts of gods and people (Jg 9:9,13; Hos 9:14). We should also mention the visits of divine messengers who regularly partake of sacrificial meals. All of this evidence is dismissed by de Vaux as ancient relics of Israel's Canaanite past. He takes no account of the fact that these terms are freely introduced into all genres of Israel's literature in almost all periods. De Vaux recalls the image of Israel's austere nomadic beginnings and suggests that some of the food images were incorporated into the cult only after the tribes settled down and fell prey to Canaanite agricultural heathenism.

The boldness of such an argument is quite clear. While he retains a few isolated poetic texts which speak of YHWH's freedom from human needs such as food, he dismisses dozens of other texts from a variety of genres as unrepresentative, or relics of an archaic past.

---

[57]The term is common in the P document and Ezekiel. It is also in the Deuteronomistic history (I Kg 7:48), the Chronicler (I Chr 28:16 among others) and the prophet Malachi (1:7).

[58]The term, along with a variant, *leḥem pānîm*, "bread of presence," is common in P. It is also in the Deuteronomistic history (I Sam 21:7, I Kg 7:48).

[59]It is extremely common in P. Also note Gen 8:21 (J). The Deuteronomistic historian uses a similar idiom, *yāraḥ minḥâ* "may he accept (lit."inhale") an offering" (I Sam 26:19).

In addition to Canaanite fertility religion, de Vaux suggests the Babylonian exile as a source for many of these "unbiblical" notions. The exilic period seems to have been most influential for the P school. [60] Thus many of the mythological references to YHWH's need for food can be traced to this pagan (i.e. Babylonian) source. The Babylonian evidence, contrary to de Vaux, presents tremendous problems for this type of comparative theory. The Babylonian view was not as crude and materialistic as biblical scholars often portray it. The interests of apologetics have again influenced the use of these data. Jeffrey Tigay's work on the development of the Gilgamesh Epic has provided damaging evidence for the simplistic comparisons made by some biblical scholars.[61]

Especially pertinent is the description of the gods during and after the flood in the Old Babylonian and Standard Babylonian versions. We follow Tigay and cite both texts in parallel columns. The translation is our own.

OB Atramhasis	SB Gilgamesh (Ninevite text)
Column iii	Tablet 11
30. $^{(d)}$Anunna ilū rabûtum	113. ilāni iplaḫū abūbam-ma
31. (waš)b(ū) ina ṣūmi	114. itteḫsū ītelū ana šamê
u bubūti	ša ^{d}Anum
	115. ilāni kīma kalbī kunnunū
	ina kamāti rabṣū
32. (ū)mur-ma iltum ibakki	116. išassi ^{d}Ištar kīma alitti
33. tabsūt ilī erišta ^{d}Mam(i)	117. unamba ^{d}Bēlet ilī ṭābat rigma
34. ūmum lidda($^{»}$im)	118. ūmu ullū ana ṭiṭṭi (eṭūṭi)
35. litūr līk(il)	lu itūr-ma
36. anāku ina puḫri ša i(lī)	119. aššu anāku ina puḫur ilāni
	aqbû lemutta
37. kī aq(bi)	
38. ittīšunu gamertam	
	120. kī aqbi ina puḫur ilāni lemutta

[60]De Vaux, *Ancient Israel*, vol. 2 (New York: McGraw-Hill, 1961), p. 447.

[61]J. Tigay, *The Evolution of the Gilgamesh Epic* (Philadelphia: University of Pennsylvania, 1982), pp. 224-28 and 293-96.

121. ana ḫulluq nišīya qabla aqbī-ma

30. The Anunnaki, the great gods,
31. sat in hunger and thirst.

113. The gods feared the flood,
114. They pulled back and went off to the heaven of Anu.
115. They groveled like dogs, crouching outside (?).

32. The goddess saw and was weeping,
33. the midwife of the gods, wise Mamī:
34. "May the day become darker and darker,
35. and change to night.
36. As for me, in the assembly of the gods,
37. how did I consent
38. with them to the final decision?"[62]

116. Ishtar was crying as in birth

117. The sweet voiced Belet-ili   cried:

118. "That day, let it return to clay / darkness,

119. because I commanded evil in the assembly.

120. How could I command evil in the assembly?
121. To destroy my people, (how) did I command battle?"

Column Four

15. ilū ittīša ibkû ana mātim

16. išbi niššatam

17. ṣamiat šikriš

18. šī ašar ušbû ina bikīti

19. ušbû-ma kīma immerī

20. imlûnim rāṭam

21. ṣamiā šaptāšunu bulḫita

22. (ina bubûti)

23. ītanarraru

124. ilāni šūt ᵈAnunnaki bakû ittīša

125. ilāni ašru ašbi[63] ina bikīti

126. šabbā (var. katmā) šaptāšunu leqâ buḫrēti

15. The gods wept with her for the country,
16. She was sated with grief,
17. while thirsting for beer.
18. Where she sat,

124.The gods of the Anunnaki were weeping with her.

125. The gods in humility sat tearfully.

---

[62]This translation follows the suggestion made be W. von Soden in his article, "Als die Götter (auch noch) Mensch waren: Einige Grundgedanken des altbabylonischen Atramḫasīs-Mythus," *Or* 38 (1969) pp. 430-31.

[63]The expected form is *ašbū*. The spelling *ašbi* is an example of sandhi writing.

they sat weeping,
19. Like sheep they filled the trough
20. Their lips thirsted feverishly,   126. Their lips burn / are covered, They
                                          are taken with fever sores.
21. They suffered hunger pains.

Column Five
                                       155. ušēṣī-ma
30. ana šār(i)....   ana 4 šārī attaqi niqa
31. (i)ttaqi (niqâm.....
32. izannun (........   156. aškun surqīnu ina muḫḫi ziqqurrat šadi
33. (....)   157. 7 u 7 (DUG)adagurrī uktīn
                                        158. ina šaplīšunu attabak qanâ
                                        (GIŠ)erīna u asa
34. (īṣinū il)ū erēša   159. ilāni īṣinū irīša
                                        160. ilāni īṣinū irīša ṭāba
35. kīma zubbī elu niqi paḫrū   161. ilāni kīma zumbê eli bēl niqi iptaḫrū
36.(ištū-m)a īkulū niqiam   162. ultu ullānum-ma DINGIR.MAḪ
                                        ina kašādīšu
37. (ᵈNin)tu itbē-ma
38. napḫaršunu uttazzam

30. To the winds...   155. I let out to the four winds
31. He offered an offering...   and I offered a sacrifice.
                                        156. I made an offering at the
                                        mountain top.
32. It rains...
                                        157. I set up cult vessels by
                                        sevens
                                        158. Under them I poured reed,
                                        cedar and myrtle.
34. The gods smelled (its) savor,   159. The gods smelled (its) savor.
                                        160. They smelled (its) sweet savor
35. and like flies over the   161. The gods, like flies, around
the offering they gathered.   the offerer gathered.
36. As soon as they ate   162. When Belet-ili arrived....
the offering,
37. Nintu rose
38. to scold to them.

The significance of the Standard Babylonian text becomes quite clear
in comparison to its Old Babylonian predecessor. Approximately a thousand years
separate the two texts. During this period of text transmission some remarkable

changes were made. As Tigay observes, in every line where the OB version describes the gods as mortals requiring human food the SB version has a deletion or new description. The gods no longer sit in thirst and hunger (OB III.31), they 'fear the deluge' (SB XI.113). The mention of the gods' hunger cramps is deleted entirely in the SB text (OB III.22-23). Most surprising is the gods' reaction to the sacrifice after the flood. No longer do the gods gather like flies around the sacrificial flesh and eat (OB III.35-36), rather they gather around the sacrificer (SB XI 161-62).

But what are we to make of the shift of focus in the transmission of this epic story? Is this text representative of a new Mesopotamian perspective on sacrificial rites? If so, what do we make of all the subsequent Mesopotamian material (like the NA and NB ritual texts) wherein sacrifices are still described as 'food for the gods'? Are these subsequent descriptions simply ancient relics? Perhaps, but this decision would be more of a guess than a firm conclusion. *Mutatis mutandis* for the biblical material. The most we can say, with any certainty, is that in both Israel and Mesopotamia, certain literate groups inveighed against overly anthropomorphic characterizations of the deity. The likelihood that this immediately became a generalizable philosophical principal in either civilization is very remote.

D. Tribal and Urban Cults

Another method used to distinguish earliest Israel's cult employs the typological contrast of nomadic and sedentary culture. This view has been championed in the work of Robertson Smith and Julius Wellhausen. It was Robertson Smith who had the greatest effect in this area.[64] He attempted to divide early Israel's cultic life on the basis of nomadic and sedentary existence. The former represented the purest form of Israelite religion, while the latter was the source of syncretistic agricultural rites.

Based on his own ethnographic research among contemporary Arab tribesmen, Smith formulated a number of hypotheses about the primitive characteristics of Semitic religion. Because he felt that the nomad and the sedentary citizen were such contrasting social types, he concluded that their religious rituals must be different as well. This impulse to understand religious

---

[64]W.R. Smith, *Lectures on the Religion of the Semites*.

practice as fundamentally related to social structure remains as one of the lasting contributions of his work. Its influence, especially among French sociologists such as Durkheim, has long been noted.[65]

For Smith, the contrast between nomad and village dweller was well displayed in their different types of sacrificial ritual. Smith argued that the zĕbaḥ or "slain offering" typified the religion of the nomad whereas the minḥâ or "tribute offering" characterized the religion of sedentary culture.[66] Behind this contrast was the assumption that nomadic culture preceded settled life. Thus the 'logical' conclusion: the zĕbaḥ sacrifice was the most primitive sacrificial type.

It was from his observations of animal sacrifice in various cultures that Smith formulated his theories regarding their meaning. The most basic characteristic of these rites was the feeling of communitas enjoyed by its partakers. These feelings were of such a profound character that the kinspeople felt that their patron deity was sharing in the meal with them. This joyous sharing of a common slain animal communally among one's kin had an ethical quality as well. Because this sacrificial meal was a communal experience, the tribesmen and women learned the value of pursuing the common good as opposed to their own individual desires.[67] The intensity of the experience fostered a commitment to the kin-group and an obligation to uphold its ideals.

It was only much later when nomads settled down, that the slain offering was replaced in importance by the minḥâ or tribute offering. Behind the idea of this tribute offering stood the image of Baal, the feudal lord of the land. Baal was inextricably tied to the growth of agriculture and the accumulation of tillable land by the ruling elite. Here, Robertson Smith rightly observed that the basic Semitic meaning of the noun *baʿl was "owner" or "lord of." The religious image of a vegetable offering due to this feudal lord, Baal, reflected the social setting of the Canaanite city-state.[68]

For Smith, the worship of Baal, with its urban, non-kin based setting was far removed from the earlier commensal feast. The very concept of a vegetable offering (minḥâ) due a feudal lord assumed a rigorously stratified

---

[65]Smith's influence on Durkheim has been well summarized by T. Beidelman, W. Robertson Smith and the Sociological Study of Religion (Chicago: University of Chicago Press, 1974), pp. 55-68.

[66]Smith, p. 244.

[67]Smith, pp. 263-68.

[68]Smith, pp. 244-47.

society. It reflected the luxurious public religion of the nobles which replaced the more spontaneous kin-based religion of earlier nomads.

The value of Smith's work is still apparent to those who choose to read him. Although his work is thoroughly ingrained with a romanticism about Semitic nomadism, he is very cognizant of the social ramifications of religious ceremony. For this reason his work continues to have a profound effect on modern anthropology.[69]   Religious ritual was not a secluded sector of ancient civilization; it was at the very heart of its existence.

At the center of Smith's concerns was the social structure of the community. His relatively sophisticated anthropological sensitivities allowed him to see how kin obligations were lessened in urban life. In the urban situation, the more egalitarian distribution systems of the extended family broke down. As a result, access to resources became unequal and asymmetrical so that craft-specialists and military and religious specialists could evolve.

For Smith, this inequitable arrangement was well demonstrated in the Temples of Syria-Palestine. He asserted that the Temple of Melcarth at Tyre was hardly different from the state treasury, and sacred offerings sent to Tyre by the Phoenicians in Carthage were the functional equivalent of the tribute won from conquered colonies. City-states claimed that their collections for public feasts and rituals were sacred donations, but Smith realized their affinity to other taxes. In a highly stratified urban setting, there were unequal levels of distribution. The vegetable offerings due Baal, the divine "feudal lord," were simply a theological legitimation for a system of exploitation in the city-state. Some gave more than they received, while others received more than they gave.

This urban "Baal religion" was in vast contrast to the kin-group celebrations of nomadic culture with its egalitarian social structure. Among nomads, only the joyous celebrations of the clan were needed to impress group obligations. In the city-state, only a monopoly of force could uphold its system of unequal distribution of resources. The prophetic critique of sacrifice, to Smith, stemmed from the realization that the earlier egalitarian kin- or clan-based festivals had turned into banquets for the urban elite. Contributions to these

---

[69]Anthropologists representing widely variant methodologies appreciate the anthropological instincts of Robertson Smith even if a number of his assertions are questioned. Among these anthropologists we would note: M. Harris, *The Rise of Anthropological Theory,* pp. 204-05, 207-08; E. Evans-Pritchard, *A History of Anthropological Thought,* pp. 69-81; and M. Douglas, *Purity and Danger,* pp.13-28.

affairs depended no longer on the voluntary generosity of the individual family unit, but on forced imposts of the king.

Our major criticism of Smith concerns his sharp distinction between nomadic and sedentary culture. Modern study of nomadism in the second millennium B.C.E. has overturned most of Smith's assumptions.[70] One can no longer assume that nomadic culture is prior to settled life on an evolutionary scale. Just the opposite pattern is documented. Nomadism develops as a specialization within village life. Nomads in the second millennium B.C.E. are dependent on the produce of the village and are bound inseparably to it. Rowton labels this type of nomadism "enclosed nomadism" because of its close ties to settled life. Because of these close ties, it is best to speak of nomads within their larger tribal framework. This tribal framework in the second millennium B.C.E. was vastly different from that of 19th and 20th century Arab bedouin. These tribes were a mixture of settled and pastoral folk. Of this mixture, only a small minority practiced pastoralism with regularity. By far the largest part of the tribe was sedentary. The tribe, then, was primarily a village-centered community, with a portion of its population practicing pastoralism.[71]

Most recent research supports the idea that early Israelite tribalism was agrarian and village-centered.[72] Roughly around 1200 B.C.E. we witness a

[70]The most comprehensive study is that undertaken by M. B. Rowton. He prefers to list his work in a logical as opposed to chronological sequence: "Autonomy and Nomadism in Western Asia," *Or* 42 (1973), pp. 247-58; "Urban Autonomy in a Nomadic Environment," *JNES* 32 (1973), pp. 201-215; "Enclosed Nomadism," *JESHO* 17 (1974), pp. 1-30; "Dimorphic Structure and the Tribal Elite," *Studia Instituti Anthropos* 30 (1976), pp. 219-58; "The *Abu Amurrim*," *Iraq* 31 (1969), pp. 68-73; "Dimorphic Structure and Topology," *OA* 15 (1976), pp. 17-31; "The Physical Environment and the Problem of the Nomads," *RAI* 15 (1967), pp. 109-21; "The Woodlands of Ancient Western Asia," *JNES* (1967), pp. 261-67; "The Role of Watercourses in the Growth of Mesopotamian Civilization," *Alter Orient und Altes Testament* 1 (1969), pp. 301-316; "Watercourses and Water Rights in the Official Correspondence from Larsa and Isin," *JCS* 21 (1967), pp. 267-74; "The Topological Factor in the ʿapiru Problem," *AS* 16 (1965), pp. 375-87; "Dimorphic Structure and the Problem of the ʿApirū-ʿIbrīm," *JNES* 35 (1976), pp. 13-20; "Dimorphic Structure and the Parasocial Element," *JNES* 36 (1977), pp. 181-98. Biblical scholars have also attempted to update the description of tribalism in the late second millennium. Two of the more important treatments are: G. Mendenhall, *The Tenth Generation* (Baltimore: The Johns Hopkins University Press, 1973), pp. 174-97 and N. Gottwald, "Were the Early Israelites Pastoral Nomads?" in J.J. Jackson and M. Kessler eds., *Rhetorical Criticism: Essays in Honor of James Muilenburg* (Pittsburgh Theological Monographs Series 1, Pittsburgh: Pickwick, 1974), pp. 223-255.

[71]The discovery that tribalism in the second millennium B.C.E. is a mixture of settled and pastoral people is very damaging for the theory of a peaceful nomadic settlement (*Landnahme*) advocated by the Alt school. As Rowton's studies show, the pastoral element within a tribe is small and does not naturally seek sedentary life. Nomadism was, in fact, a specialization away from that very way of existence. When pastoral folk do settle down, it is most often the poorest or the wealthiest who do. The notion of land-hungry tribes is a fiction of some modern historians. Outside of the imposed programs of some modern states (such as the Ottoman empire, Saudi Arabia) the ethnographic literature knows no examples of whole tribes settling down in the fashion that is sometimes proposed for the Israelite settlement.

[72]See L. Stager,"The Archaeology of the Family in Ancient Israel," *BASOR* 260 (1985), pp. 1-36. N. Gottwald, *The Tribes of Yahweh*, pp. 237-337.

sizable increase in the number and density of permanent settlements in the hill country of Judea and Ephraim. The material cause for this rapid growth was the development of terraced farming. Terracing allowed the previously unusable land of the hill country to become productive agriculturally. These terraces had their origins in Canaanite civilization, but served a special purpose in the Israelite settlements. As Stager has shown, the terraces were best suited for growth of grapes and olives. Yet in earliest Israel, the probable use for these terraces was the production of grain. Thus terraced farming in the hill country allowed Israel to set up a grain economy independent of the Canaanite grain economies of the surrounding coastal plain.[73] Israel's very existence as an autonomous political unit depended on the grain produced on these terraced fields.

The picture of earliest Israel as an aggregation of small rural villages in the hill country organized into a tribal league does not render obsolete the typological contrast Smith made between the religion of the tribe and the state. Rather, it forces us to rethink the specific methods Smith proposed for discussing this contrast. No longer can we neatly separate a tribal zĕbaḥ sacrifice from an urban minḥâ type. In earliest Israel, both existed side by side. In this respect we return to the point we made at the beginning of this chapter. Israel's sacrificial rites were, by and large, very similar to Canaanite rites. But this is not to say that the cults were identical. Our initial proposition was that the early Israelite cult was distinctive due to its limitation of cultic activity to a patron tribal deity YHWH. Now we are prepared to say a little more. Along with Smith we believe the manner by which sacred offerings were collected and distributed was vastly different in tribal and state polities. In other words the contrast is no longer to be made on sacrificial types—mĕnāḥōt verses zĕbāḥīm —but rather on the manner by which the mĕnāḥōt and zĕbāḥīm are collected and used by the community. This is the exactly the manner in which contemporary anthropologists describe the contrast between tribe and state economies.[74]

---

[73]See L. Stager, "Agriculture," in the *IDBS*, pp. 11-13.

[74]See for example: R. Firth, *Primitive Polynesian Economics* (London: Routledge and Kegan Paul, 1965); C.D. Forde and M. Douglas, "Primitive Economics," in H. Shapiro ed., *Man, Culture and Society* (New York: Oxford University Press, 1960), pp. 330-44; M. Fried, *The Evolution of Political Society* (New York: Harper and Row, 1967); B. Malinowski, *Argonauts of the Western Pacific* (London: Routledge and Kegan Paul, 1965); and M. Sahlins, "Political Power and the Economy in Primitive Society," in G. Dole and R. Carneiro eds.,*Essays in the Science of Culture in Honor of Leslie White* (New York: T.Y. Crowell,1960), pp. 390-415, and *idem*, "Economic Anthropology and Anthropological Economics," in M. Fried ed., *Explorations in Anthropology* (New York: T.Y. Crowell, 1973), pp. 274-88.

This monograph will examine the social function of ancient Israelite cult. We feel this has been a neglected aspect in recent research. We should preface our work with one demurrer. We do not believe that the cult of ancient Israel can be understood only in social terms, nor do we believe that this is necessarily the best way to understand its function. What we will assert, though, is that it provides a far better vehicle for differentiating the Israelite cult from the Canaanite cult in the early period than previous idealistic solutions which characterized the Canaanite cult as a series of magical rites in which victuals were provided for the gods.

This study will begin with an examination of the terminology used for sacrifices and offerings (Chapter 2). The interest will be in those terms which have both a cultic and non-cultic usage. In this fashion our examination will be different from previous attempts to categorize the technical terminology of the offering system. For the most part these studies have attempted to divide the terms into three categories, that of gift, communion, and atonement (or sin-offerings). Sometimes scholars have taken this even further and have tried to argue for one of these three categories as the basic meaning of the sacrificial act as a whole. We do not make such claims. Nor do we deny the importance of previous studies of these cultic terms. This study is self-consciously limited to those terms which have social and political import. The purpose is not to describe the meaning of Israelite sacrifice in all of its various permutations; but rather to examine those places where it intersects with social and political history. We assert, with Robertson Smith, that the ritual life of a community cannot be appreciated fully without an understanding of its grounding in social structure.

Our third and fourth chapters will focus on the nature of sacrifices and offerings in early Israel. These two chapters will attempt to define with more precision what the social implications of the Israelite cult were. These chapters are not period studies; they do not attempt to define the complete nature of the cult in early Israel. The aim here is much more circumscribed. Only a few texts will be examined. In each case, an attempt will be made to ascertain how the social structure of early Israel influenced the cult. Following the lead of Robertson Smith, close attention will be paid to the themes of offering collection and distribution when it is appropriate.

The last chapter will return to the issue of fertility cults. In this chapter we shall show how a sensitive appreciation of the social role of the cult can make sense of the rhetoric of the post-exilic reformers. In particular, the mythic and social role of the Temple in the post-exilic programs of reform will be studied. The problem in this period centers on the Temple rebuilding projects of the various groups who return from exile. By carefully paying attention to the symbolism of this prophetic rhetoric we hope that a new understanding of the 'fertility cult' may emerge.

CHAPTER TWO

Lexical Indications of the Cult's Social Function

A. Hebrew *Minḥâ*

The Hebrew word *minḥâ* has two very different meanings in the Hebrew Bible. On the one hand it can have a cultic meaning. In this instance it can mean "offering" in the generic sense, either animal or vegetable, or as in the case of the priestly writer it can refer specifically to the cereal offering. On the other hand it can refer to a profane gift, often with a specific technical nuance of political tribute. Before we explore this variety of meaning it would be helpful to discuss the etymology of this term.

This term has cognates in Phoenician, Ugaritic and Arabic. The word has usually been understood as derivable from a root *m-n-ḥ*. The original verb would have been **manaḥa* "to give" thus making ** minḥatu*, "gift," a related noun. But Albright derived it from the root *nḥy*, "to lead, or guide."[1] In this case the noun would refer to a gift which was led or brought forward to the altar or cult center. A parallel can be found in the Arabic term *hadīyat*, "offering," from *hadâ / yahdī*, "to guide." Support for this view comes from the attestation of *mn-ḥi-ta* **manḥiy(a)t(a)* in Egyptian syllabic orthography. Albright believes the *ḥi* sign argues for a *mem* -preformative noun from the root *nḥy*. A number of problems are raised by such an etymology of Hebrew *minḥâ*. First, the plural form *měnāḥōt* presumes a segholate singular noun from the root *m-n-ḥ*. It is not a plural form of a *mem* -preformative root. Second we should remember the Arabic cognate *manaḥa* "to give," *minḥatu*, "gift." The close similarity of this root to the Hebrew word is unassailable. Yet if the Hebrew is based on an original *nḥy*, the only way to explain the Arabic is by a late borrowing. If the latter was the case, Arabic would have borrowed the Hebrew term *minḥâ* and misanalyzed it as though from a root *m-n-ḥ*. Even if this were possible other problems arise. First, Arabic rarely forms denominatives from the G. A verb like *ra'asa*, "to be a chief,"

---

[1] W. Albright, *Vocalization of the Egyptian Syllabic Orthography* (New Haven: American Oriental Society, 1934), p. 53.

27

from *ra²su* is a rare exception. But perhaps more important, the Arabic language borrowed many items from the religious vocabulary of Jewish and Christian sources, but never altered their religious meaning. We think of such examples as *qūrbān*, "offering" and *ṣalāt*, "prayer." The word *minḫâ* had a very specialized religious connotation in late Hebrew and Aramaic and the loss of this specialization in an Arabic borrowing would be most difficult to explain. Finally we should also add that if *minḫâ* is from *nḥy* then it is quite odd that we have no cognate accusative constructions: noun *minḫâ* plus the verb *nḥy*.

In Phoenician the form is *mnḥt*. In a Punic text from Carthage it seems to refer to a cereal offering.[2]   A similar usage of *mnḥt* can be found in the Marseilles Tariff.[3]   In other texts, *mnḥt* is simply a term for general cultic gifts; see the Neo-Punic text from Tunisia (*KAI* 145:13), the Kition tariff (*CIS* I 14:5) and a text from Tyre (*ESE* I p. 16 line 1). In another Tunisian text *mnḥt* is contrasted with *ʿlt*, "burnt offering" (*KAI* 159:8). This type of contrast is found in the Bible (I Chr 21:23, Ps 20:4, Am 5:22 and Jer 14:12). The meaning of *mnḥt* in one Neo-Punic text is uncertain (*KAI* 141:2).

The Phoenician texts available to us show a clear specialization of meaning for this term. Each of the texts examined uses this term to refer to cultic offerings, often with very specific technical nuances. But one should be careful about generalizing from this epigraphic data. The absence of any literary texts in Phoenician prevents us from ascertaining whether the term might have varied according to literary genre. The most we can say is that in some circles of Phoenician and Punic culture, the specialization of the term proceeded in a cultic direction.

At Ugarit the specialization proceeded in another direction. The term occurs at least twice in economic texts referring to some type of secular payment (*CTA* 141.1 and *KTU* 4.91) and in a text from Ras Hani.[4]   The term may also appear in the Baal text. The line in question reads: "He (i.e. Baal) will bring your

---

[2]The text is found in *KAI* 74:9-10, (*qdmt) qdšt wʿl zbḥ ṣd wʿl zbḥ šmn (...w)ʿl ḥlb wʿl zbḥ mnḥt wʿl (kl zbḥ),* "...Holy (first fruits), and as to the meat sacrifice, the oil sacrifice....the milk (or fat) sacrifice, the grain sacrifice, or (any other sacrifice)." This text is a sequence of sacrificial types. The last of the series is the *zbḥ mnḥt.* It ought to refer to a particular type. A grain offering seems most plausible; it completes a natural list (*ṣd,* "game," *šmn,* "oil," *ḥlb,* "milk").

[3]*KAI* 69:14. As in the Carthage tariff, *mnḥt* appears in a list of specific sacrifice types (*bll,* "mixed offering;" *ḥlb* [1], "milk," and *ḥlb* [2], "fat"). We would expect *mnḥt,* which follows, to be a particular type of foodstuff.

[4] For the latter, see M. Dietrich and O. Loretz, "Eine Abrechnung aus Ras Hani (782)," *UF* 12 (1980), p. 401, line 9). Dietrich and Loretz also mention another occurrence of the term in *KTU* 4.709 line 6. The context is fitting but the term is spelled *mnḥt* in the text. The collation could be wrong, the scribe may have confused *ḥ* for *ḫ* or we may simply have a different word here.

tribute (ʾargmnk), verily the god will bring (your present), the sons of Qudšu, your gift (mnḥyk). "5 If this term is derived from   m-n-ḥ, this would be one example in Ugaritic where the term meant "gift." The preservation of this more generic and archaic meaning in a mythic text, as we shall see, is just what one would expect.

The term minḥâ has a variety of meanings in Hebrew. It is a favorite of the Priestly writer. The word occurs many times in this document and has a very precise technical meaning in each case. The taxonomy is highly developed. The basic meaning of the term for P is "grain offering." The minḥâ   is grain brought to the priests for sacrificial purposes. In Lev 2 the minḥâ   offering is treated as an independent rite. It includes oil, frankincense (2:1), and salt (2:13). It can be prepared in a variety of ways, either in an oven, on a griddle or in a pan (2:4-7). Part of it is burned on the altar and another part is saved for the priests themselves to consume (2:8-9). When it is not an independent offering its most common usage is an addition to the continual burnt offering (Num 28-29, passim). In this case it is offered in connection with the nesek, "libation."

Outside of P the meaning "grain offering" is infrequent, but still evident. It can be so used in the Deuteronomistic history (II Kgs 16:13), the Psalter (20:4, 40:7, 142:2), the prophets (Amos 5:22,25), and the Chronicler (I Chr 23:29, 21:23; II Chr 7:7). More notable is the use of minḥâ   to refer to sacrifices in a generic fashion. The term is used this way in the Cain and Abel story (Gen 4:3ff). This generic usage is also found in the Deuteronomistic history (I Kg 18:29,36; II Kg 3:20) and in the late prophetic book of Malachi (1:10,11,13 and passim).

The secular usage of the term as simply "gift" is found in the meeting of Jacob and Esau (Gen 32:4,19-21). But quite frequently it takes on a rather specific, technical meaning of "tribute" in secular usage. This usage is frequent in the Deuteronomistic history. There it commonly refers to tribute brought by subdued nations. When David defeats the Moabites they become bearers of minḥâ (nôśĕʾê minḥâ) (II Sam 8:2). This technical usage as tribute can also be found in the Psalter (72:10), Zephaniah (3:10), and the Chronicler. The Chronicler, in describing the tribute brought to Solomon, enumerates the minḥâ. It includes articles of silver and gold, garments, myrrh, spices, horses, and mules (II Chr 9:24).

5CTA 2.139. The question here is the yod before the suffix. There are three possible solutions. It could be an example of a rare use of a mater lectionis in the epic material (manaḥīka, "your presents"). Or it might represent the rare adjectival ending ay (minḥayaka, "your present"). Finally, it could derive from the root nḥy and be cognate to the root Albright found in Egyptian syllabic orthography (see above).

The sacred and secular usages of *minḥâ* posed problems for the earliest biblical exegetes, the ancient scholars who translated the Hebrew Bible into Greek and Aramaic. Because the semantic range of this term was so wide and the versions had no direct equivalent, they were forced on many occasions to provide an interpretation of this Hebrew word in terms of its sacred or secular usage.[6] The Septuagint is the most consistent in regard to distinguishing sacred and secular usage. In general, it uses *dōron* for secular gifts and *thysia* or *semidalis* for sacred donations.[7] The Aramaic versions use *qorbānâʾ* or *tiqrĕbûtâʾ* for both secular and sacred gifts and thus retain the ambiguity of the Hebrew original. When Hebrew *minḥâ* is clearly a flour offering (as in P) Targum Onkelos uses its semantic equivalent *minḥâʾ* while the Peshitta uses *sĕmīdâʾ*.

Let us return to the issue of the semantic variability of *minḥâ* within the Hebrew Bible. How are we to account for this great variety of meaning? It has been typical in the past to view the situation simply in historical terms. For example, Snaith, Kraus, and von Rad believe that the meaning "cereal offering" is a post-exilic development.[8] Inherent in this view is an implicit Wellhausian bias. That is, the idea that because the P document is post-exilic, most if not all of its material is late. This view has a number of problems, the most severe being the rather widespread usage of the term as "cereal offering" in the pre-exilic period.[9]

This is not to deny the influence of historical development in the usage of the term. This would be absurd. What we would like to argue, though, is that a diachronic perspective alone cannot account for the variety of meanings the term possesses at a synchronic level. At any number of times in Israelite history, *minḥâ* could refer to a tribute payment, a gift or even a cereal offering. How did these variant meanings develop and continue to exist side by side?

It is well known in anthropology that societies which have a group of highly trained religious specialists also have very learned explanations of various

---

[6]Aramaic has a word *minḥâ* but its usage is much more specialized than Hebrew *minḥâ*. It is only used to convey the technical priestly meaning, "cereal offering." The term seems to be a loan word which has only assumed one meaning from the variety found in Biblical Hebrew.

[7]On the details of Septuagintal usage see S. Daniel, *Recherches sur le vocabulaire du culte dans la Septante* (Paris, 1966), pp. 201-223.

[8]N. Snaith, "Sacrifices in the Old Testament," *VT* 7 (1957), pp. 314-16. H.J. Kraus, *Worship in Israel* (Richmond: John Knox Press, 1966), pp. 114-115. G. von Rad, *Old Testament Theology*, vol. I (New York: Harper and Row, 1962), pp. 256-57.

[9]R. deVaux, *Ancient Israel*, vol 2, p. 430, has noted the following texts which seem to presume a meaning cereal offering: I Sam 2:29, 3:14; Is 19:21; Jer 14:12; Ps 20:4; and Am 5:22. We could also add Jos 22:23, 29; Ju 13:19, 23; II Kg 16:13; Ps 40:7, 142:2. One should also note the very important article of B. Levine, "The Descriptive Tabernacle Texts of the Pentateuch," *JAOS* 85 (1965), pp. 307-18. In this article Levine argues quite persuasively that Num 7—a text in which *minḥâ* means "cereal offering"—is a very early document from a cultic archive.

ritual activities and mythic motifs. These learned explanations are often very different from those of the non-specialist or commoner. This process of developing increasingly complex and intricate systems of explanation by a class of religious specialists was called "rationalization" by Weber.[10] By this he meant that intellectuals within a society structured the meaning of religious ritual and doctrine along increasingly systematic or "rational" grounds. Recently, J. Goody has proposed another means of looking at the problem.[11] He sees the development of writing among administrators as an important ingredient in the "rationalization" of societal thinking.[12] In a provocative and influential essay he examines several examples of early writing from ancient Near Eastern sources. He includes administrative lists from Ugarit and Mesopotamia, event and lexical lists from Mesopotamia, and onomastic lists from Egypt. Like other Orientalists, Goody notes that these very lists comprise the sizable majority of the extant documentation of antiquity. He further observes that the creation of lists and records among the priests and other administrators in the ancient Near East led to highly sophisticated classification schemes. These classification schemes were necessary for Temple revenues and expenditures to be accounted for. This ability to classify allowed for more precise conceptual and lexical boundaries and gave much greater visibility to categories of items. This increased precision and visibility allowed priestly specialists to organize widely disparate pieces of information. Though these classification schemes were very important for the development of a sophisticated and well-articulated social structure, they were not always pertinent to the day-to-day affairs of the average ancient Near Easterner.

How is this relevant for *minḥâ* ? We would suggest that both the usage of *minḥâ* as tax or tribute payment and as cereal offering could co-exist at one time in Israelite culture. For the common Israelite, the term *minḥâ* would have referred to a gift, most often a gift given to the Temple cult. Because Israelite society was primarily grain oriented, the *minḥâ* payment given to the Temple was

---

[10]For a good explanation of this aspect of Weber's thought see the introduction of H. Gerth and C. Mills in their collection of Weber's essays entitled, *From Max Weber: Essays in Sociology* (New York: Oxford University Press, 1946), pp. 51-55.

[11]*The Domestication of the Savage Mind* (New York: Cambridge University Press, 1977). See especially his chapter on list making in the ancient Near East, pp. 74-111.

[12]His view allows him to get beyond the notion that primitive people think mystically while modern people think rationally.   This view was pervasive in early anthropology (Frazer, Lévy-Bruhl, etc.). It is also reflected in Weber to the degree that he distinguishes between magic and rational reasoning. Goody's perspective is that the development of writing—which allows for a manipulation of ideas and concepts unthinkable in an illiterate culture—leads to the development of an ordered schema of concepts and terms.

usually grain. This basic datum was further 'rationalized' by the priestly
specialists in the Temple.[13] For them, there was a need to organize and
categorize the variety of offering types which were received. A typical Judean
farmer need not be specific regarding these matters; he simply contributed a
tenth of whatever it was he produced. But the priests—who had to deal with a
variety of agricultural and pastoral gifts and revenues—needed a more elaborate
taxonomy to order their experience. No doubt a large impetus for this ordering
came from Temple lists and tariffs.[14] In order to deal meaningfully with the
income of the Temple, a precise lexicon of cultic contributions had to be in place.
This would explain the need to specialize further a term like *minḥâ* from "a gift"
(which was most often grain) to "a cereal offering." This is not say that the
priestly usage was wholly distinct from other usages. The textual evidence cited
above shows that this priestly usage can be found in most genres of Israelite
literature. Our argument is that the need to specialize this type of vocabulary
stemmed most likely from priestly circles. Once the new lexical meaning was
established it could be used elsewhere in Israelite society. But in other segments
of Israelite society the importance of this new taxonomy was not so great as to
expel all other meanings. This was not the case in the priestly materials. There
the specialization was so firm that a new term (*qorbān*) had to be employed for
the generic sense of "gift, offering."

This view has great advantages over the Wellhausian position. There,
one had to see the specialization as late and as due to a priestly need to substitute
legalistic sacrificial service for joyous spiritual religion.

> Centralization is synonymous with generalization and fixity, and these are
> the external features by which the festivals of the Priestly Code are
> distinguished from those which preceded them. In evidence I point to the
> prescribed sacrifice of the community instead of the spontaneous sacrifice
> of the individual. . . nothing is free or the spontaneous growth of nature,
> nothing is indefinite and still in the process of becoming; all is statutory,

---

[13]B. Levine has recognized the important role of rationalization in priestly circles. See
his article, "Priestly Writers," *IDBS,* p. 686.

[14]B. Levine has explored the importance of temple lists within the priestly corpus.
Unfortunately, these very important articles have received much less attention than they deserve.
In addition to his "Descriptive Tabernacle Texts" see "Ugaritic Descriptive Rituals," *JCS* 17 (1963),
pp. 105-11; "The Descriptive Ritual Texts from Ugarit: Some Formal and Functional Features of the
Genre," in C. Meyers and M. O'Connor (eds.), *The Word of the Lord Shall Go Forth* (Winona Lake:
Eisenbrauns, 1983), pp. 467-85; Levine and W. Hallo, "Offerings to the Temple Gates at Ur," *HUCA*
38 (1967), pp. 17-58. Also note A. Rainey's article which uses Levine's work as a point of departure,
"The Order of Sacrficies in Old Testament Ritual Texts," *Biblica* 51 (1970), pp. 485-498.

sharply defined, distinct. But the centralisation of the cultus had also not a little to do with the inner change which the feasts underwent.[15]

Of course the inner change that Wellhausen speaks of is the change from an interior religion to an exterior religion. The problem with this analysis is that it takes the intellectual task of the priestly class—to classify and order a tremendously wide variety of agricultural and pastoral gifts and offerings—as indicative of a spiritual demeanor. This inability to appreciate the systematic thinking of the Priestly code has led to some very scathing criticisms of Priestly theology. Besides Wellhausen, consider the following analysis of the "strongly systematizing" aspects of the P Code found in von Rad's influential work on Biblical theology:

> All this information about sacrifices in the Priestly Code is crudely materialistic. The reader looks in vain for firm holds to enable him to rise into the spiritual realm by way of the sacrificial concepts lying behind the sacrificial practice.[16]

The development of specialized meanings for the term *minḥâ* should be seen as both an inner-Israelite and a broad Northwest Semitic phenomenon. In its early proto-Northwest Semitic form, the root had a broad generic connotation "gift." During the Iron Age, or perhaps a bit earlier, the cultic specialists in Phoenicia and Israel used this word to express the most basic cultic offering one could offer, the cereal offering. But this specialization was uneven. Its earlier generic usage survived even into post-exilic literature in Israel. While in Ugarit, already in the Bronze Age, the prose material showed a limitation of meaning to a secular economic sense.

The specialization of meaning for cultic terms has important ramifications. In any one particular dialect the terms for sacrifice become quite specific and technical. As a result of this learned procedure of classification which occurs within the cult, the priestly vocabulary becomes quite idiosyncratic. This idiosyncratic and complex classification system is paradigmatic of all mature cultic centers in the ancient world. It does not reflect a crudely materialistic view of the cult; rather it reflects the attempt of each and every cultic center to provide order and meaning to the wide variety of gifts and offerings which it receives. The special usages of any one cult center cannot be predicted on the

---

[15]*Prolegomena*, p. 103.
[16]*Old Testament Theology* I, pp. 259-60.

basis of the archaic meanings of the pertinent cultic terms. The specialization of *minḥâ*, from "gift" to "cereal offering," is paradigmatic of this. A number of other examples could be given.[17] But not all of the priestly technical vocabulary is idiosyncratic. Some terms like *zbḥ*, (*ōbḥ), "(ritual) slaughter, sacrifice" retain a cultic nuance in all of the Canaanite dialects. Other terms, like *ʿōlâ*, "burnt offering," while not occurring in all of the dialects, have transparent semantic equivalents which reflect similar rites (cf. Ugaritic *šrp*, "burnt offering").

B. Hebrew *Šay*

One point must be stressed about this specialization process when it does occur. Often those words which were passed over by a particular cultic group were still preserved in the epic or mythic texts of that culture. An example of this would be the well-attested Canaanite root *θ-(w/y)-y* (possibly, *θy* [18]) "to donate" or "to offer."   It has a quite specific cultic nuance in the texts of Ugarit. This same cultic nuance can be found on a LB Canaanite inscription incised on an ewer from Lachish.[19] It is spelled *šay* which indicates that the phonemes and have merged in this South Canaanite dialect. Albright noted this from the manner in which Egyptian regularly transcribed *θ* and *ś* by *s* and *š* by *š*.[20] It is also found on a votive seal from Phoenicia.[21] The word also occurs in the archaic Aramaic inscription from Zinjirli as an offering the king gave to Hadad. [22] Its use in all these material is cultic in nature.

The word is found in Hebrew, but the cultic specialization is absent. It is not found in priestly texts. Instead, its usage is quite restricted. It is found in poetic texts which speak of the archaic image of Israel's deity as the Divine

---

[17]In the appendices at the end of this study we examine four such terms: *mśʾt*, *mtnʾ*, *tnph*, and *trmh*.

[18]Ginsberg, on the basis of Ugaritic evidence, believed that this root was originally *θy*. See his article, "Nwspwt Kʾlylt ʾPyn—BʿT" *Tarbiz* 4 (1934), p. 384, n.16. He compared this Ugaritic term to the Old South Arabic (Minean) terms *mθʿy* and *mθʿyt* which mean "sacrifice." He related this Semitic root to Hebrew *šay* by a process of partial assimilation. He has been followed by F.M. Cross, ("The Evolution of the Proto-Canaanite Alphabet," *BASOR* 134 (1954), p. 21 n. 19). In this article, Cross outlines the development as: *θaʿyu > *θayy > šay(y). The problem with this view is that the assimilation of ʿayin is unparalleled. Also both *θ(w/y)y* and *θy* occur in Ugaritic, an argument for two different roots, not phonetic development. The proposal of a doubly weak verb follows from the vocalization of the Hebrew *šay*, with a short a.

[19]F. Cross, *BASOR,* p. 134.

[20]Albright, "The Early Alphabetic Inscriptions from Sinai and their Decipherment," *BASOR* 110 (1948), p. 15, n. 42.

[21]N. Avigad, "Two Phoenician Votive Seals," *IEJ* 16 (1966), p. 245.

[22]*KAI* 214:19

Warrior. In these cases the mythic background is a description of the Divine Warrior receiving his tribute (Is 18:7, Ps 68:30 and 76:12). If W. Moran is correct, the term is also found in Gen 49:10. [23] In a well-received article, he argued that the *MT* text be vocalized: ʿad kī yābīʾ šay lô "until one brings him (Judah) offerings" (*MT* had read ... šīlô). This reading would be just what one would expect for the period of Judah's ascendancy wherein this poem is usually dated. When the Judahite David becomes king and Jerusalem becomes his royal and religious center, one would expect that offerings would be brought to him.

It is in these selective poetic texts of Bible, where the archaic image of the Canaanite Divine Warrior image is present, that the word *šay* is found. The presence of this term solely in mythic texts, with the archaic meaning "gift," is not accidental. This is an an example of how mythic (or, often poetic) usage preserves a meaning for a term which either is not present in the colloquial prose language or is present with a different, more specialized meaning. It was mentioned above that this could be applicable to the usage of the root *mnḥ* in the Baal text (*CTA* 2.1:37-39). In that text the term meant "gift or tribute." This would contrast with its more specialized usage in economic texts. In other words, the mythic material preserves a more archaic meaning than that which is current in the economic texts.

This phenomenon of a mythic text preserving a more archaic meaning is not limited simply to terms for sacrifice and offering. Scholars have long noted that, in general, the language of the epic and mythic texts from Ugarit differs considerably from that of the letters and economic texts.[24] With good reason, scholars have suggested that this reflects the more archaic quality of the mythic material. Some have suggested that this archaic language was a pan-Canaanite phenomenon and so was not limited to the geographical area of Ugarit. In any event, the mythic texts do not address simply the local population of Ugarit. The language is much more archaic and non-regional. A similar phenomenon existed in ancient Greece. The language of the Iliad and the Odyssey is more archaic than any of the contemporary Greek dialects. Though it had many Ionic features,

---

[23] Gen 49,10 and its use in Ez 21,32, *Biblica* 39 (1958), pp. 405-25.

[24] W. Albright, "Specimens of Late Ugaritic Prose," *BASOR* 150 (1958), pp. 36-38. He notes that the epic language is somewhat artificial and does not originate in Ugarit proper. Two major differences between the prose and epic language appear. One pertains to the vocabulary. A common, and basic term of standard LB Ugaritic is *bnš*, "man" never appears in the poetic texts! Secondly, the tense system is different. The epic texts are much more archaic in usage. For similar distinctions between the epic and prose texts see M. Liverani, "Elementi innovativi nell-ugaritico non letterario," *Rendiconti lincei* 19 (1964), pp. 173-91.

the language could not really be equated with any one Greek dialect. We now know this language was the pan-Hellenic epic speech of the bard.[25] It was a language which Greeks of all dialects could understand but which was different from each of the local dialects. The grammar and vocabulary of the epic singer was not reflective of any one historical epoch or location.

Albright and others have argued that certain aspects of Canaanite epic style are analogous to this Greek model.[26] It is the opinion of these scholars that the close connection of prosodic style, word pairs, and the technical terms of religious life between Israel and Ugarit reflect a pan-Canaanite poetic continuum which existed before the rise of individual states in the first millennium. The existence of such an epic dialect would account for the appearance of technical terms in epic texts which bear little or no relationship to the prevailing technical terms of the existing cult. To assume that there was necessarily a one-to-one correspondence between a mythic term its cultic specialization is to impose a functionalist hermeneutic on the epic text. Though mythic texts often preserve a considerable amount of data for reconstructing ancient social institutions, these texts cannot be used uncritically.[27] As classicists have seen in Homeric epic, and as other comparativists have noted in other mythic traditions, the technical vocabulary of the social, economic and religious world of the poet does not necessarily accord perfectly with the particular culture in which the poet lives.

C. Ugaritic *Šlmm* as (Cultic) Offering and (Secular) Gift

1. The Use of *Šlmm* in the Kirta Epic

Not all cultic terms possess the variety of meaning present in *minḥâ* and *šay*. One term which is more uniform over Northwest Semitic culture would be *šlmm*. At Ugarit the *šlmm* offering is one of the most common sacrificial types. Many scholars have compared this Ugaritic offering to its biblical counterpart,

---

[25]The basic study is A. Lord, *The Singer of Tales.*

[26]See "Specimens" for a brief statement. He expands the argument in *YGC* pp. 8-9 and 116-119. He compares the Canaanite epic dialect to the hymnal epic dialect in Babylon as well. The tendency to generalize dialectal features, he argues, is due mainly to the need for a common language vehicle for public recitation. Moreover, Albright notes that the pantheon of the epic genre is generalized in a similar fashion. "There is no local pantheon, any more than there is in the Homeric epic. Instead we find a selection of important and interesting deities, more of the details which would tie them down locally being omitted. And just as the language of the epics differs from the current dialect of Ugarit, so the gods named and described in the epics differ from the divinities of the city as they appear (usually in a fixed order) in the official pantheon of Ugarit and in sacrificial lists" (pp. 118-119). Also see Cross' recent treatment, "The Epic Traditions."

[27]See G.S. Kirk, "The Homeric Poems as History," *CAH* vol. II, pp. 820-50.

the šĕlāmîm offering.[28] The similarities are notable. In Ugaritic šlmm is often paired with the burnt-offering, šrp.[29] One is reminded of the common biblical pair, šĕlāmîm and ʿōlâ. In both Ugarit and Israel the šlmm offering consisted of animals. And, quite possibly, at Ugarit the šlmm offering was consumed by the worshippers, just as it was in Israel.[30] Finally, the šĕlāmîm offering in the Bible and in Ugaritic has royal characteristics.[31]

The presence of the šlmm offering is rare outside of sacrificial lists. Scholars have examined many possible references to this offering in the epic texts of Ugarit but only one text is worthy of serious consideration. It is found in the Kirta epic and must be examined in some detail. The context of this narrative is a dream of Kirta's. In the dream he receives instructions to attack the city of Udum. As the siege forces take their positions, King Pabil of Udum sends messengers to Kirta.

Pabil's Offer [32]

---

[28]The bibliography is vast on this subject. For a good summary of recent work see B. Janowski, "Erwägungen zur Vorgeschichte des israelitischen Šĕlāmîm-Opfers," *UF* 12 (1980), p. 231, n.1. We should mention the works of R. Dussaud, *Les origines cananéenes du sacrifice israélite* (Paris: Leroux, 1941); R. Schmid, *Das Bundesopfer in Israel* (Studien zum Alten und Neuen Testament, 9, München: Kosel, 1964) (cf. D. Gill, *Thysia* and *Šĕlāmîm:* Questions to R. Schmid's *Das Bundesopfer in Israel,*" *Biblica* 47 (1966), pp. 255–62; A. Charbel, *Zebaḥ Šĕlāmîm: Il sacrificio pacifico* (Jerusalem: Commercial Press, 1967); R. Rendtorff, *Studien zur Geschichte des Opfers im alten Israel* (Neukirchen-Vluyn: Neukirchener-V., 1967) pp. 119–62; W. Eisenbeis, *Die Wurzel ŠLM im Alten Testament* (BZAW 113; Berlin: de Gruyter, 1969), pp. 222–96; and B. Levine, *In the Presence of the Lord* (Leiden: Brill, 1974).

[29]The texts include *CTA* 34:4; 35:13; 36.1:15; App II.14,31; *Ugaritica* V 12.A:9; 13:10,15,28.

[30]The text here is *Ugaritica* V 11.9–10: š l ʾil bt šlmm kll ylḥm bh. The first half of the line is clear: "A sheep for the god of the house." The last half is difficult. C. Virolleaud, in *Ugaritica* V p. 586, translated it: ". . . en sacrifice pacifique; tous en mangeront." This is improbable because it assumes kll is synonymous with kl. J. Blau and J. Greenfield ("Ugaritic Glosses," *BASOR* 200 (1970), p. 15) have proposed a better solution. They suggest that šlmm kll should be compared to Phoenician šlm kll (*KAI* 69.3) and so must refer to a type of sacrifice. In making this comparison they assume that Ugaritic šlmm is in construct with kll (second mem is enclitic), like its Phoenician counterpart šlm kll. A. Rainey has suggested another plausible reading ("The Ugaritic Texts in Ugaritica 5," *JAOS* (1974), p. 191.). He takes kll as adverbial and translates, "he will eat everything from it." Levine's translation is more idiosyncratic (*Presence of the Lord* p. 10, n. 21). He describes the offered animal as a "šlmm offering in connection with the kālîl (whole offering?)." The translations of either Blau/Greenfield or Rainey are to be preferred.

[31]In line one of the text quoted in n. 5 it is said that the king performs the sacrifice (ydbḥ mlk). We assume that the woman mentioned in line 8 who eats is the queen and the man mentioned in line 5 is the king. Some prefer to see everyone eating in line 10. This would accord with the communal nature of the sacrifice as we know it from the Bible, but it would be a unique rendering of kll. On the royal aspects of the biblical šĕlāmîm, see Levine, pp 27–29. Note in particular his treatment of I Sam 11:14–15. We are not sure that the šĕlāmîm was distinctive among the various sacrificial rites in the proclamation of kingship. We are more inclined to agree with Levine's conjecture that the proclamation of kingship was connected to sacrificial rites in general (p. 29, n. 71).

[32]We shall not attempt to justify all of our vocalizations. Many of the words are subject to multiple interpretations. To comment on all of them would detract from the purpose of this study. We comment only on those readings which are novel or are pertinent to our larger argument.

qaḥ kaspa wa-yaraqa ḫurāṣi
yada maqāmiha wa-ʿabdê ʿālami
θalāθa sūsawīma markabti
bi-tarbaṣi bini ʾamati
qaḥ Kirta šalamīma šalamīma
wanaggī malku la-bêtiya
raḥaq Kirta la-ḥaẓiriya
(CTA 14.3.126-33)

Take silver and glitterings of gold,
a field hand[33] and two perpetual slaves,
three horses with the chariot,
from the stable of a maidservant.
Take, O Kirta, gifts upon gifts.
Then flee, O king, from my house,
be far, O Kirta, from my courts.

This passage has been subject to a variety of interpretations. The
graphic similarities between this *šlmm* and the *šlmm* of the ritual texts is quite
striking. Before we turn to this problem, we should clarify the overall structure of
the piece. Many scholars do not attempt to organize the lines into parallel cola
and therefore lose important evidence as to the structure and meaning. For our
purposes the important structural motif is the repetition of the imperative verb
qaḥ, "take." Note the parallel construction, "Take silver...// Take, O Kirta, *šlmm*
šlmm!" The second usage of *qaḥ* not only recalls the first, but takes its object in
what follows. As many scholars have observed, *šlmm šlmm* parallels the fuller
listing of items which follow the first *qaḥ*.

Some scholars hold that the Kirta epic, like its Greek counterparts,
was composed orally and, most likely, sung at festal occasions. [34] Its structure—
which consists of many individual formulaic units bound into a larger whole—fits

---

[33]The term is difficult and subject to a variety of interpretations. My translation
derives from a suggestion of F. Cross. The literal translation "hand of its field" recalls the English
idiom, "field hand." The writer knows of no Semitic precedents. The parallelism, field hand, slave, is
nice, as is the numeric sequence (suggested by F. Cross), 1 field hand, 2 perpetual slaves (we read
dual, but the orthography is ambiguous), three horses.

[34]On the comparison of Greek and Canaanite epic style see nn. 25-26. The basic work
is A. Lord, *The Singer of Tales* (Cambridge: Harvard University Press, 1964). Also see R. Jakobson,
"Grammatical Parallelism and its Russian Facet," *Language* 42 (1966), pp. 399-429. On the formulaic
quality of Canaanite verse, see F. Cross, "Prose and Poetry in the Mythic and Epic Texts from
Ugarit," *HTR* (1974), pp. 1-15; R. Whitaker, "A Formulaic Analysis of Ugaritic Poetry," (Ph.D diss.
Harvard, 1970) and L. Fisher, *Ras Shamra Parallels* (Analecta Orientalia 49-50 (Rome: Pontifical
Biblical Institute, 1972-81). On the biblical material see U. Cassuto, "Parallel Words in Hebrew and
Ugaritic" and "The Israelite Epic," *Biblical and Oriental Studies* II (Jerusalem: Magnes, 1975), pp.
60-109; S. Gevirtz, *Patterns in the Early Poetry of Israel* (Chicago: University of Chicago, 1963)
and S. Geller, *Parallelism in Early Hebrew Poetry* (HSM 20, Cambridge: Harvard, 1979).

nicely with the structure one would expect in orally composed literature, but one should note that written traditions can employ very similar structural features. [35] Repetition of these units is a necessary element of the composition. The artistic merit of the composition derives from the manner in which the formulaic units are put together. This aspect of its composition has not always been appreciated by scholarship.[36] Our particular passage is one such formulaic unit. It is repeated several times in the telling of the story.

One repetition derives from the structure of the narrative itself. In the Kirta text there are two levels of action. On the one hand there is the revelation Kirta receives in a dream as to how he should procure a wife (who is to bear the desired dynastic heir) from King Pabil. On the other hand there is the subsequent execution of the dream itself when Kirta awakes. This repetitive style of action described, action completed, is very common in the mythic literature of the ancient Near East.

Another repetition occurs in Kirta's response to King Pabil's offer. After King Pabil has specified his gift to Kirta, which we discussed above, Kirta responds. He does not simply answer yes or no, nor does he qualify his answer with new material as one might expect in a prose text. Instead he repeats, almost verbatim, the formulaic unit of the offer King Pabil has made. The parallel structures we described for the first unit are left intact in Kirta's response with only a few minor changes.

Kirta's refusal

lamā ʾanāku kaspa   wa-yaraqa ḫurāṣi
yada maqāmihu   wa-ʿabdê ʿālami
θalāθa sūsawīma markabti
bi-tarbaṣi bini ʾamati
pa-dā ʾên bi-bêtiya tatinu
tin liya maθata Ḫurriya

---

[35]One should be careful in speaking about *oral* Canaanite literature. Our position in this regard is provisional. The presence of poetic formulae is not limited to oral literature; indeed, it is a hallmark of most Akkadian epic and mythic poetry. The written and scribal traditions inherent in the Mesopotamian literature should lend some caution to our provisional analysis of Canaanite literature.

[36]Note Finley's comments (*The World of Odysseus* (New York: Penguin Books, 1982), p. 29) on the appreciation of Homeric poetry. "Sophisticated readers of printed books have often misunderstood the device of repetition as a mark of limited imagination and of the primitive state of the art of poetry. Thus French critics of the sixteenth and seventeenth centuries placed Virgil above Homer precisely because the former did not repeat himself but always found a new phrasing and new combinations. What they failed to perceive was that the repeated formula is indispensable in heroic poetry. The bard composes directly before his audience; he does not recite memorized lines."

naʿīmata šapḫi bukuraka

(*CTA* 14.3.137-44)

What need have I of silver and glitterings of gold,
a field hand and two perpetual slaves,
three horses with the chariot,
from the stable of a maidservant.
That which is not in my house, you shall give!
Give me Lady Hurriya,
your fairest first-born.

The structure of the two scenes match each other quite closely. We
would outline this structure as:

Pabil's offer	*Kirta's refusal*
qḥ ksp wyrq ḫrṣ	lm ʾank ksp wyrq ḫrṣ
yd mqmh wʿbd ʿlm	yd mqmh wʿbd ʿlm
θlθ sswm mrkbt	θlθ sswm mrkbt
btrbṣ bn ʾmt	btrbṣ bn ʾmt
qḥ krt šlmm šlmm	pd ʾn bbty ttn
wng mlk lbty	tn ly mθt ḫry
rḥq krt lḫẓry	nʿmt špḥ bkrk

The parallel structure continues in the four lines which immediately
follow the words of Pabil and Kirta.

Pabil's offer		*Kirta's refusal*	
ʾal tṣr ʾudm rbt	A B C	dk nʿm ʿnt nʿmh	A B C
wʾudm θrrt	B' C'	km tsm ʿθtrt ts{mh)	A' B' C'
ʾudm ytnt ʾil	A B C	dʿqh ʾib ʾiqnʾi	A B C
wʾušn ʾab ʾadm	B' C'	ʿp(ʿp)h sp θrml	A' B' C'
ʿwθθb mlʾakm lh		(*CTA* 14.3.145-47)	
lm ʾank ksp . . .]			
(*CTA* 14.3.133-37)			

(Give Hurriya . . .)

Don't besiege Udum the great,	whose beauty is like Anat,
Udum the well watered.	whose fairness is like Ashtart,
Udum is the gift of El,	whose eyebrows are lapis lazuli,
a present from the Father of humanity.	whose eyes are jeweled bowls.

Both scenes are made up of two bi-colons which are consistent in their technique of parallelism. Each of Pabil's descriptions of Udum can be outlined as A B C // B' C'; while Kirta's descriptions of Hurriya can be outlined as A B C // A' B' C'. In addition the poetic metaphors balance each other chiastically. When Pabil describes Udum, he first mentions its physical lushness and then its divine status. When Kirta describes Lady Hurriya, he employs goddess metaphors first and then physical images. We should also note the irony of the images chosen. Each of the speakers describes the element they feel is a threat to their own dynasty or royal "house." For Pabil, the fear of losing his city denotes the real possibility of his losing royal status, thus he pleads with Kirta to flee from his "house" *(ng mlk lbty)*. In this instance "house" refers to the physical structure of his palace and city. On the other hand, for Kirta, the thought of no progeny is equally troubling for the maintenance of his royal "house." Thus he commands Pabil to turn over what is not in his "house" *(pd ʾn bbty ttn)*. In this case "house" refers to his dynastic lineage. The literary play on the word *bêt*, "house," here recalls a somewhat similar word play in II Sam 7.

The overall symmetry of the two scenes is worth observing. Pabil's message is: "Take (all these items).......Don't besiege Udum," while Kirta's response is the reverse: "I don't need (any of these items)......Give me Hurriya!" As readers we know that an agreement is possible. The story has revealed to us that Kirta does not wish to conquer Udum. It has also showed us that Pabil is not a proud, recalcitrant opponent. But the heightened emotions of this particular moment prevent the needed exchange. What Pabil offers to save his own house is not what Kirta needs to form his own. Most important for our purposes is the contrast evoked by Pabil's summary plea: "Take, O Kirta, gifts upon gifts!" Kirta's response is nicely matched: "What's not in my house you shall give!" The two phrases are chiastically bound: Pabil declares, "Take *(qh)*....X" while Kirta answers, "not-X....Give *(ttn)*." The urgency of Kirta's request is perhaps reflected in the strong alliteration of labials and dentals *(pa-dā ʾēn bi-bêtiya tatinu)*.

We have given two arguments in favor of interpreting *šlmm* as "gift." One is that of the parallelism within the offer of Pabil ("Take silver, etc." // "Take gifts upon gifts"). The other is the parallelism between Pabil's offer and Kirta's reply ("Take gifts upon gifts" // "What's not in your house, give (to me)"). Other arguments for this position will be presented in the course of evaluating past scholarly opinion on this passage.

Many scholars accept this view of the *šlmm*. But a few have proposed alternate readings. Ginsberg translates "Take it Keret, in peace, in peace."[37] This is difficult because *šlmm* is in the plural. One could say that each *mem* is enclitic but this would be unusual. Also, the *šlmm* lacks a prepositional modifier, though the forms could be analyzed as adverbial accusatives. Ginsberg's translation has not been followed by others, even those who believe the *šlmm* does not consist of Pabil's gifts.

Caquot proposed that the first *šlmm* is a D imperative and the second is the noun "peace" (both, presumably with enclitic *mem*).[38] The translation proposed is "Prends Keret et accorde en échange la paix." But this translation does not follow from the use of *šlm* in the D as Caquot proposes. The verb connotes the compensation or requital of something owed. The exact opposite meaning is found in this text. Kirta is not the one who is to provide compensation or payment! Also the verb takes a concrete object (to fulfill a vow or pay a fee); the abstract object proposed here, "en échange la paix" would be odd.

Fensham feels the passage has a treaty background.[39] Drawing on the work of Munn-Rankin, he suggests the Akkadian root *salāmu* is the proper cognate for *šlmm* .[40] The verb *salāmu*[41] ("to form a treaty, be friends") and noun *salīmu* ("friendship") have a covenantal background. Moreover, the treaty nuance is used in some of the Akkadian documents found at Ugarit.[42] Fensham's argument suffers from a lack of parallel occurrences. After presenting the lexical evidence, he translates *šlmm šlmm* as "a treaty of friendship," a use unparalleled in the comparative material. Janowski follows Fensham's proposal of a treaty background, but improves his argument.[43] He notes the Akkadian construction *salīma leqû*, "to accept (covenantal) friendship" which nicely parallels *qaḫ...šlmm*.

[37]H. Ginsberg, *ANET*, p. 144.

[38]A. Caquot, M. Sznycer, A. Herdner, *Textes Ougaritiques, I: Mythes et légendes* (Littératures anciennes du Proche-Orient 7, Paris: Les Editions du Cerf, 1974), p. 523.

[39]F.O. Fensham, "Notes on Treaty Terminology in Ugaritic Epics," *UF* 11(1979), pp. 265-74.

[40]J.M. Munn-Rankin, "Diplomacy in Western Asia in the Early Second Millennium B.C." *Iraq* 18 (1956), p. 85.

[41]According to von Soden, *AHw*, p. 1013, the root is a secondary formation from *šalāmu*.

[42]See J. Nougayrol, *PRU* IV, p. 35, *riksu u salāmu KUR Ḫatti*, "treaty and friendship of the Hittites." Compare this to *CTA* 64.12, a Ugaritic treaty text where *šlm* is used to connote a friendship or a covenantal accord.

[43]B. Janowski, "Erwägungen zur Vorgeschichte des israelitischen *Šelāmîm*-Opfers," pp. 241-45.

In both cases the word friendship would imply a covenantal relationship.[44] Two problems arise from this view. If it is accepted that the second imperative, *qaḥ*, introduces a new item offered by Pabil, then Kirta's response becomes quite problematic. Since he clearly refuses each of the other items Pabil offers, why would he neglect the treaty offer? The parallelism of the formulae make this a difficult suggestion to accept. Kirta's response assumes only one thing was offered, the items of tribute. Moreover the repetition *šlmm šlmm* is problematic for Janowski. As de Moor[45] and Levine have noted, the repetition is emphatic, "Take O Kirta, *šlmm* upon *šlmm*." Janowski understands the repetition in the same way. But if *šlmm* is translated as an abstract accord of peace, this repetition becomes difficult.[46] To take friendship in great amounts is awkward.

If we reject these views which would see *šlmm* as different or separate from the items offered by Pabil we are still left with the problem of translation. De Moor suggested "gifts that are offered in order to obtain peace." The translation of Driver and Gibson, "peace offerings," is similar.[47] Both translations implicitly link the use of *šlmm* in this passage to the occurrence of the word in cultic texts. De Moor suggests that this context might disclose the original purpose of the *šlmm* rite itself: "If we may draw a parallel between this usage and the *šlmm* -offering it is conceivable that in the cult the *šlmm* were offered as a kind of tribute to prevent the deity from raging against his worshippers and to guarantee the people a peaceful existence."[48] We would not want to be quite that speculative.

Dietrich and Loretz provide another view. They also argue that *šlmm* means "gift" but they do not feel it is in any way related to the cultic term *šlmm*.[49] They argue this because the cultic *šlmm* consists of items which are different from those listed by king Pabil. The cultic *šlmm* consists of animals, while the *šlmm* offered to Kirta is similar to an inventory of tribute or greeting gifts. But we would disagree with this. As noted in the first section, one has every reason to believe that a technical term for an offering in the cultic sphere could have a

---

[44]See W. Moran, "A Note on the Treaty Terminology of the Sefire Stelas," *JNES* 22 (1961), pp. 173-76.

[45]J.C. de Moor, "The Peace-offering in Ugarit and Israel," in *Schrift en Uitleg* (Kampfen: J.H. Kok, 1970), p. 117. De Moor translates the term in accord with the root *šlm*, "gifts that are offered in order to obtain peace."

[46]See F.E. König, *Lehrgebäude der hebräischen Sprache II: Syntax* (Leipzig: Hinrichs, 1897), §§ 85-90; also see *GKC*, § 123 c-e.

[47]See J.C. Gibson, *Canaanite Myth and Legends* (Edinburgh: T & T Clark, 1977), p. 86.

[48]De Moor, p. 117.

[49]"Neue Studien zu den Ritualtexten aus Ugarit," *UF* 13 (1981), pp. 82-83.

different meaning in an epic or mythic text. In fact, to demand that the technical term *šlmm* retain its specialized cultic nuance in an epic text would be wrong. One could as well demand that the phonology and grammar of everyday speech be found in these literary texts as well. In sum, *one cannot simply assume that the culture-specific meaning of a cultic technical term retains its specialized meaning in an epic text.*

This insight into the semantic variability of cultic terms according to literary genre has been noted by B. Levine.[50] He has argued in a fashion very similar to our own that the term should be rendered as "gift or tribute." Unlike Dietrich and Loretz, Levine does not think the cultic and secular usages of this term are so unrelated. Yet he does not follow Driver, Gibson and de Moor by translating the secular usage in the Kirta text according to its cultic meaning (i.e. "peace offering"). He is content to translate this usage in the Kirta epic as simply "tribute." Levine argues that the "lexicon of the cult. . .appears to be largely derivative, taking its terminology from other spheres in the life of a society, and attributing specialized meanings to terms and concepts of broader application." [51] The usage of *šlmm* in the Kirta text provides "a singular instance in Ugaritic of what was the basic sense of the term *šlmm*, whereas in the descriptive ritual texts we have the specialized cultic appropriation of that term, used to designate a type of sacrificial rite."[52] His arguments will require some examination.

2. Akkadian *Šulmānu* and the Use of Cultic Terms in Mythic Paradigms

Levine uses Mesopotamian evidence to suggest that the earliest meaning of *šlmm* is "gift."[53] The Akkadian word *šulmānu* is described as a semantic equivalent of the biblical *šĕlāmîm*. The Akkadian word is most common in the correspondence of the Amarna period. This correspondence covers almost every part of the ancient Near East. We have references to *šulmānu* gifts from Egypt up to Ugarit and Asia Minor and even over to Assyria and Babylonia. It is best translated "greeting gift" and constitutes a symbolic (often diplomatic) present exchanged among the kings of this period. The word derives from a *qutl*

---

[50]B. Levine, *Presence of the Lord*.
[51]Levine, p. 17.
[52]Levine, pp. 17-18.
[53]In doing this, Levine is following G.B. Gray (*Sacrifice in the Old Testament* (New York: KTAV, 1971, reprint of the original 1925 edition). Gray's general theory was that sacrifices were best understood as a gift to the deity. Gray did not include the *šĕlāmîm* offering in this theory.

noun *šulmu* "peace, well-being" with an *ānu* ending. The noun *šulmu* is used often in the beginning of letters. It is what one king wishes on behalf of another. The formation *šulm* + *ānu* suggests the literal rendering "an instance of well-being" or "that which pertains to well-being." The gift, then, has an important symbolism. It is a token of the good will and beneficence existent among the kings.

Levine's interest is not in this common diplomatic usage. Instead he examines the (rare) use of the word *šulmānu* in the *Königsritual* [54] and the corresponding usage in the Enuma Elish. In the latter, a *šulmānu* gift is given to Marduk after he slays Tiamat (IV.134). In the *Königsritual*, the *šulmānu* is a gift given the king by his subordinates at his festival of investiture. The king, in turn, gives this gift to the Temple where the priests appropriate their own share. Levine concludes that "the gift to the hero (Marduk) becomes, in another context, the ordained ritual offering to the ruling god of the city, presented to him by the king of the city who rules in his name. . . . In this ritual we observe the step-by-step process by which a present to the king becomes an offering to the god, and is then appropriated by the priesthood."[55]

Levine finds evidence of a biblical parallel in the narrative of I Sam 11:14-15. In this text, Saul, having returned as a victor from battle, is made king amid the festive warriors. At Gilgal, where the victory feast occurs, the *šĕlāmîm* offering takes place: "they performed the *šĕlāmîm* offering there before YHWH." From this brief narrative summary Levine asks if "it is not possible that the *šĕlāmîm* were, in the first instance, gifts presented to Saul on the occasion of his victory and investiture as king over Israel, and that he, in turn, offered these very gifts as sacrifices to the God in whose name he ruled?"[56]

Many of Levine's observations are quite sensitive and perceptive. Yet there are several details in his analysis which are not quite accurate. Our analysis will begin with the Akkadian material.

The attempt to connect events of the cosmogonic myth with those of the royal cult is a well accepted method in scholarship. This is most evident in the myth-and-ritual school. This school believes most myth has an explicit cultic reflex. But even if one is uncomfortable with this broad generalization, it is difficult to deny that some connection is present. At the conclusion of the text of

[54]K. Müller, *Texte zum Königsritual* (MVAG 41/3, Leipzig: Hinrichs, 1937).
[55]Levine, p. 30.
[56]Levine, p. 32

the Enuma Elish itself we find the injunction that an equal of what has been established in the divine sphere be established on earth.[57]

At first glance Levine's connection of the *Königsritual* to the Enuma Elish is appealing. The parallel realms of divine order and earthly order are set forth quite clearly in the ritual text. In column one we find the cultic cry "Aššur is king, Aššur is king" as the divine patron of Assyria assumes his heavenly office.[58] In response, the king offers gifts to the statue of Assur (which become the priest's share); he prostrates himself *(šukênu, garāru)* before the statue and then provisions the offering table of Assur.[59] In column two the ritual activity is reversed; the king becomes the subject of adoration. He is formally crowned by the chief priest and Assur and Ninlil are called upon to bless his reign and solemnize the king as the true *sangû*, that is, "priest" of Assur.[60] Finally in column three the palace officials appear before their newly enthroned king. The activity of column I is recapitulated with two important changes. Now it is the earthly king who is honored with gifts by various palace officials. The latter do obeisance to their sovereign by prostration *(šukênu, garāru)* and by gift offerings.[61] These gifts to the king are then turned over to the Temple where they become the priest's share.[62] In return, the enthroned sovereign formally reappoints the subordinates to official posts within the kingdom.[63]

The most important aspect of this text for our purposes is the subordinate's gift to the king. The gift is called *šulmāna pānīa*, "a first *šulmānu* gift."[64] Levine is not interested in the formal parallels we have noted between columns one and three, where the king's gifts to Assur are analogous to the palace officials gifts to the king.[65] The parallel he finds illuminating is from the Enuma Elish as noted above.

But there are problems with this use of the Enuma Elish. To be sure, Marduk does receive a *šulmānu* gift after he slays Tiamat, and in view of the fact that Marduk does become the king of the pantheon later in the epic, one is

---

[57]Tablet 6:112: *tamšīl ina šamê īteppūšu ina erşētim līpuš-ma* (text has *lippuš-ma*), "a counterpart of everything he made in heaven, let him make on earth."

[58]K. Müller, pp. 8-9, line 29.

[59]lines 30-40.

[60]lines 25-36.

[61]Lines 1-6.

[62]Line 6.

[63]Lines 7-14.

[64]Line 5. In line 7 it is summarized as *nāmūrātē* gifts.

[65]The gift-giving is similar but the terms for the actual gifts is different.

tempted to interpret this gift as a token of homage. But gift-giving, in and of itself, is not always a token of homage. This is especially true for the *šulmānu* gift. In the correspondence of the Amarna age the term denotes a greeting gift which kings exchanged among themselves.[66] Its use in the first millennium is exceedingly rare.[67] The term seems most appropriate to an age when kings were "brothers" (*aḫḫū*) and international relations were regulated by diplomacy rather than imperial supremacy.[68] The *šulmānu* gift was a sign of the beneficence and wealth of an individual king. The expected return of a gift of similar quality from the recipient is good evidence for the equal standing of the two kings.

In some ways the *šulmānu* gift parallels Hebrew *minḥâ*. Although *minḥâ* is usually used in the sense of a tribute gift, it can simply mean "present" or perhaps even "greeting gift." P. Artzi compares the usage of *minḥâ* as "present" in the confrontation between Jacob and Esau as a functional equivalent to the Akkadian *šulmānu*.[69] An even better functional equivalent in our opinion is the *minḥâ* the king of Babylon sends Hezekiah in 2 Kgs 20:12 (= Is 39:1). The gift was sent with letters and messengers when Hezekiah became ill. We should also observe that this functional equivalence is noted in Targum Jonathan. In the Targum to I Sam 10:27, the translation given to the Hebrew *wě-lōʾ hēbîʾû lô minḥâ* ("and they did not bring him a gift") is *wě-lāʾ ʾětô lě-miśʾal bi-šlāmêh* ("and they did not come to inquire about his well-being"). Quite obviously, the Targum preserves the symbolic meaning of the gift-giving scene, symbolism which is as old as the LB period. Not to give a gift is to be unconcerned with another's well-being.

We are not attempting to equate Hebrew *minḥâ* with Akkadian *šulmānu*. We are merely saying that in certain cases they are functional

---

[66]The term has been subject to considerable examination. We would mention P. Artzi, "The First Stage in the Rise of the Middle-Assyrian Empire, *EA* 15," *Eretz Israel* 9 (1969), pp. 26-27; M. Liverani, "Elementi 'irrazionali' nel commercio amarniano," *OA* 12 (1972), pp. 297-317, and the important, comprehensive work of C. Zaccagnini, *Lo scambio dei doni nel Vicino Oriente durante i secoli XV-XIII* (Orientis antiqui collectio 11, Rome: Centro per le antichità e la storia dell 'arte del Vicino Oriente, 1973). We should also mention the specialized juridical usage of the term found in *MA* legal documents. These have been examined by J. Finkelstein, "The Middle-Assyrian *Šulmānu* Texts," *JAOS* 72 (1952), pp. 77-80.

[67]H. Tadmor and M. Cogan, "Ahaz and Tiglath-Pileser in the Book of Kings," *Biblica* 60 (1979), p. 500.

[68]Our sketch is subject to some exceptions. As one kingdom would become more powerful than another, the *šulmānu* gift would be less motivated by free will and more subject to enforcement. Thus Hittite kings reprimanded subject kings for sending *šulmānu* gifts to other kings beside themselves (*CAD* vol E, *šulmāna epēšu*). But even in this instance, when the *šulmānu* gift became a symbol of loyalty to a sovereign, it never replaced *mandattu* as the regular term for "tribute."

[69]"The First Stage," p. 25, n. 13.

equivalents. But the difference between Hebrew *minḥâ* and Akkadian *šulmānu* is small; it is primarily one of emphasis. Most often *minḥâ* refers to a tribute payment, rarely does it mean just "present," while *šulmānu* almost always means "present" though it occasionally refers to tribute.[70]

Let us return to the Enuma Elish. In tablet 4, line 134, where we see *šulmānu*, the context is one of message-sending. The context seems more appropriate to a gift of greeting than to formal homage. The gift of greeting is sent to Marduk along with an *igisû* gift, through an unmentioned envoy, after the wind has borne the "(good) news"*(busrāti)* [71] of Marduk's victory to the council. The gift is not formally presented by the donors themselves; Marduk is still at the battle site while the council remains waiting in assembly. The parties have merely exchanged messages regarding the outcome of the battle. Marduk's elevation to supreme king must await his fashioning the cosmic order and the building of Babylon. To be sure, the gifts sent by the council in response to Marduk's message of good tidings are weighted with perhaps a proleptic accolade for his awesome deed, but the formal execution of this accolade is still to come. What we see in lines 4:133-34 is best described as an exchange of messages between Marduk and the council, one which conveys the results of the battle.

The formal execution of the council's homage toward Marduk appears in 5:77-88 after Marduk fashions the universe from Tiamat's carcass. When the gods take note of this handiwork they praise Marduk and give him gifts. The gods are presented in the same chronological order as they were created in tablet one.[72] The creation of the gods themselves is recapitulated in the order in which they present themselves to the Divine Warrior. The adoration given Marduk is described in general terms. Some of the gods prostrate themselves or give other physical demonstrations of subservience while others give gifts. These gifts are called *qīšātu* and *igisû*.

What is important to the text is the mythic pattern: victory of the Divine Warrior, creation, and then formal homage. Levine errs in seeking to

---

[70]In addition to noting its symbolic importance as a means of expressing loyalty (see note 52) we would mention a *NA* text where Sargon II describes Ashdod's gifts to Egypt in request of aid as *šulmānu* (in H. Winckler, *Die Keilschrifttexte Sargons* (Leipzig: Pfeiffer, 1889), 188:33-36). For Hebrew *minḥâ* we should probably also mention the royal wedding Psalm (45:13). Here the gifts are best described as presents not tribute.

[71]Our reading differs from that of the common translations. We read *busrāti* "good news," following the *CAD* vol. B *(bussurtu).* Earlier translators had read *puzrāti,* "secret places." *Busrātu* is preferred because one would expect the victor to send back the good news of his victory. Why the victor would hide such an event *(puzrāti)* is difficult to explain.

[72]The order is Laḫmu, Laḫāmu, Anšar, Anu, Enlil, Ea, Damkina and the Anunnaki. Enlil, Damkina and the Anunnaki are not listed in tablet 1.

identify specific gift types as the central concern. One could say the same for the Assyrian *Königsritual.* The important pattern in this text is not the comparison of the divine council's gift of *šulmānu* to Marduk with the palace officials in column III of the *Königsritual.* Rather the pattern is in the *Königsritual* text itself. The gifts in column III offered by the palace officials to the king parallel the gifts made by the king to the city-god Assur. [73] The terminology is not the significant item. The gifts given to Assur by the king are not the same as the gifts given the king.

3. Hebrew *Šĕlāmîm* between Tribe and State

Levine has suggested that the *šĕlāmîm* may have played an important role in the nexus of monarchy and cult. In view of I Sam 11:14-15 when Saul returns victoriously to Gilgal to renew his kingship with a *šĕlāmîm* offering, Levine wonders if these gifts were not first turned over to Saul by his warriors and then, in turn, offered by Saul to the divinity by whose name he ruled. In the fashion, the biblical *šĕlāmîm* would closely parallel the *šulmānu* gifts of the Assyrian *Königsritual.*

We would reject this argument on the same grounds we rejected his connections between the *šĕlāmîm* of the *Königsritual* and the Enuma Elish. Levine is correct in perceiving a nexus of monarchy and cult, but again the issue is that of a mythic or ritual pattern, not the specific offering of *šĕlāmîm.* The parallel images of king serving his patron (national) god // people serving their king is present in biblical literature. But here, as in the *Königsritual* , the language is most often variable.

In the Deuteronomistic history the *šĕlāmîm* offering plays a strong role in the national, or covenantal festivals of Israel. Deut 27:7 specifies its explicit role in the context of covenantal renewal. Because this sacrifice is so closely tied with eating and festal celebration, its role in covenantal ritual is to be expected. In the ancient Near East there are many examples of covenants being

---

[73]We might also mention the contrast the text makes between the king's priesthood and that of the other priests. The king is the one who attends to Assur's offering table (lines 39-40 *paššūra rakāšu*) while the other priests concern themselves with the other gods. In Assyria, the king was the true priest of Assur. Thus there are at least three types of service in this text: the king in respect to Assur, the priests toward the other gods, and the people in general to the king.

sealed through a shared meal.[74] In Jos 8:31 the šĕlāmîm rite is associated with Israel's first covenant ceremony in the promised land.[75]

In the tribal period the rite served as a regular festival offering (I Sam 10:8) and as a special sacrifice in times of war. It was used as a means of calling the troops to battle (I Sam 13:9) and as a means of celebrating a victorious return (I Sam 11:15). Because of its political importance in militia musters and harvest festivals (where agricultural produce was collected and distributed),[76] it became important for kings to control. But the tragic figure Saul is mercilessly reprimanded for attempting to do so in I Sam 13:9. Nonetheless David twice offers šĕlāmîm (2 Sam 6:17, 2 Sam 24:25) in the process of solidifying his claims to royal control.[77] He is never reprimanded. By the time of Solomon, the king regularly offers šĕlāmîm three times a year (I Kg 9:25).[78] By this time the offering of šĕlāmîm becomes not as much a pan-tribal gathering as a festival for the palace entourage.[79] This is exactly the type of change in festal practice Robertson Smith observed in the transition from the tribal period to the era of the royal state. It is also a major theme in the prophetic critique of royal religious festivals.

---

[74]Cf. ARM VIII:13 and EA 162:22-24. Also see Ex 24, a text often cited by scholars who feel the šĕlāmîm rite was basically a covenantal one. We should also mention that other nominal and verbal uses of the root šlm in Hebrew are explicitly covenantal. See Jos 9:15, 10:4, 11:19; Jg 4:17, 6:24 among others.

[75]Its covenantal character might also be present in Jos 22:23,24. This difficult narrative about the Transjordanian tribes needs further study. The text cannot simply be concerned with the religious problem of a new altar. In the tribal period the cult served as the focal point of the muster and produce (as well as booty) collection. It seems very probable that the "sin" of the Transjordanian tribes was the installation of an independent cultic system that would not acknowledge the covenantal obligations of the Cis-Jordanian league. Other biblical narratives describe the fear that the Transjordanian tribes will not show up at the (cult site of the) muster. Most likely, the cultic site described in Jos 22 represented an attempt by the Transjordanian tribes to write their own covenantal charter separate from the Cis-Jordanian one. All of this, though, needs further study.

[76]Our best evidence for this is in the Covenant Code (Ex 23:14-17). There Israel is enjoined to send all her men to the three pilgrimage festivals with produce in their hands. These injunctions are missing from the latter priestly redactions of this festival laws (Lev 23 and Num 28-29). Also note I Sam 1-3. In I Sam 1:21 the LXX (both LXX [b] and LXX[l]) states that the tithes were paid at this tribal festival. McCarter (I Samuel (AB 8, Garden City: Doubleday, 1980), p. 55) assumes the validity of this longer reading but does not include it in his translation. We would read with the Greek.

[77]Note that in 2 Sam 6:17 David distributes food at the festival as a sign of his beneficence. As we know from I Sam 9:22-24, the festal meal was very important for demonstrating social standing within the community. These features of food collection and distribution have gone unnoticed in most treatments of the biblical cult. Note also the importance of offering sacrifices as a symbolic claim to kingship in the Panammu inscription (KAI 214). In this text to offer sacrifices to the royal patron, Hadad, is to claim kingship in the land (line 15).

[78]"Solomon offered the holocaust and the peace-offerings three times a year on the altar which he built for YHWH."

[79]See I Kg 3:15: "Solomon offered the holocaust and performed the peace-offering rite and made a feast for all his servants."

In sum, the festive offering of šĕlāmîm is very important in the royal period, but not because the rite is uniquely associated with kingship. On the contrary, the rite is a major league institution which the royal interests seek to take over. Moreover, the important detail in I Sam 11 is that Saul *does not* usurp control over this rite. This narrative, which has strong continuities with the old savior-figure stories from Judges, emphasizes Saul's place within this tradition. His power is charismatic yet circumscribed; Saul seeks no more power than what the people and YHWH grant him. This strongly contrasts with the picture of Saul in chapters 13 and 15 where he is actively seeking a cultic role. In this instance, he is subject to stern rebuke.

4. The Semantic Development of Šlmm in the Kirta Epic

We have argued at length against the hypothesis that šlmm has an original sense of "gift" or "present." But we have not accounted for how this meaning developed in the Kirta epic.

The term šlmm / šĕlāmîm is usually analyzed as an "intensive" or "emphatic" plural, an unclear and unhappy designation at best. The exact purpose or function of the intensive plural is not known. The Hebrew vocalization of this plural is based on a segholate pattern. Thus, it is commonly thought that it is derived from a singular noun *šalmu. Support for this can be found in the usage of this singular form as a cultic term in Amos 5:22 and well as in Phoenician epigraphic materials. This qatl noun, as well as its Akkadian counterpart, šulmu (qutl), derive from an original stative-adjective base šalim(a). This stem is common-Semitic and means: "healthy, complete or sound." The expected original meaning for this noun would be "health, completeness or well-being." Its related qatāl noun became the standard salutation in Hebrew and Arabic; while in Akkadian, this noun of greeting derived from the qutl stem, šulmu (šulmānu ; e.g. ana šulmānīka ašpuram).

The šĕlāmîm offering is best defined as a festive meal. It was noted earlier that this offering was consumed at Ugarit as well. It presumes an environment of friendly accord as the participants share a common meal. It would seem that this very environment of friendship and harmony allowed this sacrificial feast to assume a covenantal quality. As has so often been observed, the terminology of covenantal partnership presumes such an environment. The covenanters employed kinship terminology to express their close bond. These partners often exchanged their daughters and sons in marriage to concretize their "kin" relations. The alliance itself was sealed through a common meal. Most importantly, they also shared their most precious possessions in a highly symbolic gift-exchange.

The forming of any friendship or covenantal pact most likely presumed an act of gift exchange. In Akkadian, this is precisely how *šulmānu* acquired its meaning "gift." It is not original to the root, as Levine has presumed. Rather, it follows from the greeting formulas of friendly (royal) correspondents. When a messenger brought word from one king to another, he almost always brought a corresponding gift. This gift was an expression of both the well-being one king hoped for another and the well-being which existed between them.[80]   These gifts were not trivial. In vassal relationships, to not send a gift, or worse, to send a gift to a third party was to abrogate the accord *(salmu / šalmu)*; enmity *(nakru)* was the result.

A similar linguistic development in West Semitic is not impossible. It was noted above that agricultural produce was collected and often distributed at festal meals (see nn. 76-77). New relationships or covenants were cemented with a shared meal and an exchange of gifts.[81]   Moreover, the Targum to I Sam 10:27 is very important in this regard. This text shows us how deeply ingrained was the connection between gift-giving and the salutation of well-being. This was not simply an accident of the Amarna age, nor a peculiarity of Akkadian epistolary practice; it was constitutive of West-Semitic thinking too, well into the Common Era. In sum, the creation of "accord, or well-being" *(šalmu)* necessitated some type of symbolic act. We suggest that Pabil's offer of gifts to Kirta is an example of such an act. In the ancient Near East, one did not simply *wish* well-being *(šalmu)* for another, or between two parties. This desire for accord was most often accompanied by a symbolic act.

Our conclusion has some similarities to Janowski's proposal mentioned above.[82]   He connected Pabil's plea to *qaḥ . . .šlmm*, "take . . . *šlmm*," to the Akkadian idiom *salīma leqû*. Thus, he argued that Pabil is offering the possibility

---

[80]The close relationship between "gift" and "well-being" is exemplified in the use *šulmānu.* On one hand, an individual can both give and receive a *šulmānu-* gift *(šulmānu epēšu; šulmānu magāru),* while on the other hand one can hear *(šemû)* a *šulmānu-*greeting. The greeting, or sign of peaceful relations, was often inseparable from the physical gift.

[81]Cf. Akkadian *šulmānu ša isinni,* "the isinnu festival gift" *(EA 3.20).*

[82]See n. 43.

of a covenantal pact. This is not to retract our earlier arguments. It is quite unlikely that Pabil is offering a new item, an actual treaty proposal, in his plea to Kirta. But the close relationship between gift-giving and treaty-making should not be forgotten. Perhaps the poet is playing on this double meaning. Pabil's gifts were offered to obtain šalmu, that is, peace or accord. In this instance, for Kirta to take these gifts is to assume a friendly disposition toward king Pabil and his royal city. The acceptance of such a gift was a highly symbolic affair. It was a concrete manifestation of the peace or accord which was to exist between the two parties.[83]

D. Conculsions

This chapter has examined several cultic terms which also have very clear social and political meanings. It would be helpful to summarize the several ways in which these cultic terms reflect social and political realities and indicate how this information will be used in the following chapters.

1. The discussion began with the terms minḥâ and šay. In respect to etymology, both of these terms have a very broad and generic original meaning of ˈgift.ˈ In the course of time, several local dialects chose to specialize and narrow the meaning of these terms. The specialization and classification of cultic vocabulary which took place in the P document is not reflective of a crudely materialistic view of the cult as Wellhausen and von Rad intimated. Rather, this learned process of structuring cultic terminology is part and parcel of each and every cultic center in the ancient Near East. Although each Canaanite cultic center drew originally on a common pool of terms, the process of specialization in each specific cultic center led to a dramatic narrowing of meaning for many of the individual lexical items. This process of cultic specialization illustrates quite nicely the insight of Levine, who argued that the lexicon of the cult ˈattributes specialized meanings to terms and concepts of broader application.ˈ

Not all terms for ˈgiftˈ were specialized. In Hebrew, the term šay never developed the technical cultic usage it acquired in other Canaanite circles (Lachish ewer, Ugaritic sacrificial lists) or in the archaic Aramaic text from

[83]In a future monograph we hope to explore how two other Semitic lexical items have concrete cultic or gift-exchange meanings. The first concerns the root kbd. In the D, it is usually translated ˈto honor.ˈ In both Akkadian and Hebrew this act of ˈhonoringˈ can have a concrete association, the giving of a gift. The second term is Hebrew šamēaḥ, Akkadian ḫadû, both meaning ˈto rejoice.ˈ These terms do not imply so much a mental state (ˈhappiness, joyˈ) but rather a (festal) meal (see, provisionally, I Sam 11:15).

Zinjirli. The Hebrew word *šay* retained its archaic and more general sense of "gift." Quite different is the development of the term *minḥâ*. Priestly circles in Israel specialized this term quite narrowly; yet the broader more general sense was preserved in other spheres of life. In the Deuteronomistic history both usages are found. The term *minḥâ* offers a good illustration of how political and cultic spheres intersect. The double meaning of the term is reflective of the social structure of ancient Israel. Its political meaning "tax or tribute payment" reflects the perspective of the Israelite commoner (or subjugated foreign nation) who must regularly turn over a percentage of his produce. The cultic value "cereal offering" reflects the perspective of the priestly specialist who offers part of this produce as a cereal offering to God and then consumes the rest. In chapter three we will examine how this dual usage is employed literarily in an early Israelite narrative of social revolt.

       Other terms of the cult have a linguistic history similar to that of *šay* and *minḥâ*. For two more examples, see appendices A and B for a study of the terms *maśē't* and *mtn'*. *Těnûpâ* and *těrûmâ* might also be applicable to this category, but one should note the problems of etymology as discussed in appendices C and D.

       2. *Šlmm* represents a special case in the development of the cultic lexicon. This term exhibits a strong lexical uniformity among the cultic centers of Israel, Phoenicia and Ugarit. The political function of the term is also explicit in the Ugaritic Kirta epic. The political value of this term is clear from its context in the epic, but the question of how the political and cultic meanings are related is a somewhat difficult one. Scholars in the past erred in their study of this relationship. More often than not, they too closely associated the epic usage of the term with its usage in ritual texts. For scholars who denied any relationship between the two the reason given was that the constituent elements of the political and cultic *šlmm* were different. Thus they could not be relatable phenomena (so Dietrich and Loretz). Others, who felt the two were related erred in the opposite direction. They over-specificied the definition of the term in the cultic materials on the basis of its epic usage (so de Moor). A better methodological assumption would be to recognize that cultic terms and their social/political reflexes—though ultimately related as to etymology—need not be simple equivalents in everyday usage. Epic and mythic texts often exhibit meanings which are not reflected in the specialized and technical vocabulary of the local cult centers. In chapter four of this study, we will note how the usage of

maᶜăśēr, "tithe," varies in a similar way in epic and cultic texts. Some scholars in the past have rigidly attempted to align epic and cultic usage for this term. This has led to a number of distortions.

CHAPTER THREE

Ehud's Delivery of *Minḥâ* to Eglon of Moab: Tribute Offerings in Tribal Perspective

A. Introduction

The nature of the cult in the tribal period is much debated. It would be presumptuous to think that a new synthesis is readily at hand. In this chapter and the next, our aim will be closely circumscribed. We wish to probe just a few dominant issues regarding the place of offerings and gifts in the tribal cult.

As Robertson Smith observed the nature of sacrificial activity changes quite abruptly during the transition from tribal league to city-state.[1] Along with the arrival of a king and urban social structure came a sophisticated symbolic system of social hierarchy. The most important feature in the symbolic system is the parallelism between the divine king and his human counterpart. The prophet Malachi (1:7-8) makes this association undeniable when he states that sacrificial gifts to YHWH were analogous to gifts due a political overlord.[2]

In the ancient Near East these symbolic gifts had strong cultic and political functions as was observed in the last chapter. As a symbolic action, the act of formalized gift-giving communicated one's status within a given social group. When the two parties involved in such an exchange were not equals, the act of formally turning over a gift became an onerous affair. This meant that periodic gift or tribute delivery required both political and ideological sanctions. On the political level there was the suzerain's army which enforced proper delivery of gifts. On the ideological level there was the doctrine of divine kingship. This doctrine presumed that the divine king had a human counterpart,

---

[1] See our discussion in chapter one. We do not follow Smith's arguments as to what the exact changes were.

[2] See the recent work of J. Tigay, "Some Aspects of Prayer in the Bible," *AJSR* 1 (1976), pp. 363-72. Also note M. Greenberg, "On the Refinement of the Conception of Prayer in the Hebrew Scriptures," *AJSR* 1 (1976), pp. 64-70.

and thus, a gift given to this human king was understood to be at the same time a gift to the king's patron god.

In tribal Israel the idea of a human king ruling on behalf of a divine patron was not accepted. And herein lies the distinctiveness of the earliest Israelite cult. It was not the case that its worship alone was ethical, or that Israel alone denied the mythic motif of the deity's appetite for savory viands; rather Israel's cult was distinctive in that it was oriented around YHWH, the divine king, alone. Though this distinctiveness seems colorless at first, it had very important ramifications. By denying the right of human kings to "stand in" for their divine patron, Israel set herself apart from at least some of her neighbors. Many of the stories of early Israel's wars and conflicts with her Canaanite neighbors were focused on this very issue. When the opportunity presented itself, one Canaanite king after another would attempt to assert a territorial claim on Israel. If successful in his invasion, the king would then attempt to exact tribute payments from this new vassal in the name of the king's patron god.[3]

The symbolic act of formally turning over a tribute gift to an overlord is well known in the Canaanite materials. The formal process of this ritual has recently been examined in some detail by M. Gruber.[4] The periodic appearance of a vassal before his overlord was a well-known event in ancient Near Eastern affairs.[5] The motif of subjugation and formal gift-presentation is the nucleus of the story of Ehud (Jg 3:15-29). In this narrative, Ehud is appointed by his fellow Israelites to bring an offering of tribute (minḥâ) to the king of Moab.[6] We can visualize the scene as follows: the king of Moab sits on his royal throne with attendants on the right and left. Ehud along with his fellow tribute-bearers (nôśĕʾê minḥâ) stand before this king ready to turn over their gift. They bow

---

[3]See J. Roberts' article, "The Davidic Origin of the Zion Tradition," *JBL* 92 (1973), pp. 341. He observes how religious ideologies parallel underlying political realities. For example during the Sargonic empire of Akkad the patron god Ištar is elevated in importance, during the first Babylonian dynasty Marduk rises in stature, while in some copies of the Assyrian Enuma Elish, Asshur replaces Marduk as the hero of the epic.

[4]*Aspects of Nonverbal Communication in the Ancient Near East* (Studia Pohl 12, 2 vols, Rome: Biblical Institute Press, 1980), pp. 182-320.

[5]See the dozens of texts cited in Gruber, *Aspects of Nonverbal Communication*, as well as Tigay, "Some Aspects," p. 374, n. 13.

[6]The archaic nature of many of the stories about Israel's judges is well accepted in recent scholarship. For a summary of the research see A.D.H. Mayes, "The Period of the Judges and the Rise of the Monarchy," in J. Hayes and J. Miller (eds.) *Israelite and Judean History* (Philadelphia: Westminster, 1977), pp. 285-93. The Ehud story is considered by all modern commentators to be one of the older narratives in this genre. On the antiquity of this narrative see J. Soggin, *Judges* (Philadelphia: Westminster, 1981), p. 53.

before this sovereign and perform their formal homage by presenting their gift to him.

The Ehud story begins with a situation not unlike one episode within the Baal cycle. In this scene, Baal is subordinated to his rival Yamm/Nahar. He must bear tribute as a sign of his status as a subject. We join the narrative with El's speech:

> O Yamm, Baal is your vassal,
> (O Nahar), Baal is your vassal,
> The son of Dagan is your prisoner.
> He will bear your tribute,
> certainly this god (or these gods) shall bring (your gift),
> certainly the sons of Qudšu, your present.[7]

With the aide of two divinely fashioned weapons Baal drives his nemesis from his throne *(la-kussiʾihu)*, the seat of his royal dominion *(la-kaḥθi darkatihu)*. [8] Presumably in the midst of this fray, the tribute is not turned over. The scene ends with the two combatants reversing their original roles. Yamm/Nahar becomes the captive of Baal, and Baal assumes kingship.

The Ehud story, though, acquires a specifically Israelite flavor. For tribal Israel, only YHWH was king. To recognize the office of human kingship on Israelite soil or in a foreign land was, implicitly, a form of idolatry. [9] It implied a recognition not simply of a human king, but of the patron god by whom he ruled. Specifically, in Jg 3 this meant that Israel's tribute-gift to Moab was a sign of the subject or vassal status of Israel's own divine patron. In Israel the claim that YHWH alone was king necessitated that only YHWH could receive Israel's tribute. YHWH's ultimate power as king depends on this type of cultic exclusiveness. Thus, the zealous limitation of Israel's cultic life to one patron deity had important social implications. Our thesis is that the Ehud story is a satiric description of the symbolic act of periodic tribute delivery. The story reaffirms the true character of YHWH's kingship by carefully denying Eglon the symbolic actions of subservience which earthly monarchs thought were their due.

---

[7]*CTA* 2.1.36–39.
[8]*CTA* 2.4.12–13 and 19–20.
[9]This is also observed by J. Levenson, *Sinai and Zion* (Chicago: Seabury Press, 1985), p. 66.

B Literary Structure of the Ehud Narrative

1. Outline of the Four Scenes

Following W. Richter we feel that vv. 12-15a are not part of the original Ehud narrative but rather constitute a deuteronomistic addition. Within the original Ehud unit (vv. 15b-29) four separate scenes can be found which, in turn, are divided by a series of three *waw* + noun (or, as we prefer to call them, disjunctive *waw-*) clauses.[10] The *waw* clause is a syntactical feature of biblical Hebrew grammar which often serves a major literary purpose: it demarcates narrative units.

The first scene describes the formal presentation of tribute to Eglon (vv. 15-19).[11] It ends with Ehud's request for a private audience with the king. Verse 20 marks the boundary of scenes one and two and is disjunctive in terms of syntax: "Now when Ehud had come to him, he was seated in the timbered [12] upper chamber all alone." Scene two is a description of Ehud's slaughter of Eglon (vv. 20b-23). It too is separated from scene three by a marked disjunction: "Now when Ehud had gone forth, then the servants came in (v. 24a)." Scene three (vv. 24b-25) describes the foolish delay of the Moabite royal guard. They do not immediately perceive what fate has come upon their king. In scene four (vv. 26b-29) the Israelites quickly answer the summons to war given by Ehud. They take their positions by the Jordan river and slay the hapless Moabites. Again the last two scenes are separated by a marked disjunction: "But as for Ehud, he escaped while they tarried, and he crossed over (to Israel) at the place of the sculpted stones (v. 26a)."

---

[10]This is very similar to the proposal which W. Richter developed in his, *Traditionsgeschichtliche Untersuchungen zum Richterbuch* (Bonn: P. Hanstein, 1963), pp. 13-20. His analysis differs in that he sees the first three *waw* clauses as the central structural features of the narrative. Richter labels some of these *waw* clauses, *ḥāl*, 'temporal" clauses. While he is correct in doing so, the use of Arabic grammatical terminology is not helpful. Hebrew has fewer particles than Arabic to indicate a specific manner of subordination. Hebrew is much more reliant on word order to convey this information. Thus, while *waw* + noun grammatically marks a temporal (*ḥāl*) clause in Arabic, only the context would suggest such a translation for Hebrew. Although the Arabic *ḥāl* clause is related to the Hebrew *waw* + noun clause historically, the use of Arabic terminology is misleading. Whereas the Arabic clause is grammatically marked as temporal, in Hebre, *waw* + noun clauses can have other syntactical functions. This problem of terminology serves to highlight the need for a better description of Hebrew syntax. Richter is to be applauded for his efforts, even if we quibble with his choice of terms.

[11]Verses 12-15a are part of the deuteronomistic redaction. Cf. W. Richter, pp. 1-13.

[12]On this translation of *mqrh*, see Stager, "The Archaeology of the Family in Ancient Israel," *BASOR* 260 (1985), p. 16.

The disjunctive clauses are not the only signs which mark the four scenes as integral units. Within the scenes themselves we have signs of literary integrity. Scene three opens with the Moabites' appraisal of the situation: "They noticed right away that the doors were locked." It ends with a similar construction, "they opened the door and right before them was their lord, fallen to the ground, dead." Both sentences use the Hebrew particle *hinnēh*, a word that is common in clauses related to perception, but one that is difficult to translate.[13] It emphasizes the immediacy or the here-and-nowness of the situation. At the beginning and the end of this scene the Moabites are observing. In both instances, one with the doors locked, the other with the doors opened, the Moabites have little control over what is in front of them. They are helpless as well as foolish.

Scene four is similarly bound by its opening and closing lines. The section begins with Ehud's escape *(mlṭ)* to *Śĕ'îrâh*. It closes with the notice that no Moabite escaped *(mlṭ)* Israel's act of war.[14]

2. Scenes One and Two

Let us now turn to the first two scenes of this story (vv. 15-19 and 20b-23). These two scenes have the most relevant events for our study: the delivery of *minḥâ* and slaughter of Eglon. The description of this process has surprisingly little interest in character development. In fact, the verbs used in the beginning of the story serve only to describe the movement of the principal characters *(šālaḥ, yāṣā', bā', šāb, qām)*. In this manner, the story of Ehud is very different from those of other northern savior figures like Deborah, Gideon and Jephthah. The latter give us much more detail especially in regard to their summons to deliver Israel. In contrast to this the Ehud story puts special emphasis on several parenthetical physical descriptions. These include the sword of Ehud, the slaughter of Eglon (both are described in detail), and the physical appearance of

---

[13]Alter's translation 'and, look' is most inelegant (p.40).

[14]Biblical scholars in the past (G.F. Moore, *Judges* (ICC 7, Edinburgh: T & T Clark, 1895), pp. 90,102 and C. Burney, *The Book of Judges* (New York: KTAV, 1970), p. 67) have described the double use of *mlṭ* "to escape" in verse 26 as evidence of a doublet. They see no logical explanation for mentioning Ehud's escape twice. Our own analysis of the structure of the Ehud narrative as a whole would make such an hypothesis unnecessary. Both usages would be structurally important. The first use of the verb *(nimlaṭ)* marks the initial verb in the disjunctive sequence. The second use of the verb *(wayyimmālēṭ)* begins the narrative sequence of converted imperfects. This second narrative use is picked up again at the end of this section with the notice that no Moabite escaped *(wĕlō' nimlaṭ 'îš)*. This is a common idiom of holy-war narrative, though, and may not be of any literary significance.

both Ehud and Eglon. We would argue that this lack of character development serves a narrative purpose. The writer is not interested in Ehud and Eglon as individuals, but rather as symbolic role-players in an act of formal homage. This will become clear in the course of our exegesis.

The narrative begins with a typical motif. Israel is to bring tribute to Moab. Nothing in this description of the delivery is out of the ordinary. Ehud is commissioned as the messenger. He is accompanied by fellow Israelites who do the actual carrying of the gift.[15] And he, in fact, turns the gift over to Eglon. From an examination of the ancient Near Eastern iconography one could (as could any Israelite) fill in this picture of presentation. [16] Eglon was seated on his royal throne as Ehud and the Israelites came before him.[17] As in all other messenger scenes in Canaanite literature, no doubt Ehud performed the proper genuflections before the king as a sign of his obeisance and servanthood.[18]

But alongside this rather banal description are points of tension. The story begins with the standard motif of Judges: YHWH has raised up a savior (môšîaᶜ), Ehud, one of the great left-handed Benjaminite warriors.[19] But immediately juxtaposed to this reference to a divine commissioning is a most unusual statement: "And the Israelite sent tribute by his hand to Eglon, king of Moab (v. 15b)." This is certainly an odd mission for a savior of Israel! No sooner has YHWH raised up a savior, then Israel sends him off to Moab as a tribute bearer. Why would this renowned warrior and savior be sent with tribute symbolic of subjugation?

Sandwiched between this commission to bear tribute and the actual delivery is the rather unusual and not so brief mention of Ehud's sword (v. 16) and his act of fastening it to his right leg underneath his garment. Finally when the narrator tells us of Ehud's actual presentation of tribute (wayyaqrēb) he includes the parenthetical remark: "now Eglon was a very fat man (v. 17)." Both of these details, the sword and the mention of corpulence have no narrative role in this

---

[15]The idiom nāśā' minḥâ, "to bear tribute," is common in the Bible. The Akkadian equivalent is bílta našû.

[16]Compare the Ahiram sarcophagus (ANEP 456-58) or one of the Megiddo ivories (ANEP 332). In both cases the king is seated on a cherub throne with supplicants bearing gifts.

[17]Almost all commentators recognize the iconography or "picture" which this narrative assumes. See for example, G. Moore, Judges p. 93; C. Burney, The Book of Judges, p. 71 and A. Penna, Giudici e Rut (Turin: Marietti Editioni Ltd., 1963), p. 71. The scene is conventional in all respects.

[18]This procedure is common in Israelite, Canaanite and Mesopotamian literature. We will examine some examples below.

[19]Cf. Jg 20:16. We believe that the mention of Ehud's left-handedness is an allusion to this apparently well-known warrior group.

first scene. These details, together with the tension created by a great savior and warrior bearing tribute, await further explanation.

Each of these details is taken up in scene two and their ultimate purpose is made clear. Whereas earlier Israel had sent *(wayyišlĕḥû) minḥâ* through the hand of Ehud *(bĕyādô)*, now Ehud sends forth his hand *(wayyišlāḥ ʾet yād šĕmōʾlô)* to slay the enemy king. The passive role of Ehud's "hand" is replaced by an active one.[20] This active role is much more becoming for a left-handed Benjaminite warrior. Through this act of slaughter, the purpose of Yahweh's raising up a left-handed savior becomes clear. Likewise, the description of the sword and the fat king now finds an explanation. The sword bound to Ehud's right thigh (v. 16) is unsheathed (v. 21) and used to slay this foreign suzerain who would claim kingship over Israel.

Several other narrative elements of scene one are paralleled in scene two. One would be the ruse Ehud employs to gain access to Eglon's private chamber. In the first scene, Ehud approaches Eglon, after sending the Israelites away, and says "I have a secret matter *(dĕbar sēter)* for you, O king." When the next scene opens, Ehud reformulates his request: "I have a word from God *(dĕbar ʾĕlōhîm)* for you." The use of *dābār*, "word, matter, thing" is deliberately ambiguous. What Ehud possesses, Eglon will not hear.

The formula of address is also significant in both scenes. Ehud initially addresses the king with what appears to be a rather colorless vocative "O king." But a closer inspection reveals that this expression lacks the usual accompanying honorific term *ʾădōnî*, "my lord."[21] In excluding such an honorific, Ehud is denying his allegiance to Eglon. In the Bible, as well as in extra-biblical sources, one always uses the two together.[22] This neglect to address the king as "my lord" alerts the reader to Ehud's rebellious attitude. Also one should note that Ehud refers to himself in the first person. This is uncharacteristic of formal addresses.

---

[20]This was noted by L. Alonso-Schökel,"Erzählkunst im Buche der Richter," *Biblica* 42 (1961), p. 152.

[21]R. Alter, *The Art of Biblical Narrative* p. 40.

[22]For the Bible see I Sam 24:9; 2 Sam 3:21, 4:8, 9:11, 13:33 and *passim*. We have counted over 50 occurrences of the two and none of simply *hammelek*. Note also the Amarna correspondence. The standard formula of address in these letters employs both *bēlu*, "lord" and *šarru*, "king."

One would expect Ehud to refer to himself elliptically, in the traditional manner, as "your servant" *(ʿabdĕkā)*. [23]

This motif is continued in the second scene when the "secret matter" turns out to be a word from God. In this instance Ehud drops the honorifics altogether. His diction matches his action. Ehud is no longer a humble supplicant to the king; rather, the king is about to become an "offering" for Ehud's patron deity. These small narrative details are excellent examples of Ehud's role as a symbolic figure. The formula of address given by a messenger bearing gifts or tribute was well known. As noted in the last chapter, such gift-giving activity had a highly symbolic role in the culture of ancient Near Eastern city-states. Our writer clearly has this symbolic role in mind, only he uses Ehud's peculiar manner of formal address to besmirch Eglon's royal status.

We have mentioned the important role several physical descriptions play in the narrative: the description of the sword, the physique of Eglon, the arm of Ehud and the extensive account of the actual murder. Another important element is the physical positioning of the two principal characters. In scene one Eglon was most likely seated while his attendants stood beside him and Ehud stood before him. In a similar fashion scene two begins with Eglon seated *(yôšēb)* in his upper chamber. As was probably typical in all messenger scenes, Ehud approached the seated king and stood before him. The physical position of each individual participant describes the hierarchy of social structure. Even the biblical idiom reflects this important fact: to stand before someone *(laʿămōd lipnê PN)* is to be in service to him, while to be seated *(yôšēb)* can refer simply to acting as king.[24]

In this respect the response of the king to Ehud's announcement, "I have a word from God for you," is significant. The king promptly rises from his chair, and then Ehud kills him. We read the text as follows:

wayyāqōm mēʿal hakkissēʾ (wĕʿeglôn qārôb ʾēlāyw
wayhî kĕqûmo)[25] wayyišlāḥ ʾēhûd ʾet yād śĕmōʾlô......

---

[23]See for example 2 Sam 9:11. It is a standard means of talking about oneself in the Lachish letters (2:3-4; 3:1; 4:3 and *passim*, my thanks to S. Olyan for these references). Perhaps this is another symbolic statement concerning Ehud's true mission. YHWH alone is his lord *(ʾādōn)* and only to YHWH is Ehud a vassal *(ʿebed)*.

[24]For *yôšēb* as a metaphor for "ruler," see N. Gottwald, *The Tribes of Yahweh* (Maryknoll: Orbis Books, 1979), pp. 512-30.

[25]We read with the LXX, but with some reservations. The MT is haplographic, perhaps by *homoioarkton*, but this is difficult. The only similarity is with the initial waw: wĕ-ʿeglôn ... wayyišlāḥ. One would like to see a bit more similarity as an inducement for a haplography.

And he rose from his chair (throne).
(Now Eglon was close to him.[26]
And upon his arising,) Ehud sent forth his hand.....

Rabbinic midrash interpreted this arising as a sign of reverence by Eglon for Ehud's God.[27] Even though this midrash may appear too pious for modern scholars, it does show sensitivity to the symbolic importance of Eglon's movement in the narrative. His arising from his seat showed respect for Ehud's mission.[28] What was a symbolic role of subordination in scene one becomes an act of rebellion in scene two.

As in other cultures, the rules of etiquette regarding social hierarchy and its symbolic expression were well known. In the Baal cycle this topos of using non-verbal expression as a means of narrative development is quite pronounced.[29] We think here of the sending of messengers by Yamm/Nahar to the divine assembly. There, the gods sat in council. El, the leader and head of the council was seated while Baal stood by his side. Yamm/Nahar emphatically instructs his servants how to position themselves in front of the council before they speak.

taba‘ā ǵalmā(-mi ʾal taθibā)
ʾidaka pānīma ʾal tatinā
‘im puḫri môʿidi
tôka ǵūri lvlv
la-pa‘nê ʾili ʾal tappulā
ʾal tištaḥwiyā puḫra (môʿidi)
(qāmā-mi ʾammiru ʾammiȓā
θiniyā da‘takumā

[26]If this reading is original then the comments of many commentators about Ehud's "left-hand" are misplaced. Many feel that Ehud's left-handedness in our narrative allows him to slay the king by surprise. His reaching into his garment with the left-hand is not perceived as dangerous by the king. But if the king is already close to Ehud, such a narrative device is not needed. The action would have occurred too quickly for the king to respond. We believe the initial mention of Ehud's left-handedness is an allusion to his membership among a Benjaminite warrior clan. The mention of his sending forth his left hand in this verse corresponds to the passive role of that very hand in the first scene. The element of surprise seems less than likely if Ehud is already standing next to Eglon.

[27]Ruth's entrance into Israel and her subsequent role in the genealogy of David was later seen as a reward for the piety displayed by her fellow Moabite Eglon (*Ruth Rabba* on Ruth 1:4).

[28]A similar motif is found in Is 49:7. There, foreign kings are said to arise and then prostrate themselves before the servant of the Lord. Presumably the action envisioned would be the rising from a royal throne in recognition of the superiority of the Lord's servant.

[29]See Mark Smith, "Divine Travel as a Token of Divine Rank," *UF* 16 (1984), p. 359. Also see Gruber, pp. 301-03.

(*CTA* 2.1.13-16)

"Leave, lads, (do not tarry (lit. sit down))
Now, set your faces[30]
to the assembled council
in the midst of the mountain *lvlv.*

At the feet of El do not fall!
Do not bow before the assembled (council!)

(While standing, give your spe)ech,
repeat your knowledge.

One should contrast this with a more typical appearance of a messenger or supplicant before El. Usually such a person would bow and do obeisance before conveying a message. Asherah's appearance before El is typical.

la-pa꜄nê ꜄ili tahburu wa-tiqalu
tištaḥwiyu wa-takabbiduhu
(*CTA* 4.4.25-26)

At the feet of El she bows and prostrates herself,
she prostrates herself and honors him.

This same picture obtains in the Amarna and Ugaritic correspondence. The proper physical comportment of a subject king is a major literary motif of the letter form.[31] The subject says that he falls seven times to the ground before the king in the initial address (*ana šēpē šarri bēlīya 7 u 7 amqut*, "Seven by seven times I hereby fall at your feet").[32] Often there is reference to the footstool of the king, perhaps a hint of the picture of such a visit.[33] The sovereign king would

---

[30]The use of *꜄al* is difficult. Standard translations do not assume a negative. Gordon (*UT* 9:19) explained the usage of *꜄al* as asseverative. F. Cross has proposed emending the text to *l*, asseverative *lamed.*

[31]Gruber, pp. 201-31. This motif is found in both the Canaanite and Akkadian materials from Ugarit.

[32]For example, see *EA* 136:3-5. It is a standard formula. One should note the special use of the preterite in this sentence. It is translated in the present tense. It indicates action which is taking place 'right-now' from the perspective of the reader or hearer of the text. See W. Mayer, *Untersuchungen zur Formensprache der babylonischen 'Gebetsbeschwörungen,'* (Studia Pohl, series maior 5, Rome: Pontifical Biblical Institute, 1976), pp. 183-201 for a discussion of this usage of the preterite in Akkadian and other Semitic languages.

[33]Cf. *EA* 141:39; 195:9-10 and *passim.*

have sat on his throne while the messenger (representing the servant king) would prostrate before him. The Bible also has many references to YHWH seated on his throne as king,[34] replete with his own footstool [35] and humble worshippers bowed low or standing before him.[36] No doubt this image came from the royal court.[37]

The name attributed to this Moabite king suggests the motif of sacrifice. As commentators have noticed, the name Eglon is built on the noun *ʿegel* or ˙calf.˙[38] In this story, as will be shown below, the name assumes the meaning ˙the calf-like one.˙[39]

Support for this can be found in the very description of the king. He is called a *ʾîš bārîʾ mĕʾōd* ˙a very fat man.˙ The diction is significant. The adjective *bārîʾ* is used 12 times in the Bible, only 2 apply to humans.[40] The term most commonly refers to animal fatness rather than human. The more common term for human fatness is *šāmēn* which, curiously, is used in just this fashion in v. 29. The choice of our writer to describe Eglon's fatness as *bārîʾ* is unexpected and extraordinary.

The extraordinary character of the diction is reflected in the difficulty the ancient versions had with this word. The Greek *anēr asteios sphodra*, ˙he was very handsome,˙ takes the description as a positive one. A rather unusual choice

---

[34] I Kg 22:19 and Is 6:2.

[35] Ps 99:5; 110:1 and 132:7.

[36] Ps 99:1-5 and Ps 96:7-8.

[37] We might add that the notice about Eglon's posture, ˙he was fallen on the ground, dead,˙ may be important too. The Hebrew idiom, *nōpēl ʾarṣâ*, is used elsewhere in the Bible only for describing adoration of a superior, it is not used to describe the dead men. Many Hebrew idioms for falling down dead occur in the Bible but none use the adverbial element *ʾarṣâ*. The Peshiṭta and the Targum curiously use the verb for prostration (*rĕmî*, passive participle) to translate Hebrew *nōpēl*, not their semantic equivalent *nĕpal*. If the diction is significant then the reversal is complete. Eglon abdicates from his position of authority by first rising to meet Ehud and then falling to the ground, the position of a humble supplicant. On the formulaic association of rising (*qûm*) and falling in prostrating (*nāpal, hištaḥăwâ*) see Gruber, p. 292-320.

[38] For example, see R. Alter, *The Art of Biblical Narrative*, pp. 37-41. See also L. Alonso-Schökel who first noted the folkloristic level of meaning in this name, ˙Erzählkunst,˙ pp. 148-51.

[39] This definition does not correspond to the onomastic type that Eglon represents. Properly the name should be parsed as *ʿegel* ˙calf˙ plus the hypocoristic *ʿôn* (< *ān*) ending (contra Soggin, *Judges*, p. 49, who says it is a diminuitive; he takes the folkloristic meaning as grammatical). A comparable name, *ʿglyw*, is found in the Samaria ostraca, (*41 line 1). The most likely meaning of the name would be *ʾDN* is a young bull.˙ In the Ehud story, the name has a folkloristic value and so denotes a ˙calf-like˙ individual. But perhaps the *DN* element was present in the audience's mind as well. The slaying of Eglon frees Israel from service toward both the divine and human king of Moab! One should also note that personal names which use animal terms are common in West Semitic. These types of names are often used for designations of the military elite or the nobility. See P.D. Miller, ˙Animal Names as Designations in Ugaritic and Hebrew,˙ *UF* 2 (1971), pp. 177-86.

[40] The term *bārîʾ* refers to humans in Ps 73:4 and Dan 1:15. The other occurrences are: Gen 41:2,4,5,18,20; I Kg 5:3; Ezek 34:3,20 and Zech 11:16. Alter compares this term with the more common biblical term for fatling, *mĕrîʾ*. The term *mĕrîʾ* is used always in a cultic context, cf. 2 Sam 6:13; I Kg 1:9,19,25; Is 1:11; Ezek 39:18 and Am 5:22.

since the fatness of the king has such a gruesome narrative use in the second scene. But the rarity of this expression in the LXX reflects the fact that the Hebrew is peculiar.[41] The Syriac *dabrîr ṭāb*, "(He) was a very simple man," translates the expression in negative terms, but assumes this adjective is used metaphorically so as to refer to the king's character rather than his physical corpulence. The Targum reflects the exact sense for which we are arguing. It translates Hebrew *bārîʾ* by the term *paṭṭîm*, "fatling." This is the the very term Targum Jonathan uses on other occasions to translate the unambiguous Hebrew expression of animal fatness.[42] The animal imagery is quite evident to the Targumist.[43]

One argument against this understanding of Eglon as a "fatted calf" is that it serves to portray Ehud's act of political assassination as a human sacrifice. This would seem to be a repugnant literary image for Israelite culture which harshly criticized the sacrifice of humans among her neighbors. But usage of sacrificial imagery in narratives of holy war is not rare in biblical literature or in the Pseudepigrapha. In fact, Hebrew idiom contains the expression *hikkâ lĕpî ḥereb* which is used countless times in the Bible. [44] The idiom is best translated "to smite according to the mouth of the sword," or more elegantly, "to smite that the sword can devour."[45] The image does not seem to be an archaic linguistic vestige of a primitive stage of pre-biblical culture. The image of the sword consuming its sacrificial victim is found in many poetic and prose texts throughout the history of the biblical period.[46]

Other biblical texts are even more explicit. They characterize the slaying of enemies in holy war as nothing other than sacrificial activity. An excellent example can be found in Is 34:5-7.

> For my sword is filled in heaven,
>   now it shall descend upon Edom,
>   for judgment against a people doomed by me.

---

[41]It is used only four times in the Hebrew Bible: Ex 2:2; Num 22:32; Jg 3:17 and 11:23.

[42]For example, see I Sam 28:24 (*ʿegel marbēq*), II Sam 6:13 (*mĕrîʾ*, and I Kg 5:3 (*bāqār bĕrîʾîm*).

[43]Vulgate *crassus* is ambiguous. It refers to corpulence, but it can apply to animals or humans.

[44]Over 20 times in Joshua and Judges. Its also found J and E. It is not used by P.

[45]As is stated in *BDB* (p. 352). This idiom was not pleasing to all the ancient versions. Though the Syriac recreates it faithfully, the Targum translates *lĕpitgam ḥarbāʾ*, "according to the law of (war)." The LXX has both a literal rendering *en stomō machairas* and an interpretative rendering *en ponō machairas*.

[46]Dt 32:42; II Sam 2:26, 11:25, 18:8; Is 1:10; Jer 2:30, 46:10; Nah 2:14.

> YHWH's sword is filled with blood,
>   it is engorged with fat.
> The blood of lambs and goats,
>   the fat of the bowels of rams.
> For YHWH has a sacrificial feast in Bozrah,
>   a great (cultic) slaughter in the land of Edom.
> Wild oxen shall go down with them,
>   Cows amid the mighty steers.
> Their land will be filled with blood,
>   their soil engorged with fat.

Note the diction of holy war. The victims are given over to total destruction *(ḥrm)* and treated as slain animals *(ṭebaḥ)*. Moreover, the victims are none other than the leaders of Edom, here characterized as animals bound for slaughter. This holy war is none other than a sacrifice for God *(zebaḥ la-YHWH)* whose sword consumes blood and fat just as the earth does. The same theme of holy war as sacrificial slaughter is found in Ezek 39:17-20. Again the victims of this slaughter are the leaders of the foreign nations who are characterized as animals. Most revealing as a parallel to our narrative is Jer 46:10,20-21. In this narrative YHWH's war against Egypt is not only described as a sacrificial slaughter (v. 10), but the victims of this slaughter are none other than Egypt's military elite characterized as fatted calves (vv. 20-21, *ʿeglê marbēq*). YHWH's sword is said to consume (v. 14). It is important to note the interest these narratives show in regard to the Divine Warrior's sword. Both Ezekiel and Isaiah describe it with some care. For the latter two, *the most significant aspect is its hunger for fat.* The parallels to Ehud's sword could not be closer. Our author seems to have set in prose narrative a motif of broad mythic dimensions.

   If there are literary resonances in the narrative that Eglon is a fatted calf, some other details in the narrative might be significant. It is important to note when the writer chooses to describe Eglon as an *ʾîš bārîʾ mēʾōd*. Significantly, he does not choose to do so when he first introduces him in v. 15. Instead, the parenthetical remark is inserted just as Ehud presents the *minḥâ:* wayyaqrēb ʾet hamminḥâ lĕʿeglôn melek môʾāb, wĕʿeglôn ʾîš bārîʾ mēʾōd, "And he offered the *minḥâ* to Eglon, king of Moab. Now Eglon was a very fat man." Why place the description here, just as Eglon turns over the *minḥâ*, rather than when Eglon is introduced as a character in the narrative? Perhaps the writer wishes to juxtapose the offering of *minḥâ* with the description of Eglon as "a fatted calf." We have noted the semantic range of the term *minḥâ*. The term can refer either to a tribute payment or a cereal offering. Perhaps our author is playing with the meaning "cereal offering" in this usage and thus the association of *minḥâ* with fatted calf becomes quite understandable.[47] The association of the two types of offerings has many biblical parallels in all periods of biblical history and in most literary genres.[48] It was a standard and formulaic association.

The idiom *lĕhaqrîb minḥâ*, "to offer or present *minḥâ*," is a common construction for conveyance of a cultic offering.[49] It refers to the formal presentation of the grain before Yahweh. The verb *lĕhaqrîb* is not limited to grain offerings; it is common with animal offerings as well. It should be noted that the verb of presentation *lĕhaqrîb* can refer to the formal presentation of a gift to the king outside of the cultic matrix.[50] But the cultic nuance cannot be excluded from our narrative. This would appear to be justified by the close association of *minḥâ* offerings with slaughtered offerings.[51]

In summary, we see how the literary details of scene one are systematically picked up and completed in scene two. Many of the narrative details of scene one only find an explanation in scene two: the description of the sword, the corpulence of Eglon and the left hand of Ehud. Moreover, several narrative incidents are paralleled and contrasted between the two scenes. For example we have compared Ehud's "being sent" with tribute and Ehud's "sending" forth his hand, as well as Ehud's "secret matter" (v. 19) which becomes a "word from God" (v. 20).[52] We also described how the narrative dismantles the symbolic structure of the tribute presentation ritual. The narrative begins with a very stereotypical description of this motif. The social hierarchy is acted out symbolically, by the physical activity of the participants. The first sign of tension

---

[47]Penna *(Giudici e Rut)* notes the ambiguity of the term. Soggin *(Judges,* p. 50) suggests that this ambiguity might be relevant for the story. Targum Jonathon chooses to retain the ambiguity even though it had other expressions which would have made the sense "tribute" undeniable. The Targum's retention of an ambiguity here, though, does not necessarily mean that the Targumist was interpreting along the lines we are suggesting.

[48]I Sam 2:29; I Kg 18:29,36; Jer 14:12; Am 5:25; Ps 20:4, 40:7; Dan 9:27 and I Chr 21:23.

[49]See especially the many references in P: Lev 2:8, 6:7, 7:12, 23:16; Num 5:25, 6:16, 15:9 and *passim.*

[50]Ps 72:10.

[51]Additional support for this view may come from the Targum and Peshitta. In the case where *minḥâ* has an unambiguous political value, Peshitta and the Targum will often reflect this in their translation. This occurs in I Sam 8:2 and 6 in which case David makes Israel's neighbors bearers of *minḥâ*. In I Sam 8:6 the Peshitta use *maddattā*, a technical term for political tribute. The Targum uses *pĕrās* for both I Sam 8:2 and 6. In Judges 3:18, though a very similar sort of narrative, both Targum and Peshitta opt for the more ambiguous term "gift" (Peshitta— *qorbānā*, Targum— *tiqrûbĕtâ*). Perhaps both Targum and Peshitta realized that the bearing of *minḥâ* in Judges 3:18 had cultic resonances which were not present in I Sam 8:2 or 6.

[52]On these parallel features, see Alonso-Schökel, "Erzählkunst," p. 157.

in this symbolic form comes through the atypical address of the king by Ehud. Finally, the social hierarchy is overturned in scene two as Eglon rises to stand beside Ehud, receives the blow from the sword and collapses, prostrate on the ground, dead.

This narrative began with an unusual description of YHWH raising up a savior who thereupon set out to deliver an offering of *minḥâ* to a foreign suzerain. The narrative ends with the description of a radically different type of offering, the sacrificial slaying of the illegitimate foreign king.[53] No longer is Eglon's kingship a threat to YHWH's suzerainty. Israel's period of vassalage is about to end.

3. Scenes Three and Four

Scenes three and four continue to develop this theme of sacrifice. R. Alter has argued that Ehud's assassination of Eglon is an emblematic prefiguration of the eventual slaughter of the Moabite militia. He feels this link is reinforced by two punning verbal clues.

> "Ehud thrusts *(tqᶜ)* the dagger into Eglon's belly (v. 21) and as soon as he makes good his escape (v. 27) he blasts the ram's horn--the same verb, *tqᶜ* - to rally his troops. The Israelites kill 10,000 Moabites, "everyone a lusty man and a brave man" (v. 29), but the word for "lusty," *shamen*, also means "fat," so the Moabites are "laid low (or subjugated) under the hand of Israel (v. 30) in a near parallel to the fate of their fat master under the swift left hand of Ehud.[54]

Let us first discuss the use of the word *tāqaᶜ* . One might suggest, against Alter, that the double occurrence of this term is accidental or incidental and of no literary significance. But the first use of *tāqaᶜ* —to describe a sword thrust—is unique in the Bible. Why would the writer use the term in an unparalleled fashion? To answer this question it would be helpful to clarify the semantic range of this term.

Tāqaᶜ , has three basic meanings. It can refer to the striking or clapping of hands (Ps 11:15,17:18, 22:26, 47:2), the blowing of the shofar (Jos 6:4

---

[53]Alonso-Schökel, "Erzählkunst," p. 152, also notes the parallels between these two actions. In regard to the slaying of Eglon he writes: "Und die eigentliche Gabe ist das Schwert! Der Tribut wird nicht nur zum König hingebracht *(hiqrîb),* sondern in ihm hineingesteckt *(tāqaᶜ).* Was zunächst ironisch anklang, klingt nun tragisch aus."

[54]R. Alter, *The Art of Biblical Narrative,* p. 41. See also L. Alonso-Schökel who first noted the *tāqaᶜ* word play, "Erzählkunst im Buche der Richter," pp. 152-154.

and *passim*) or the driving of a tent peg into the ground (Gen 31:25; Is 22:23,25; Jer 6:3). It is used three times to describe a violent act. In Jg 4:21 Yael murders Sisera by putting a tent peg in his skull *(titqāʿ ʾet-hayyātēd bĕraqqātô)*; in I Sam 31:10 (I Chr 10:10) Saul's body is fastened to the wall of Bet Shan *(wĕ–ʾet gĕwîtô tāqĕʿû bĕḥômat bêt šān)* and finally, in II Sam 18:14 Joab kills Absalom thrusting darts into his heart *(wayyitqāʿēm bĕlēb ʾābšālôm)*. The first example is easily understood as a variant of driving in a tent peg. The mounting of Saul's corpse on a city wall is not dissimilar. The thrusting of darts into Absalom's heart is more difficult. Presumably the use of *tāqaʿ* here emphasizes the fact that the darts were *sunk* into Absalom's body. This would contrast with the normal sword thrust which would often impale the victim and then be pulled out for further use. The usage of the term in Mishnaic Hebrew would support this hypothesis.[55]

The preferred term to describe a sword thrust would be *dāqar*. This is the verb one would expect to be used for Ehud's action. Quite clearly the usage of *tāqaʿ* to describe Ehud's sword thrust is unusual. Is it the author's intention to link this act of slaughter with the following blow on the Shofar? There is additional support for such a linkage. In Israel as elsewhere in Canaan and even Greece a sacrifice was a necessary component in the muster of the militia. This theme is well-illustrated in the Kirta epic. In this text, El instructs Kirta to prepare for war. His instructions first call for a sacrifice before the troops are mustered.

> Enter (into the shade of the tent,)
> take a lam(b in your hands,)
>
> a sacrificial lamb in your right hand,
> a kid (in both hands.)
>
> a whole offering, your succulent food,
> take a *mas(rura)* bird of sacrifice.
>
> Pour wine into a silver (bow)l,
> into a gold bowl, mead.
>
> Ascend to the (tow)er top,
> mount the shoulders of the wa(ll,)
> raise your hands to heaven.
>
> Sacrifice to the Bull, your father, El,
> serve Baal with your sacrifice,

---

[55] *Y. Soṭa* 9. 23c, "knife sticking in his heart," or b. *Yebamot* 54a, "His membrum was inserted."

the son of Dagan with your game.

··········

··········

Provision the Southland that they may go forth,
the best troops of the south.

Let them go forth, provision (them)
your troops are a very great host. (*CTA*   14.1.65-86)

Burkert has observed a similar pattern in ancient Greece.

> Among the Greeks, a military expedition was prepared and
> ended by a sacrificial ritual. There was a sacrifice before
> setting off, then adornment and crowning with wreaths before
> the battle—all as if it were a festival. A slaughtered victim
> introduced the subsequent deadly action.[56]

There is a similar pattern in the Bible. The connections between
religious festivals and military musters are exceptionally close. Cross has called
them variants of one another.[57] Each was summoned by a trumpet blast. Each
was the occasion of sacrificial offerings, tribal feasting and the presentation and
distribution of offerings.

The clearest biblical text in this regard is I Sam 13:8-12. The text is a
description of Israel gathering before Saul at Gilgal. Saul had been strictly
admonished by Samuel to wait until he got there before proceeding to war.
Samuel is delayed and Saul subsequently feels constrained to go ahead with the
sacrifices. The tension Saul experiences in Samuel's delay presumes the necessity
of the sacrifice before the war. Without a sacrifice to YHWH, the participation of
YHWH in the sacral war is not assured. So important is this ritual act, that Saul
proceeds to take matters into his own hands and offer the sacrifices himself.

In an earlier narrative, Samuel as well had offered sacrifices before he
sent the troops to battle (I Sam 7:9-10). Other narratives of holy war do not
mention an explicit use of sacrifices, but they do mention the gatherings of militia

---

[56]W. Burkert, *Homo Necans: The Anthropology of Ancient Greek Sacrificial Ritual
and Myth* (Berkeley: University of California, 1983), p.47.

[57]"Epic Traditions of Early Israel," p.37.

at cult sites.[58] It is most likely that sacrifices were offered before these sacral wars began as well.

Let us return to the Ehud story. It can hardly be accidental that the author linked Ehud's slaughter of Eglon *(tāqaᶜ)* with the summons to war *(tāqaᶜ)*. Temporally, the summons to war follows immediately upon the act of slaughter. This is somewhat obscured in the text by the description of the Moabites standing beside the locked door. Yet, if one notes Ehud's movement, the close temporal sequence of first a slaughter followed by a muster of the troops becomes clear. Verse 24 states that Ehud has gone forth *(yāṣāʾ)* while the Moabites enter *(bāʾ)*. Ehud's action is picked up again in verses 26-27 where one learns what Ehud had done while the narrative had focused on the Moabites. He had escaped while the Moabites tarried by the door. He entered Israel *(bāʾ)* and sounded the trumpet. Ehud's activity can be summarized as (1) slaughtering *(tāqaᶜ)* Eglon, (2) escaping to Israel and (3) blowing *(tāqaᶜ)* the trumpet. The "sacrifice" of Eglon becomes a prelude for Israel's sacral war.

The intervening material in the temporal sequence of Ehud's escape is of tremendous literary value. The dilatory and obtuse actions of the Moabites are contrasted sharply with the resolute and obedient behavior of the Israelites. Moab is bereft of king, while Israel marches as one behind her deliverer.[59] YHWH has decreed a victory. Even the slaughter of the Moabites recalls the slaughter of their king. Some of these Moabites are called "robust," or "fat" *(šāmēn,* v. 29) in quite the same manner as their now-dead "fat" king.

The contrast of Israel and Moab is made more effective by the fact that scenes three and four are partially congruent in terms of their time-framework. While the Moabites delay and stand outside the room of their dead king, Ehud escapes and musters the militia. The attack itself is described as a surprise. Evidently Israel had come upon the Moabites before the royal guard could ready a response. Israel took its position along the Jordan and rather than meeting Moab in pitched combat, they slaughtered the Moabites in their attempt to make a hasty retreat. The delay of the Moabites allowed them no time to repel the hasty Israelite onslaught; their only recourse was to flee.

---

[58]Num 1-10 and Dt 20 are programmatic statements to this effect from two different circles, the priestly and Deuteronomic. In Judges, wars are commonly called for and begun from cult sites (4:6; 10:17 and 20:2). Even Joshua, which presumes one large pan-tribal conquest of the land, mentions several forays from and returns to Gilgal.

[59]The emphatic word order *(wĕhûʾ lipnêhem)* of the narrative emphasizes that Ehud is at the lead.

The literary structure of scenes three and four is parallel to that of one and two. Within both of these pairs we find stark narrative contrasts. In the last two scenes this contrast is made all the more effective by the temporal overlap of some of the activity. While the Moabites foolishly delayed outside the door of their dead king, the obedient Israelites hastened to their savior Ehud. In the first two scenes the contrast is not temporal, but rather symbolic; what appeared to be a tribute delivery on the part of a vassal became an offering of a wholly different nature.

In all four scenes one sees allusions to sacrifice and offering. These themes were central to the beginning of the narrative but were picked up in the closing two scenes as well. It has been noted how this binding was effected by common diction *(tāqaʿ)* and the historical pattern which was presumed therein. Eglon is satirized as an obtuse, rotund king who must be slaughtered. But, there are literary resonances of another type of deed in this act of political assassination. In some senses, Eglon becomes the "fat young bull," prepared for sacrifice.

The image of the human king as one to whom gifts and offerings are due is satirized in this narrative. The tribute delivery scene was used by king Eglon as a time for demonstrating his claims to power. In this ritual, there was a public demonstration of the power Eglon's god had bestowed upon him. Like the divine king, he too sat on a throne with attendants surrounding him while loyal supplicants honored him with gifts. Unfortunately for Eglon, tribal Israel could recognize no human pretender to kingship. Thus, Ehud's initial delivery of the *minḫâ* offering becomes a prelude to a dramatically different type of ritual act. The slaughter of the "fat young bull" (Eglon) initiated a holy war which abruptly ended the Moabites subjugation of Israel.

CHAPTER FOUR

Sacred and Secular Evaluations of the Tithe

A. Israel between Tribe and State

1. Introduction

The cult of earliest Israel experienced at least two types of social and political tension. On the one hand there were the encroachments of neighboring Canaanite kings who attempted to deprive the league of its autonomy by extracting regular *minḥâ* gifts. This is a socio-economic explanation of the danger of "serving other gods." To become a vassal to a neighboring king entailed a covenant which declared the supremacy of the sovereign king and the god by whom he ruled.[1] Israel was not to enter into any such covenant. Israel's cultic dues were to be given to YHWH alone.

Another equally important concern had to do with the process of collecting (and sometimes, re-distributing) the offerings. One first reads of this concern in the Covenant Code. In this document each male is required to present himself before the patron deity three times a year with an offering (Ex 23:14-17). Because these festivals constituted the only "routinized" (to use Weber's term) mechanism for gathering the tribal clans, they also provided the only means for gathering and re-distributing agricultural goods on a pan-tribal basis.

For our purposes, it is important to note that the gathering of agricultural goods and the appearance of all males before the patron deity occurs without the enforcement of a strong, centralized institutional structure. Moreover, the contributions required could not have been large because the requirements of the pan-tribal religious and political institutions were few. Such was not the case with the onset of the monarchy. The acquisition of a standing

---

[1]J. Levenson, *Sinai and Zion* (Chicago: Winston Press, 1985), p. 86.

army, the building of major cities and military installations required much larger sources of revenue. No doubt much of this revenue came from the indigenous population. In addition, the state could no longer depend on the more voluntary (and hence less enforceable) mechanisms for collection of grain from the tribes. Instead, the state instituted programs of forced conscription and more regular, enforceable tax collection.

During the transition to statehood, Israel became more and more like the Canaanite city-states which surrounded her, both in terms of social structure and in religious ideology. She borrowed extensively from this sophisticated and literate culture. She not only copied the physical architecture of the Canaanite Temple, but much of its descriptive vocabulary was incorporated into Israel's Psalmody and mythic lore. As one could expect, there was much resistance to many of these changes. In particular, we are interested in the changes which occurred within the system of cultic offerings, specifically that of the tithe. To isolate these changes, we have chosen to examine two biblical texts (Gen 14:18-20 and I Sam:10-17) from the same era which comment on this new institution of the state. Before we turn to these texts, some preliminary remarks about the nature of the tithe in Northwest Semitic culture will be helpful.

2. The Tithe in Canaanite Culture

The tithe was the central means of revenue collection in the Canaanite world. Unlike other offerings and imposts, the tithe did not consist of luxury goods, nor did it always include livestock.[2] It consisted primarily of grain, but also included olive oil and wine. The grain as well as "the products of the vat" were the very staples of the diet and economy. But its banal nature masks its major significance. The importance of the tithe for the basic maintenance of the economy more than made up for its lack of ostentatious qualities.

The position and evaluation of the tithe in biblical culture cannot be fully appreciated without a clear understanding of its seminal importance in the basic economy of Canaan. Our best sources for documenting its position come from the Ugaritic economic texts, the P document and the Chronicler. One problem in comparing the biblical and Ugaritic material is the different

---

[2]For Ugaritic examples, see the discussion below. In the Bible, the tithe is variable as to its makeup. In Num 18:27 and Dt 14:22-23 the tithe consists of grain and products of the vat. In Lev 27:30-33 the tithe includes livestock as well.

evaluations made of the tithe by the two cultures. In much of the biblical material the tithe is treated as a sacred donation to the priestly class while at Ugarit the tithe is most often a secular impost due to the king or one of his servants. We will examine the problems this variability provides later. [3] For now, it is important to see the similarities. In both Ugarit and Israel the tithe consisted of the grain, oil and wine, the staples of the Levantine economy.   In both cases it was the responsibility of the central authorities to collect, store and redistribute it.[4]

In Ugarit, as elsewhere in the ancient world, the village is the unit of primary production. The agricultural surplus it produces is conveyed to urban centers. Within the urban center the surplus allows a degree of economic differentiation. Specialists in crafts, the military, and administrative and cultic personnel all subsist to some degree on this surplus which is taken from the village as its tithe (Akkadian *eširtu*, Ugaritic *ma'śaru*). In Ugaritic these royal dependents are called *bnš mlk*, "men of the king" (cf. the Akkadian counterpart *ardē šarri*, "slaves of the king") and include priests *(qdšm, khnm)*, traders *(mkrm)*, homebuilders *(ḥrš bhtm)*, chariot makers *(ḥrš mrkbt)*, warriors *(θnnm)*, and administrators *(mru' skn)*.

The treatment of priests is noteworthy. In texts which itemize payments *(ḥpr bnš mlk)*, the priests are not differentiated from other specialists. They are subsumed under the rubric *bnš mlk* for accounting purposes.[5]

These same economic texts, on the other hand, treat the population of the villages very differently. In contrast to the interest in the royal dependents as individuals, the urban scribes perceived the village as a collective unit both in regard to taxation and conscription. This perspective is made clear by several documents. In *PRU* V.58 we have a tribute payment list to the Hittite king *(spr 'argmn špš*, "document of the tribute to the Sun"). Lines 70-80 list the various villages which must send tribute; while on the reverse, the individual royal dependents *(bnš mlk)* are itemized along with their tribute. In other taxation documents (*CTA* 69 and *PRU* II.176) the villages are always mentioned as a unit. There is never a mention of an individual villager paying a tithe. The same is true

---

[3]There are other problems the tithe presents for the biblical scholar. For example, some scholars are puzzled by the fact that the Holiness Code discusses the tithe in the context of votive offerings. Is the tithe a votive or obligatory gift? Kaufmann has argued that the tithe was originally a votive offering and remains so in the P document (see his *Religion of Israel* (Chicago: University of Chicago Press, 1960), pp. 190ff.). This view is nicely refuted by J. Milgrom in his book *Cult and Conscience* (Leiden: Brill, 1976), pp. 55-63. Another problem concerns the status of the tithe in Deuteronomy. On this subject, see Weinfeld, "Tithe," *EJ*, pp.1160-61.

[4]Lev 27:30-33; Num 18: 21-32; I Sam 8:15; Neh 10:39-40, 12:44, 13:5,12; II Chr 31:4-11.

[5]*CTA* 74,75,76,113,173, *PRU* 2.44, *KTU* 4.609 and 4.745.

for conscription. In several texts the number of men or days for which labor or military service is required is apportioned to villages as a whole but to the *bnš mlk* as individuals.[6] We should also note the practice at Ugarit as well as in Alalakh of giving a village as a gift to a son or daughter of a neighboring king.[7] What is emphasized in these documents is the agricultural yield (explicitly, "its tithe"). Another text records the gift of a city by king Ammistamru to Yasiranu.[8] The gift of the city includes: *šešu sikaršu ša   ma'sarīsa u immerātu maqqadu*, "its grain and beer, i.e. its tithe together with its sheep, i.e. its *maqqadu* tax."[9] Therein lies the value of the village as a gift.

In one such royal grant text from Ugarit, we might have an allusion to a priestly share in the tithe.[10] In this text king Niqmaddu gives his daughter and a certain KAR-kušuḫ the village of Ahnabi. The formula of the gift reads: *RN ittadin GN ana PN u PN qadu ZAG.10 ša qadu miksīša qadu širkīša. Mamma ana GN lā iraggum*, "The king has given the village Ahnabi to KAR-kušuḫ and Apapa, the daughter of the king, along with its tithe, and its *miksu* and *širku* tax." Later the text records that the recipient, KAR-kušuḫ, is free *(zaki)* of all claims. J. Nougayrol has read the last line as: *É ^dBaal ḫuršān (Ḫazzi) u LÚ.kum(rūsu) ana PN lā utebbū*, "The temple of Baal and its pr(iests) shall have no claim on KAR-kušuḫ." Unfortunately the restoration of *kumrū*, "priests," is difficult. This word for priest is not found elsewhere in Ugarit. If the reading is correct, then the priests must have had some prior interest in the produce from this village.

Elsewhere in Canaanite culture, the Temple did have a share in tithe collection. Diodorus mentions such a process in his description of the Punic community in Carthage. He mentions that it was their custom to send the city god a tenth of all that was paid to the public revenue.[11] He connects the religious tithe to the basic taxation system of the city.

---

[6]*CTA* 65,71, *PRU* III.11.790 (p. 189) and 11.830 (p. 190).

[7]For Alalakh, see D. Wiseman, *The Alalakh Tablets* (London: British Institute of Archaeology in Ankara: Occasional Publications, 1953), texts 52-58; also note text 42 where a village is said to go into debt rather than the expected individual(s).

[8]*PRU* III.16.153, lines 10-12 (pp. 146-47).

[9]The word *ma'saru* is a Canaanite gloss. Normally we would expect the Akkadian equivalent *eširtu*, sometimes written with the logogram, *ZAG.10*.

[10]*PRU* III 16.276 (pp. 69-70).

[11]*Diodorus of Sicily*, Book 20.14.

3. The Tithe in Israelite Culture

A similar treatment of the village can be found in ancient Israel. Like other Canaanite kings, Israelite kings could sell a whole village to a neighboring monarch (I Kgs 9:10-14). In the Arad letters there is a text which itemizes localities in Judah which supply grain to the royal fortress at Arad (25:2-4).[12] The same phenomenon of collection can be seen in an ostracon found at Beer Sheba.[13]

Aharoni believes that the consignment lists which are found at Arad were records of tax or tithe payments for a large area in southern Judea.[14] If Aharoni is correct, then this would would be an excellent example of how a royal fortress was administered by priests loyal to the king. In the case of these particular payments—speaking from the perspective of the tax payers in the countryside—any distinction between secular and sacred would be of little practical value. Like the situation at Ugarit, villages contributed to the central stores within the city as a unit. It was only when the contributions were in the urban confines, that administrative officials redistributed them to various urban specialists.

The sacred or secular quality of the tithe must be understood in terms of the means by which is was collected and distributed. Just as the semantic variability of the Hebrew term minḥâ cannot be understood simply in terms of diachronic development, so also for the sacred and secular nuances of the tithe. That is to say, the move from a sacred to a secular nuance (or vice versa) need not necessarily be historically conditioned. One must be sensitive to the function of tax collection lists compiled by urban administrators. Once the tithe is collected and in the city, urban elites take special care to classify its subsequent distribution. This classification as to which individuals would receive what was very important within the city. In the city, the royal dependents and other elites are treated individually in regard to taxation. A clear picture of secular and sacred usage can be found. In the village the picture is much different. Such specificity as to classification was of much less value. In the village, as the texts plainly show, individual distinctions were not made; the farmers of a given area were subsumed under the rubric of their particular village. For these individuals the tithe represented income over which they had no control. For them, the tithe

---

[12]Y. Aharoni, *Arad Inscriptions* (Jerusalem: Bialik Institute, 1981), pp. 52ff. See also the article by A. Rainey, "A Hebrew 'Receipt' from Arad," *BASOR* 202 (1971), pp. 23-9.

[13]See Y. Aharoni, *Beer-Sheba I* (Tel Aviv: Tel Aviv University, 1973), p. 71.

[14]Aharoni is followed in this respect by A. Lemaire in his *Inscriptions Hébraïques* I (Paris: Les Éditions du Cerf, 1977), pp. 119-20, 196-97.

is simply a fixed agricultural quanitity which must be surrendered to urban authorities.

The close interconnection of royal and priestly interest has been noted by Milgrom[15] and Weinfeld.[16] Both claim that the tithe has both sacred and secular referrents because the Temples which received the tithes were royal Temples. The royal nature of the Temple is explicitly declared in Amos 7:13. Other biblical (and Ugaritic) texts speak of the royal responsibility for the maintenance of the Temple.[17]   And still other biblical texts describe the royal control over Temple treasuries.[18] The different means of talking about its sacred or secular quality do not reflect different tithes, but rather, different estimations of the nature of the tithe.

With these prelimary remarks about the tithe behind us, we are ready to examine two texts which address the issue of the tithe and date to the early monarchical period.

B. Genesis 14:18-20

Genesis 14 has long troubled commentators.[19] The picture of the patriarch Abraham as a warrior is not in keeping with his other roles in Genesis. There is also disagreement concerning the text's date. In spite of the detailed descriptions of several kings and their respective countries, no satisfactory temporal or political *Sitz im Leben* has been agreed upon by scholars. Yet within this chapter there is one narrative which is generally recognized to be a creation of the United Monarchy. [20] We speak of the scene described in vv. 18-20 where Melchizedek, the king of Salem (Jerusalem) and priest of El Elyon comes forth to greet the victorious patriarch Abraham. He brings forth from his city bread and

[15]*Cult and Conscience* (Leiden: Brill, 1976), p. 57.

[16]"Tithe," *EJ*, pp. 1156-1162 and "The Royal and Sacred Aspects of the Tithe in the Old Testament," *Beer-Sheva* I (1973), pp.122-31 (Heb.).

[17]II Kg 12:7-17, 22:3-7, and II Chr 31:3ff; for Ugarit see *PRU* 2.10.

[18]I Kg 15:18; II Kg 12:19 and 18:15.

[19]The literature on this chapter is enormous. For a summary of past work see the recent commentary of C. Westermann (*Genesis*, (BKAT I/2, Neukirchen-Vluyn: Neukirchener Verlag, 1981), pp. 213-46 and the two important articles of J. Emerton, "Some False Clues in the Study of Genesis XIV," *VT* 21 (1971), pp. 24-47 and "The Riddle of Genesis XIV," *VT* 21 (1971), pp. 403-39.

[20]So Westermann and Emerton. Also see J. Bowker, "Psalm CX," *VT* 17 (1967), pp. 31-41. Von Rad, *Genesis*, H.H. Rowley, "Zadok and Nehustan," *JBL* 58 (1939), pp. 113-41 and "Melchizedek and Zadok (Gen 14 and Ps 110)," in *Festschrift für Alfred Bertholet* (Tübingen: Mohr, 1950), pp. 461-72.

wine and pronounces a blessing on Abraham, invoking the deity by his archaic epithet, El Elyon. Abraham responds by paying a tithe of all he has to the priest, Melchizedek.

Literarily, this narrative is intrusive in the chapter, as almost all commentators admit. It breaks the narrative flow of the story. One could read verse 21 immediately after verse 17 and not lose any necessary narrative elements for the remainder of the story. Only the repetition of the epithet $^{\jmath}\bar{e}l$ *'elyôn qôneh šāmayim wā-$^{\jmath}$āreṣ*, "God Most High, who creates heaven and earth," (Gen 14:22, cf. v. 19) binds the general story of Gen 14 to the unit in vv. 18-20. Also one should note the problem v. 20 provides for vv. 21-23.[21] In the latter, Abraham declares that he will return to the king of Sodom what he has taken in battle, yet in the former, Abraham states that he will give a tenth of all he has won in battle to Melchizedek. This contradiction demonstrates that the story as we have it now comes from at least two sources.

The narrative found in vv. 18-20 shows some independence from its immediate context. Its concerns do not quite match those of the larger chapter. Instead of the issues of war and fraternal obligation we read of a cultic meal and an offering to the patron deity. Yet, in spite of these different concerns, the narrative is not understandable outside of the framework of chapter 14. Because these verses require the context of chapter 14 to make sense, most commentators argue that this unit is secondary to the larger chapter.

But at least three commentators have argued that it is original to the chapter. They in turn argue that vv. 17 and 21-4 are an intrusion.[22] The strongest argument for this position is the presence of the formula $^{\jmath}\bar{e}l$ *'elyôn qôneh šāmayim wā-$^{\jmath}$āres* in v. 22, which is dependent on the use of the divine title $^{\jmath}\bar{e}l$ *'elyôn,* in v. 20. But, as Emerton asserts, the formula found in v. 22 could have appeared secondarily as an act of assimilation by the editor who inserted vv. 18-20. Or, just as possible, the formula found in v. 22 could have been original to chapter 14 and so provided a lexical link to the independent narrative about Abraham's encounter with a priest-king of $^{\jmath}\bar{e}l$ *'elyôn.* The biggest problem with the minority viewpoint is the fact that if 17, 21-24 is a late redaction and 18-20 is original, why is the former so close in content to the rest of chapter 14 while vv.

---

[21]See Emerton, p. 408.

[22]M.C. Astour, "Political and Cosmic Symbolism in Genesis 14 and in its Babylonian Sources," in A. Altmann ed., *Biblical Motifs* (Cambridge: Harvard University Press, 1966), pp. 65-112, esp. 67-8, O. Procksch, *Die Genesis* (2nd ed. Leipzig: A. Deichert, 1924), pp. 509-10, and E. Sellin, "Melchizedek," *Neue Kirchliche Zeitschrift,* 16 (1905), pp. 929-51.

18-20 is so different? It would seem much easier to see 18-20 as the editorial intrusion.

This narrative is built on a curious juxtaposition. The deity is invoked by his archaic title of the patriarchal period, *ʾēl ʿelyôn*, yet his cult site is the more recent royal city of Jerusalem.[23] Most scholars have explained this curious mixture as the result of the etiological function of the narrative.[24] The patriarch is offering cultic service to *ʾēl ʿelyôn* (the archaic element) via the mediation of the priest of Jerusalem (the subsequent capital of Israel) and thereby sets up the precedent for all Israel to recognize this city as a legitimate place of worship. The fact that Abraham offers a tithe is very significant. This term usually implies more than simply a token gift. It is used most often to designate a routinized system.[25] Therefore, there is an implied regularity to the act and so the narrative has a legitimizing function. Abraham's single act of patronage is a precedent for later Israel. Jerusalem is understood to be worthy of regular cultic attendance.

Previous scholarship has advanced three possible dates for this etiological narrative. The oldest theory, and one which finds almost no adherents today, dates the narrative to the post-exilic period. This position was based on several discredited arguments. First was the dating of Ps 110—which also refers to Melchizedek—to the second century.[26] No one dates the Psalmic materials this late anymore. Secondly, there was the problem of some rare lexical items in this unit including the divine epithets, *ʿelyôn*, ("Most High") *mgn* ("shield" or "Benefactor") and *qôneh šāmayim wā-ʾāreṣ* ("Creator of Heaven and Earth"). Prior to the modern epigraphic discoveries, most of these terms were believed to be of recent origin. Now, of course, these terms are known to be quite archaic and can be documented in other Northwest Semitic materials. The one, still plausible, reason for a late date would be the characterization of the priest as one who gets the tithe. This is exactly the situation in P and the Chronicler. But, as Emerton notes, there is no evidence which denies that the tithe would have been treated differently before the exile.[27] Moreover, Melchizedek is portrayed as a priest

---

[23]On the archaic nature of this epithet, see Cross, *CMHE*, pp. 1-76.

[24]For example, see the work of Emerton and Westermann cited above and M. Weinfeld, "Tithe," *EJ*, p. 1158.

[25]Westermann's comment (p. 244) is appropriate. "Der Zehnte ist eindeutig und unbestritten eine stetige Abgabe. Er begegnet nur im Zussammenhang des seßhaften Kultes und bedeutet hier immer die Abgabe des zehnten Teiles des Ertrages in stetiger Folge, von Jahr zu Jahr. Niemals aber wird vom Zehnten als einer aus einem einmaligen Gewinn erwachsenden Abgabe gesprochen."

[26]For example, see B. Duhm, *Die Psalmen* (2nd ed., Tübingen: Mohr, 1922).

[27]"The Riddle of Genesis XIV," pp. 416-19.

and king. There is no evidence of any priest making claims to royal symbols until the Hasmonean period.

Another theory is that of H. Schmid who dates the text to the period of Jeroboam.[28] He feels the text serves as a polemic against the competing claims of the Bethel shrine in the north. Though this is plausible, why does the competing claim arise so late in the history of Israelite cultic practice? Did not Jerusalem require legitimation at an earlier date? Why compose a narrative asserting the sanctity of the site well after its founding, especially when its founding was the subject of some mixed feelings? Also problematic for Schmid's position is the narrative of Jacob's founding of Bethel in Gen 28. In this text, Jacob, upon founding the cult site, vows to give it a regular tithe. In both Gen 14:18-20 and Gen 28:22 a major Israelite cult site is endowed by a patriarch. Significantly these are the only two narratives which speak of the patriarchs funding a cult site. It would be most unusual and awkward to see the two texts functioning at cross purposes.[29] It is better to see their function in accord; they legitimate the two major cult centers at the time of the United Monarchy. This is exactly what we would expect from the J source.

Emerton argues that the passage is best dated to the time of David because it was precisely then that the cult center needed legitimation. Jerusalem was not a tribal possession. It was a Canaanite city-state in the midst of the Israelite tribal coalition. The attempt to transform Jerusalem into a *royal capital with a Temple* met with considerable opposition (cf. II Sam 7:4-7). These political and religious institutions had no prior place in Israelite tradition and thus, required legitimation.

Emerton advances two other arguments for a dating to the Davidic period that are not as persuasive. He believes that this text serves to unite the separate cults of YHWH and El Elyon. The former, he asserts, is the God of Israel, the latter, the patron deity of Jerusalem. We would rather see this text as identifying the national God, YHWH, with an archaic epithet of God of the fathers, El.[30] Emerton also believes the text served to unite the Canaanite subjects of the city-state of Jerusalem with the Israelites. We think such ethnic distinctions are of little value in Israel's early history. Such distinctions connote harsh ethnic and

---

[28]H. Schmid, "Yahwe und die Kult Traditionen von Jerusalem," *ZAW* 67 (1965), pp. 168-97.

[29]The linkage of these two etiological narratives is noted by Westermann and Weinfeld.

[30]See Cross, *CMHE*, pp. 1-76.

linguistic differences between Israelites and Canaanites that remain assumed but unproved.   Apart from these minor differences, we believe Emerton's argument for a date to the United Monarchy is well founded. If this date is accepted, its purpose as legitimating the new cult center becomes clear. The bringing of one's tithes to the newly built Temple in the royal capital is given an archaic precedent. Just as Israel's revered ancestor, Abraham, contributed to a priest-king of Jerusalem's cult, so now all of Israel was called to do the same.

C. I Samuel 8:10-17

The Melchizedek narrative is not the only perspective we have on the institution of the Temple and king in Jerusalem and their requirement of a tithe. The tithe is mentioned in another contemporary text, that of Samuel's remonstrance against kingship (I Sam 8:10-17).[31]   In this text, which is contemporary to the Melchizedek text of Genesis, the tithe is described as the fixed exactions the king will *force* on the people. The text declares that Israel's future king would take a tenth of the agricultural produce and a tenth of the flock for his own use.

> wĕzarʿêkem wĕkarmêkem yaʿśōr
>   wĕnātan lĕsārīsāyw wĕlaʿăbādāyw (v.15)
> ṣōʾnĕkem yaʿśōr   wĕʾattem tihyû lô laʿăbādîm (v.17)

He will take a tenth from your grain and your vineyard
   and give it to his courtiers and servants.
He will take a tenth from your flock. As for you, you will become his
   slaves.

The grant formula found in verse 15, *yaʿśōr wĕnātan*, is one of many such

---

[31]The dating of this text to the early monarchical period is hardly novel. As F. Crüsemann notes (*Der Widerstand gegen das Königtum* (WMANT 19, Neukirchen-Vluyn: Neukirchener Verlag, 1978), pp. 66-73), the text, in order to work as a polemic against Israelite kingship, must reflect familiarity with the burden of taxation imposed by such a king.

formulae in this narrative. The Canaanite background of this vocabulary has been well documented in a recent study by J. Greenfield.[32]

Greenfield observes that in the Akkadian texts of royal grants from Ugarit, a favorite means of expressing the conveyance and transfer of property is the *našû—nadānu* formula.[33] The clause of property conveyance would typically read: *šarru rabû iššī-ma ana PN iddin*, "the great king has taken and given (X) to PN." The formula is also present in Anatolia (in Akkadian and Hittite documents) and the Canaanite cuneiform texts of Ugarit. Most important, in these texts from Anatolia, the idiomatic use of *našû* is not always employed. In the Akkadian from Anatolia two variant expressions occur, *leqû—nadānu* (Canaanite *lqḥ*) and *nadānu—šakānu*. Indeed, some Akkadian texts from Ugarit employ *leqû* instead of *našû* in some grants. Greenfield suggests that the *našû—nadānu* formula is replaced in some cases by *leqû—nadānu*. This represents a (perhaps colloquial) preference of the Ugaritic scribe; presumably they felt uncomfortable with this usage of *našû*. This would seem a likely explanation, because the grant texts presume a situation where property is taken *(leqû)* from one party and given to another.

Greenfield, building on the work of Güterbock,[34] suggests three separate functions for the three variant formulae, (1) *našû—nadānu*, (2) *našû—sakānu*, and (3) *leqû—nadānu*. The first is used to describe property given to a person, the second, property given to an institution and the third, a person given to an institution. With these distinctions in mind, Greenfield outlines I Sam 8:10-16 as follows:

formula of grant	items of transaction
(1) v. 11 yiqqaḥ wĕśām	conscription of males
v. 12 wĕlāśûm	continuation of above
v. 13 yiqqaḥ	conscription of females
(2) v. 14 yiqqaḥ wĕnātan	fields, vineyards, olive groves confiscated and given to royal courtiers

---

[32]"*Našû—nadānu* and its Congeners," in *Essays on the Ancient Near East in Memory of Jacob Joel Finkelstein*, ed. by M. Ellis, Memoirs of the Connecticut Academy of Arts and Sciences, 19 (Hamden: Archon Books, 1977), pp. 87-91. His study presumes the work of C.J. Labuschagne, "The Formula *našû—nadānu* and Its Biblical Equivalent," in *Travels in the World of the Old Testament, Studies Presented to Prof. M.A. Beeks at the Occasion of his 65th Birthday* (Assen: van Gorcum, 1974), pp. 176-80.

[33]Greenfield also assumes the important work of E.A. Speiser, "Akkadian Documents from Ras Shamra," *JAOS* 75 (1955), pp. 154-65.

[34]H. Güterbock, *Siegel aus Bogazköy* 1 (AfO Beiheft 5, Osnabrück: Biblio Verlag, 1942), pp. 47-55.

(3) v. 15 ya'šōr wĕnātan   granting tithes to courtiers

(4) v. 16 yiqqaḥ wĕ'āšā limla'ktô   confiscation of staff, servants, and beasts for
                                    royal use.

In the Samuel text *lāqaḥ wĕnātan* is limited to the transfer of land to the royal courtiers. In this respect it matches the *našû—nadānu* formula found at Ugarit. The formula *lāqaḥ wĕšām* is used to describe the grant of people to an institution. This usage closely parallels *našû—šakānu*, *šām* being a semantic equivalent in Hebrew to Akkadian *šakānu* "to place or set." The formula we are interested in, *ya'šōr—wĕnātan*, "he will take a tenth and give," has no clear parallel in the Akkadian texts of Ugarit. But there are attested uses of the formula *našû—nadānu* which describe the royal grant of a tithe to a royal courtier.

Mendelsohn was the first to show clear parallels between the text of Samuel and legal documents of Ugarit.[35] Greenfield's work only strengthens his conclusions. This anti-kingship narrative in Samuel shows a sophisticated understanding of the royal economy and its attendant system of grants and contracts. The social background of this text is quite clear. The author is describing the tithe as it actually was practiced in the Canaanite city-state. In contemporary usage, the tithe was a fixed levy of the king. It represented the most basic type of tax in the economy of Syria-Palestine. It was levied on the produce of native agriculturalists, and so constituted the most important staple of the village economy.

Genesis 14:18-20 does not describe the royal tithe as a tax. The contrast to I Sam 8 could not be more complete. In the epic text found in Genesis, the tithe was a vowed, or voluntary offering to the patron deity.

How do we account for these vastly different usages of the tithe in this period when Israelite society was evolving toward kingship? Is one strictly a cultic term and the other a term of the secular economy?[36] This would be one

---

[35]I. Mendelsohn, "Samuel's Denunciation of Kingship in the Light of Akkadian Documents from Ugarit," *BASOR* 143 (1956), p. 20. Also see the remarks of A. Rainey in *Ras Shamra Parallels*, vol 2 (Rome: Pontificium Institutum Biblicum, 1975), pp. 93-98. He believes Mendelsohn's parallels can be made even more exact.

[36]This has been a common conclusion. It can be found in one of Eissfeldt's earliest works. See his, *Erstlinge und Zehnte im alten Testament*, (BWAT 22, Leipzig: J.C. Hinrichs, 1917). He argues that in early Israel the tithe was a voluntary and sacred gift; it became a fixed obligation or tax late in the biblical period. In regard to the evidence of I Sam 8 he asks (p. 154: Warum sollen nicht beide Zehnten, ein staatlicher und ein kultischer nebeneinander bestanden haben?" This type of thinking can be found in the most recent scholarly literature. See H. Jagersma, "The Tithes in the Old Testament," in *Remembering all the way...* (OTS XXI, Leiden: Brill, 1981), pp. 116-28, esp. p. 121. He asserts that the tithes spoken of in Gen 14 and I Sam 8 are two different types.

solution, but it is rather artificial. It reflects an exegetical method which does not respect questions of genre and literary usage. It assumes, in a very functionalist manner, that epic language must parallel common usage. This view is fraught with problems. Those who insist that the tithe mentioned in Gen 14:18-20 fits an actual historical context often assert a post-exilic dating because only then does the biblical text regularly require the tithe be turned over to the priests. The Gen 14 text would reflect the common usage of only the post-exilic period. But this argument from common usage is flawed. As Emerton notes, not all of the details fit. For one, the priest in the post-exilic period was not seen as a king. Also the tithe spoken of in P pertains to agricultural yield, not the spoils of war as seen in Gen 14.

Another attempt to fit Gen 14:18-20 neatly into a historical time frame is that of Fisher. He does not believe the text reflects post-exilic practice; rather he argues it reflects the usage of the tithe we have documented in the Ugaritic and related materials. His exegetical presupposition is that the patriarchal story should fit the common usage of the tithe in the patriarchal period (an assumed historicity of the narrative). To do this, he asserts that Abraham was a merchant prince hired by Melchizedek and *paid* a tithe "as an expected obligation to his king."[37] This argument must be rejected. Nowhere in the text is Abraham said to be a merchant prince. This is simply another attempt to force the epic text into a particular historical model. This LB model overlooks the priestly and religious quality of the narrative completely. But Fisher's argument does have one thing in common with those who argue that Gen 14 reflects post-exilic social practice. It must ignore one component of Melchizedek's priest-king role. Fisher emphasizes the royal to the exclusion of the priestly, whereas those who argue for a post-exilic dating must emphasize the priestly to the exclusion of the royal. The details, when taken as literal exemplars of social praxis, cannot be made to fit one specific period.

In an epic story it would be quite appropriate for the patriarch to offer homage to the priest-king of Jerusalem through the cult. To recognize the cult of a city as legitimate and worthy of one's offerings and maintenance is tantamount to recognizing its political power as well. As we shall observe in our next chapter, the prologue of Hammurapi's Code often describes Hammurapi's control over the cities of his Mesopotamia in terms of his cultic responsibility to

---

[37]L. Fisher, "Abraham and his Priest-King," *JBL* 86 (1962), pp. 246-70.

their shrines. Many of the various epithets of benevolence toward the cult have non-cultic parallels. To be the one in charge of the city-god's cult implies a parallel authority over the other affairs of the city as well.

In short, the epic description of Melchizedek as a priest-king fits the larger Semitic mythic picture of the king as priest or intercessor for the people. This does not imply that in everyday affairs of the cult the king played a major role. The epic description is meant to be impressionistic and mythic, not realistic and mundane. It is neither the function nor the interest of epic narrative to describe the actual secular or sacred nature of tithe collection in everyday affairs.

In the Samuel text, the author has dispensed with the mythic portrayal of the king. This is not unparalleled in the ancient Near East. In the economic texts from Ugarit we see the tithe functioning in a very secular fashion. There the tithe is a fixed payment due the king from the villages of Ugarit. The king, in turn, can hand these villages along with their tithes over to servants within his kingdom, including the priests. The Samuel text describes the tithe in a basically similar fashion. But, unlike the economic and juridical texts from Ugarit, the Israelite author evaluates these royal exactions as despotic acts. The sardonic flavor of this text becomes most dramatic when one reads it as contemporary to the Genesis tithe narratives. The Samuel text describes the same act, which in Canaanite royal ideology is most sacred (Gen 14:18-20 and Gen 28:22), but evaluates it in a completely negative fashion.

CHAPTER FIVE

Temples and Fertility:
A Reconsideration of the Rhetoric of Post-Exilic Prophecy

A. Introduction

The rhetoric of post-exilic prophecy poses tremendous problems for those who wish to believe Israel's cultic service is radically different from Canaanite 'fertility' practices. As D. Petersen has observed, there are few places in ancient Near Eastern literature where the causal connection between Temple building and fertility of the land are so explicitly drawn out.[1] To make the point even more emphatic, Haggai associates this arrival of fertility with the very day on which the Temple is re-established (2:18). Ackroyd observes that in this passage one sees the biblical writer "anxious to show the precision of the divine blessing."[2] Von Rad observes that the rebuilding of the Temple in the minds of these post-exilic authors becomes a necessary precondition for the return of the biblical deity to the land.[3] It is this fact, von Rad notes, which has proved embarrassing for a number of commentators.

The source of this embarrassment stems from the strong contrast previous scholarship has tried to draw between Canaanite and Israelite cultic life. This contrast is dependent on a common evaluation of the fertility theme in Canaanite religion. This common evaluation consists of several parts. Firstly, it characterizes Baal as a vegetation deity who dies and rises in accord with the seasons of nature. Secondly, the benefits this god provides are described as magical in nature. Finally, these magical traits of Canaanite religion are compared with the ethical and historical traits of biblical religion. The end result is a dramatic theological contrast between the ethical deity of Israel and the magical god of Canaanite paganism. Once these positions are assumed to be normative expressions of the respective religions, the biblical scholar is forced to

---

[1] D. Petersen, *Haggai and Zechariah 1-8* (Philadelphia: Westminster Press, 1984), p. 54.
[2] P. Ackroyd, *Exile and Restoration* (Philadelphia: Westminster Press, 1975), p. 159.
[3] G. von Rad, *Old Testament Theology*, II (New York: Harper and Row, 1965), p. 281.

conclude that fertility interests, when they appear in the Bible, are vestigial remains of a discredited, magical, nature deity.

This common characterization of the relationship of Canaanite to Israelite religion makes the interpretation of Haggai and Zechariah very difficult. One must explain in some fashion the reason why these post-exilic prophets could so easily accommodate themselves to these purported Canaanite ideas. Had they forgotten the most salient features of their ancestral religion and 'returned' to a magical fertility cult? This would be a Wellhausian answer, but few modern scholars would wish to describe the end of the biblical period in such a negative fashion.[4] As has been often observed, such a description too easily fits the needs of Christian apologetics wherein the decline of late and post-biblical religion is used as a foil for the triumphant rise of early Christianity. In order to avoid this, many modern scholars have sought to interpret late biblical prophecy in a more positive fashion. But significantly, these positive treatments--in order to be positive-- have *to ignore or explain away* the fertility themes of late prophecy. For example, von Rad says that it is not the case that pre-exilic prophets are more spiritual than Haggai and Zechariah. Rather, the difference between the former and the latter can be attributed to the spiritual condition of the peoples addressed. Haggai and Zechariah appear less spiritual because of their audience's interest in economic concerns. It was these economic concerns which "prevented them from looking any higher" and so "the question of the rebuilding of the Temple (became) *status confessionis.*"[5] Ackroyd, on the other hand, discovers a symbolic element in this prophetic rhetoric. He argues that the demand for rebuilding is necessary for the removal of impurity or sin. Thus, the call to rebuild is tantamount to a "recognition of the nature of God, for whom acceptability on the part of his worshippers is essential." Thus, the point of Haggai's rhetoric is not an instrumental one—that somehow the human activity of Temple building could effect change on the natural environment—but rather a symbolic one. In Ackroyd's terms: "The emphasis is not thereby placed upon human endeavour, but upon the recognizable danger of treading unwarily into the

---

[4]But some biblical scholars have done this very thing. See E. Hammershaimb, *Some Aspects of Old Testament Prophecy* (Copenhagen, 1966), p. 105, who states that all ethical considerations are lacking in Haggai. Or see F. Hesse, "Haggai," in A. Kuschke (ed.), *Verbannung und Heimkehr* (Tübingen, 1961), pp. 109-34, who says that Haggai is not a forerunner of Christ; rather he is a forerunner of Judaism. Also see J.D. Smart, *History and Theology in Second Isaiah* (Philadelphia: Westminster Press, 1965), pp. 284, who says that Haggai's promise to the people is that a better time awaits them *simply* upon completion of the Temple.

[5]von Rad, p. 281.

presence of holiness."[6] We are not attempting to argue that Ackroyd is wrong. On the contrary, in many respects his analysis is sensitive and perceptive. What we wish to illustrate is that Ackroyd's attempt to describe Haggai's rhetoric sympathetically *necessarily ignores or downplays* the instrumental quality of that rhetoric. The association of Temple rebuilding and fertility is simply a symbolic metaphor in this analysis.

If we return to the issue of magic and fertility without the prejudice against Canaanite culture, perhaps a new understanding of the role of Temple building in the rhetoric of post-exilic prophecy can be better understood. As we shall see below, these prophets are most emphatic in their belief that the physical reconstitution of the Temple building will assure new vigor for fertility in the agricultural sphere. How are we to interpret such a statement? Is this language to be understood in an instrumental fashion? That is, did these post-exilic prophets think that simply laying stone upon stone on the Temple mount within Jerusalem could open the sluice gates of Heaven? Or is this language to be understood as symbolic speech; speech which attempts to draw a metaphoric correspondence between heaven and earth? Before we can begin to answer such a question we must examine, in some detail, the basic outline of this prophetic language.

B. Covenantal Curse Formulae and the Absence of YHWH's Presence

The overriding theological issue for the early post-exilic community is that of YHWH's presence. More specifically the concern is with the perceived absence of this presence while Jerusalem and the Temple remain in ruins. While YHWH is absent from his Temple the land languishes. Several different proposals are made by post-exilic writers which seek to restore the presence of YHWH to the Israelite community and so assure a renewed fertility for the soil. Each of these proposals presumes a particular theological position which, in turn, is expressed by means of a very technical vocabulary. Some of these theological positions and technical terms are shared among the various post-exilic writers, while others are the exclusive domain of an individual author.

---

[6]Ackroyd, p. 160.

For Ezekiel, the important concept is that of the return of YHWH's *kābōd*, "presence".[7] In his work, the return of YHWH's presence to Jerusalem is predicated on a properly built Temple administered by Zadokite priests.[8] A detailed prescription for the actual restoration of Jerusalem, and the hoped for return of YHWH's presence, is outlined in Ezek 40-48. Particularly crucial for this prescription is the erection of an altar and the establishment of proper sacrifices. Ezekiel's vision begins with a description of the architecture of the new Temple (40-42). At the end of this description, YHWH's *kābōd* makes its triumphal return to Jerusalem (43:1-5). Once God is again present with his people, the sacrifices of consecration for the altar can begin. These sacrifices are offered up for seven days (43:18-26). Then on the eighth day, in what is certainly one of the thematic highpoints of Ezekiel's message, the regular sacrificial system is re-instituted.[9] This regular, properly performed, liturgical ritual is a necessary, though not sufficient, means for assuring YHWH's presence among the biblical community. Once this is accomplished, Israel's suffering under the curse of covenantal disobedience is ended. YHWH declares: "On the eighth day and thereafter, when

---

[7]For authors other than Ezekiel, at least two other technical terms come to mind which concern themselves with YHWH's former absence and his hoped for return. One is the favorite term of the priestly school *šāken*, "to abide, dwell." The importance of this root for the priestly theology of God's presence has been amply discussed by Cross *(CMHE,* p. 299). Another important term is *bāḥar*, "to choose." It is often used with the technical sense of divine election and is a favorite of Zechariah (1:17, 2:16, and 3:2). See the discussion of D. Petersen, p. 184.

[8]In an earlier part of the book (chapters 10-11) the *kābōd* left just before the destruction of the Temple. The departure of a god or goddess from his or her city which is about to be destroyed is a common motif in Mesopotamian literature. This motif is found in the "Lamentation over the Destruction of Ur," "Lamentation over the Destruction of Sumer and Ur," and in "The Curse of Agade." The first two are translated by Kramer in *ANET,* pp. 455-463 and 611-619. The latter has recently been investigated thoroughly by J. Cooper, *The Curse of Agade* (Baltimore: Johns Hopkins University Press, 1982). But biblical descriptions of YHWH's departures are not exactly paralleled by the Mesopotamian examples. As J. Roberts and P. Miller point out *(The Hand of the Lord* (Baltimore: Johns Hopkins University Press, 1977), p. 42 and n. 12), in the Bible, the deity does not choose to go into exile. The departure is a compelled one, occasioned by the military defeat Israel suffers due to her disobedience.

[9]Two scholars have questioned the authenticity of vv. 25-27. See Zimmerli, *Ezekiel* II (Philadelphia: Fortress Press, 1983), p. 435 and W. Rautenberg, "Zur Zukunftsthora des Hesekiel," *ZAW* 33 (1913), pp. 92-115. Zimmerli believes that vv. 25-27 are the result of a redactor who wishes to harmonize the cultic ordinances of Ezekiel with those of P.

the priests offer on the altar your holocaust offerings (ᶜōlōt) and your peace offerings (sělāmîm), then I will accept you (wěrāṣîʔtî) (43:27)."[10]

Once the Temple and its cult have been reconstituted, Ezekiel, later in his work, describes the return of fertility to the land. The source of this fertility is the stream of 'living' water which shall emanate from the Temple threshold itself (47:1-12). This image of the Temple mount providing fertile waters has roots in the cosmic mountain myth of ancient Canaan and in the pre-exilic Zion imagery of biblical religion.[11]

Ezekiel's program of restoration is a technical and learned one. It is replete with difficult terminology and detail. To be sure, this detail served a very important theological purpose in Ezekiel's program. For Ezekiel the Temple architecture was a type of non-verbal expression of the nature of God himself. As Levenson has observed, "the architecture of Zion, like the history of redemption, is a public testimony to the nature of God."[12] As a program of restoration, Ezekiel's detailed description is unambiguous as to its intent. But one must wonder how functional such a program would have been as a rhetorical vehicle, or text for popular oration. Ezekiel's learned disquisition is hardly the stuff of a popular plea to the post-exilic community.

For the latter we must turn to Haggai and Zechariah. As Hanson has argued, their interest in the Zadokite priesthood and a properly functioning post-exilic cultus cannot and should not be disassociated from Ezekiel's message.[13] All

---

[10]The root here is rḍw (cf. Hebrew rṣh, Aramaic rᶜh, Arabic rḍy). Fitzmyer discussed the root as it appears in Sefire (The Aramaic Inscriptions of Sefire (Rome: Pontifical Biblical Institute, 1967), pp. 109-110). He concluded from the form rqw (rḍy) found there and the South Arabic form rḍw that it must be originally a final waw root. Such evidence merely supplements the Arabic data which show us that the root must be final waw on the basis of the maṣdar riḍwān. The G form is raḍiya/yarḍā, but here a regular Arabic sound change iw>iy is in evidence. Such interference is missing in the qitlān maṣdar pattern. In Sefire the forms are in the D with a factitive sense meaning "to make acceptable" or "to prevail." Its G form must have been similar to the G in Hebrew, "to be acceptable." In Hebrew this G form often has the technical meaning of God's acceptance of sacrifices (or the sacrificer). In P, though, this technical meaning is limited to the N stem while the G has a secondary meaning of "making acceptable" or more specifically "paying off a debt (Lev 26:34,43)." Deutero-Isaiah uses the N stem in his stirring opening address (40:1): "(Israel's) service is completed, her iniquity is pardoned (made acceptable)." The technical meaning of accepting a sacrifice was not limited to the Hebrew. This exact technical sense is found in the archaic Aramaic inscription of Bir Hadad (yarḍay bih, "(Hadad) shall accept it," (KAI 214:18)).

[11]See the discussion of J. Levenson, Theology of the Program of Restoration of Ezekiel 40-48 (HSM 10, Missoula: Scholars Press, 1976), pp. 7-19.

[12]Levenson, p. 16.

[13]P. Hanson, Dawn of Apocalyptic (Philadelphia: Fortress Press, 1975), pp. 228-262.

three, though having distinct emphases, envision similar ends. [14] In fact, the ends are complementary. Haggai and Zechariah, because of their rhetorical interests, search for themes which will motivate their hearers. They eschew the technical details of Ezekiel's description not because they view them as unnecessary or superfluous, but because they do not serve the needs of popular oration. Haggai and Zechariah required a language more general in scope which would achieve the same political and religious ends.

The message of Haggai and Zechariah is straightforward: *build the Temple and the fertility of the land will ensue.* Haggai opens his case not with the problem of the absence of the divine *kābōd,* but with the mundane implications of this absence.

kōh ʾāmar YHWH ṣĕbāʾôt
śîmû lĕbabkem ʿal darkêkem
zĕraʿtem harbēh wĕhābēʾ mĕʿāṭ
ʾākôl wĕʾên lĕśobʿâ
šātô wĕʾên lĕšokrâ
lābôš wĕʾên lĕḥōm lô
wĕhammiśtakkēr miśtakkēr ʾel ṣĕrôr nāqûb

Thus says the Lord of Hosts:
"Take consideration of your plight;
you sow much but bring in little,
you eat but without satisfaction,
you drink but without inebriation,
you clothe yourselves but have no warmth,
the wage earner earns wages to a bag with holes."
(Haggai 1:5-6)

---

[14]As we will argue in the conclusion of this chapter, the different styles of language used by Ezekiel on the one hand and Haggai and Zechariah on the other does not imply widely variant programs of restoration. The different descriptions are better explained by the contrasting audiences these prophets address. Still, one contrast does seem quite apparent. This is in regard to kingship. Ezekiel is most concerned to keep the power of the royal office closely circumscribed in his new constitution (see Levenson, pp. 55-101). The best evidence of the underlying suspicion toward this office is the conscious preference for designating the secular ruler by the archaic tribal league term for a chief, *nāśīʾ*. Haggai on the other hand had a much more developed royal ideology. His hope seems to be for nothing less than a return to the grandeur of the Davidic house with all its mythic associations (2:21-23). If Hanson is correct ("Zechariah" in the *IDBS,* pp. 982-983), the debate between these conflicting perspectives on the royal office are displayed in the redactional history of Zechariah 1-8. In the last phase of this redaction (stratum II) Hanson claims that the diarchy of priest and king is superseded by a hierarchy of priest (Zadokite in this case) alone. This intriguing hypothesis will require more extensive documentation before it can be evaluated.

Although the images here are concrete, *the language is highly formulaic.* Individual elements in this text find parallels elsewhere in the Bible and are best understood as covenantal in background.   As Hillers has observed, the use of covenantal or treaty curses within prophetic speech is quite common.[15] This text in particular seems to fit Hillers' rubric of the "futility curse." This rubric is well documented in the ancient Near East and finds abundant expression in the Sefire treaty as well as in the newly discovered bilingual inscription of Tell Fakhariyeh. At Sefire a typical example is: "And though seven cows suckle a calf it will not be filled" (Sefire I A: 22-23). This curse, like our Haggai text, is concerned with fertility, though the specific images are different.

Closer parallels to our passage are found in the Bible itself. Of these perhaps Micah is the best, "You shall eat but not be sated...You shall put away but not save... You shall sow but not harvest, you shall tread olives but not anoint with oil, (you shall tread) new wine but not drink wine" (6:14-15).[16]   Other, similar examples are found in Dt 28:38-42; Hos 4:10, and Am 5:11. Because the ordering of biblical curses varied from one text to another, one should not expect the whole curse oracle of Haggai to be duplicated elsewhere in order to assert its formulaic nature. It is enough to show that its constituent parts find parallels in other biblical curse lists. Haggai's ordering of these elements was his own creative endeavor.

Other texts in the book of Haggai fit the curse form as well. One thinks of Haggai's reference to YHWH's smiting the land with "blight and mildew" (*šiddāpōn* and *yērāqōn*) (2:17).   These two are always paired in the Bible. Significantly, they are mentioned as punishment for irreverent behavior toward YHWH's Temple in Solomon's prayer (I Kg 8:37 = II Chr 6:28). This is exactly the error Haggai attributes to the post-exilic community.

---

[15]The major work on this area is D. Hillers, *Treaty Curses and the Old Testament Prophets* (Rome: Pontifical Biblical Institute, 1964). In this work he argues that biblical curses are not directly derivable from their Assyrian counterparts, even where close connections are apparent.   One of the unique elements of the biblical curses is their poetic nature; the Akkadian curses are all prose.   Poetic elements can be found in the curses listed in this chapter and have been highlighted.

[16]The Greek lacks the word "wine" in the phrase "but not drink wine." Hillers says that this is because the LXX has already used *oinos* to translate *tîrôš* in the first part of the bi-colon (*Micah* (Hermenia, Philadelphia: Fortress Press, 1984), p. 81). This is not entirely convincing. Certainly the LXX could have made a distinction if this was the intent of the translator. In general, the LXX is not so useful in the minor prophets and its witness should not be overly trusted. Although the text is very mutilated, a Qumran fragment seems to support the MT (see D. Barthélemy and J. Milik, *Qumran Cave I* (Discoveries in the Judean Desert I, Oxford: Clarendon Press, 1955), p. 79 and plate XV).

The use of these descriptive formulae should alert the reader that the prophet is not necessarily referring to everyday affairs.[17] These formulaic descriptions have literary and theological functions which exist outside the realm of mundane reality. In this regard, the remarks of G. Mayer are quite instructive: "(Pestilence) is not used in a secular setting in the OT. According to the usual translation, pestilence is a divinely sent punishment for disobedience." [18] Mayer's study serves to emphasize the formulaic character of much of the pestilence and famine language in the Bible. Moreover, Mayer observes that these formulae are concentrated in prophetic and late deuteronomistic texts.[19] Most often these threats of pestilence and famine occur in covenantal contexts (like the Micah text cited above) in the form of curse formulations for disloyal behavior.

The perception that Israel was abiding under the curse is a pervasive theme in most post-exilic writings. Its extensive reach is very understandable. Already among many pre-exilic prophets there was a frequent use of these curse formulae. These earlier prophets used these curses as a threat, to Israel first, and then to Judah, to induce covenantal faithfulness. As the history of pre-exilic Judah drew to a close, deuteronomistic writers found the threat of the curse particularly important theologically. For these individuals, the contrast between blessing *(běrākâ)* and curse *(qělālâ)* became the *leitmotif* of an entire theological program (cf. Dt 11:26,28; 23:6, and 30:1,19). This rich tradition developed by Israel's prophets and deuteronomistic circles provided a groundwork for exilic and post-exilic theological expression. The objective datum of the Babylonian advance seemed to provide final confirmation of earlier prophetic admonitions; Israel had fallen under the curse. The exilic redactor of the Deuteronomistic history (Dtr[2]), in fact, described the Babylonian advance as one of the covenantal curses about which Israel had been forewarned (Dt 28:47-68). Other exilic and post-exilic writers share this theological viewpoint. Zechariah concluded that Israel in exile was under the curse, while the hoped-for restoration was to bring

---

[17]D. Petersen has noted this feature as well (pp. 49-51, 91-93). Other scholars have not appreciated the formulaic quality of this speech and have consequently used this material for the purposes of a social description of post-exilic Judea. For example, see H. Kreissig, *Die sozialökonomische Situation in Juda zur Achämenidenzeit* (Berlin: Akademie Verlag, 1973), pp. 39-56, esp. 41.

[18]G. Mayer, 'Debher,' in G. Botterweck and H. Ringgren eds., *Theological Dictionary of the Old Testament* (Grand Rapids: Eerdmanns, 1975), p. 126. See also the discussion in note 54.

[19]Mayer postulates that the threat of pestilence was such a rhetorical figure in biblical writings that its could be used to describe a wide variety of calamities. For example in Ezek 5:1-11 a variety of punishments are listed which are then summarized in verse 12 by the formulaic triad of pestilence, famine and sword. Ezekiel is not bothered that this triad does not exactly match the earlier list of punishments.

an age of blessing (8:13). So also Ezekiel declares that a restored Israel will become a blessing (34:26).

Israel's coming under the curse meant that the land had lost its fertile nature. The descriptions, then, that Haggai provides of exilic Judah (1:5-6) were founded in the covenant theology of his time. Haggai, though—unlike Ezekiel—does not dwell on the origins of the curse nor describe in any detail YHWH's consequent departure from Jerusalem. In an earlier time, Jeremiah speculated that the punishment for covenantal disobedience would last 70 years (25:12), a concept Zechariah accepted (1:12). Haggai's explanation of the present distress is much simpler. He offers no insights as to why YHWH originally left nor for how long he shall remain absent. The land languishes for one simple reason:

"Because of my house that lies in ruin...." (Haggai 1:9).

The solution then for Haggai is rather straightforward.

> Go up to the hills and fetch wood!
> Build the house!
> Then I will accept it (ʾerṣeh)
> and I will be glorified (ʾekkabĕdā).
> (Haggai 1:8)

The theological interests of Haggai are similar to those of Ezekiel. YHWH's acceptance and glory are sought (rāṣôn and kābôd). But Haggai's theological program, in contrast to Ezekiel's, is reduced to its barest essentials. Haggai's vocation as a popular orator limits the scope of his message. His address to the people is brief: rebuild the Temple.

We have noted that Haggai's description and explanation of Israel's plight is more mundane than that of Ezekiel. Our choice of words here was quite intentional. The images are more mundane but not mundane altogether. Haggai's description of the land's impoverishment is formulaic. We have noted its affinities to the treaty-curses, but another perhaps more important source for Haggai's description of the land is the mythic imagery of Canaanite literature. [20] Consider this description Haggai provides of the land while the Temple is in shambles.[21]

ʿal-kēn[22] ʿălêkem

kālᵉʾû šāmayim[23] miṭṭal[24]

wᵉhāʾāreṣ kālᵉʾâ yᵉbûlâ

wᵉʾeqrāʾ ḥōreb ʿal hāʾāreṣ wᵉʿal hehārîm

wᵉʿal haddāgān wᵉʿal hattîrôš wᵉʿal hayyiṣhār

wᵉʿal ʾăšer[25] tôṣîʾ hāʾădāmâ

wᵉʿal hāʾādām wᵉʿal habbᵉhēmâ

---

[20]Hillers has noted that curse-language is not limited to treaty documents. Because of their formulaic quality curses could be inserted by poets into a variety of texts as the document required. Hillers provides a remarkable parallel between two curses found in the mythic lore of Ugarit and the royal inscription of Ahiram.

lyhpk ksa mlkk	Verily (El) shall overturn your royal throne
lyθbr ḥt mθptk	He will break your juridical sceptre
(CTA 6.6.28 and 2.3.18)	
thtsp ḥṭr mšpṭh	Let his judicial staff be broken
thtpk ksʾ mlkh	Let his royal throne be overturned
(KAI 1:2)	

It is not our concern here to decide the exact literary precursor of each curse found in Haggai or Zechariah. Because curses can be found in a variety of genres, such an attempt at precision would be necessarily artificial. Our main concern here is to show the formulaic quality of these curses.

[21]The text here is fairly secure, but some difficulties exist. In general, one should distrust the versions in the minor prophets because they do not preserve a text type which is significantly different than the MT. Barthélemy (Les devanciers d'Aquila (Leiden: Brill, 1963), pp. 266-70) argued that the LXX of the minor prophets is of the kaige type, in other words, a text which was systematically corrected to the proto-Rabbinic text. As can be seen below, many of the alternate readings are expansionistic and so we opt for the briefer reading.

[22]ʿl kn ʿlykm] The Syriac omits ʿl kn, while the Greek and the Old Latin omit ʿlykm. The Hebrew is perhaps expansionistic here (though some explain the Hebrew as an imperfect dittography) but the original reading is difficult to assess. It would be just as easy to explain the versions abbreviated readings as due to haplography.

[23]šmyml The LXX and some Hebrew mss. read hšmym. This is perhaps a harmonization toward hʾrṣ. Though one should also note that while Hebrew grammar allows the absence of the article in archaic and archaizing poetry, proper Greek grammar is not so flexible.

[24]mṭll The min must be privative not partitive. To balance the suffix on yebûla some propose emending to ṭlm. This is supported by Zech 8:12, which balances a similar bi-colon this way. If this is accepted, the MT reading would be the result of a dittography (šmym ṭlm), but the subsequent loss of the suffixed mem would still be unexplained. We prefer the MT (also supported by the Greek). The lack of a corresponding suffix in one colon of a bi-colon is not uncommon in poetry. The suffix in one colon does double duty (see M. Dahood, Psalms III (AB 17a, Garden City: Doubleday, 1970), pp. 429-33 for examples).

[25]ʾšr] In some Greek mss. as well as in the Syriac and Vulgate the reading kl ʾšr is found. The kl could have dropped out of the MT by homoioteleuton (ʿl kl ʾšr)but its inclusion could just as well be expansionistic.

wĕʿal kol-yĕgîaʿ kappāyim[26]

Therefore, on your account:
The heavens have withheld the dew
and the earth has withheld its produce
and I have called for a drought in the land and hills
concerning the grain, the wine and oil,
and what the ground produces,
and concerning people and animals,
and on all the toil of hands.
(Haggai 1:10-11)

Zechariah's description is slightly different. He does not describe the land's barrenness in quite the same fashion as Haggai.[27] But he uses similar mythic motifs to describe the land's bounteous restoration upon completion of the Temple and YHWH's return to the land. Upon completion of that Temple he asserts,

kî zeraʿ haššālôm
haggepen tittēn piryâ
wĕhāʾāreṣ tittēn ʾet yĕbûlâ
wĕhaššāmayim yittĕnû ṭallām

---

[26]*kpyml* The versions read with a suffix, *kpyhm*. Many prefer this reading, but one must remember that the supplying of suffixes is a very common expansionistic device. None of the scholars who prefer the versions bothers to explain the origin of the MT reading, but there is an explanation if MT is secondary. In the Aramaic scripts of inter-Testamental times, there is ample room for confusion of *heh* and *mem*. For example, in the third century scripts such as 4QSam(b), the bottom stroke of the *mem* does not touch the left vertical. In this case the MT corruption would be haplographic, a very common error.

[27]The significance of this will be examined in the third section of this chapter. For now it should be noted that Zechariah does not emphasize the barrenness or infertility of the land. The only allusion he makes in this regard is to the "desolateness" of the land, but the root employed (*šmm*) most often implies military destruction (7:14). This is in line with Zechariah's description of the land's barrenness. He alludes to the loss of population in Jerusalem and Judah, rather than to crop failure (7:7). To be sure, he believes the rebuilding of the Temple will bring fertility to the land, but he does not describe the pre-Temple period as one of drought or natural disaster. The problems the land faces before Temple building, in Zechariah's mind, are best described as socio-economic: "For in those days there was no wage for man nor a wage for the beast. There was no safety from the adversary in traveling, for I set each man against his fellow" (8:10).

> For there shall be a peaceful sowing[28]
> the vine shall produce its fruit
> and the earth shall produce its yield
> and the heavens shall give their dew
> (Zechariah 8:12)

The motifs found in both of these passages have striking similarities to Canaanite literature. It is a commonplace that Baal's fecund powers are dependent upon his recognition as king and his acquisition of a Temple. A standard example of the link between Temple building and fertility is found in the poem recited upon El's granting a Temple to Baal.

wên ʾap ʿaddini maṭarīhu baʿlu

yaʿaddina ʿaddinu[29] θarra bi-galθi

wa-yatāni[30] qālahu bi-ʿarapāti

šarrihu laʾarṣi baraqa-mi

bêta ʾarazīma yakālilanhu

himma bêta libānati yaʿmusanhu[31]

---

[28]The RSV translates this very woodenly as "a sowing of peace." This is a good example of how a word-for-word translation can not only be imprecise but also dead wrong. The genitival construct formation in Hebrew (and in other Semitic languages) has many nuances, to which the translator should be sensitized. Here we would argue for an adjectival nuance, "a peaceful sowing," or perhaps "a safe sowing" as in har-haqqōdeš, "holy mountain," not "mountain of holiness." The best argument for this translation is the context given by the previous verses (8:10-11 and see n. 17) where šālôm has the sense of safety. The JPS translation is possible too, though it is a bit freer and avoids the construct formation altogether. This is perfectly acceptable since the segholate noun zeraʿ appears the same in any case. It reads: "but what (this people) sows will prosper."

[29]We have vocalized the case ending of the infinitive absolute with an u when it is used as an adverb. When it is used as a verb, we use i. This is based on a distinction used in the Amarna texts. For an explanation of this, see W. Moran, "The Use of the Canaanite Infinitive Absolute as a Finite Verb in the Amarna Letters from Byblos," JCS 4 (1950), pp. 169-172. The meaning of the root ʿdn is now clear from the Tell Fakhariyeh inscription. In the Aramaic section this root is used as an epithet for Adad to describe his fertile powers. The reading of θarra was first advanced by Driver (Canaanite Myths and Legends, (Edinburgh, T. & T. Clark, 1956)). The root is found in Arabic and connotes abounding waters. Herdner reads kt which is much more difficult. The cuneiform is of no assistance because the plate is too dark to read. The reading θr in place of θkt is very plausible epigraphically. Also in its favor is the reading of glθ in parallel to θr in Ugaritica V.3.1.7.

[30]The verbs yatāni and šarri are infinitive absolutes. It has become more and more apparent that the infinitive absolute had a widespread use as a narrative tense in Canaanite; here it continues a string of jussive clauses. See Moran, "The Use of the Canaanite Infinitive Absolute," and J. Wevers, "The Infinitive Absolute in the Phoenician Inscription of Azitawadd," ZAW 62 (1949), pp. 316-317.

[31]Most read lbnt as "bricks." This is unlikely for two reasons. First, Temples were not built of bricks in Syria-Palestine, but rather of hewn stone and wood. Second, the meaning "perfume" seems best read in another passage where again "bricks" has been the preferred reading: Himma ʾamatu ʾaθirati talbunu libānata, "Am I a maidservant of Asherah who mixes perfume" (CTA 4.4.61). A reading "bricks" here would be most unlikely for a goddess.

Let Baal make fertile with his rains.
Let him make fertile with ground water and torrents.
Let him set his voice in the clouds.
Let him blaze to the earth lightning.
Let him complete for himself a house of cedars.
Let him construct for himself a sweet smelling house.
(CTA 4.5.68-73)

Elsewhere Baal's powers of fertility are demonstrated in his struggle with Mot. In this section of the Baal cycle, Baal's death brings sterility, while his return to life brings fertility. Accompanying his victory is the cry, "Let the heavens rain down oil, let the wadis run with honey" (CTA 6.3.6).

It has long been recognized that the Baal cycle, with its strong interest in kingship and Temple building among the gods, intends to reflect the institutions of earthly kingship and Temple building as well. This is also true for the Akkadian Enuma Elish. Baal's (or Marduk's) investiture as king and his request for a Temple have direct parallels in the liturgical life of ancient Canaan (and Mesopotamia). It should not surprise us then that outside of the mythic Baal cycle we see similar patterns in the epic stories of Canaanite kings. Because human kingship has a divine prototype, the human king is heir to many of the traits of the divine king. Important among these is that of fertility. Just as Baal's proper execution of his royal office brought fertility to the land, so the same could be said for the earthly king. In particular, one can see in both the Aqhat and Kirta narratives how the fertility of the natural order depends on the health of the king or king's son. In the Kirta text there is a lament over the king's loss of health and his inability to rule properly.[32]   As is expected, the land begins to languish and the formulaic triad of bread, wine and oil (lḥm, yn , and šmn) disappear. This triad should be compared to their biblical counterparts (dāgān, tîrôš, and šemen / yiṣhār).

naša'ū ra'ši ḥāriθūma

---

[32]Admittedly the connection in the Kirta text is a bit difficult to substantiate due to the fragmentary condition of the tablets and the question of the order in which they should be read. H.L. Ginsberg doubts whether the drought spoken of here has any connection with the king's illness (ANET, p. 148 n. 31). We feel this is too cautious. We know from the Aqhat text that Canaanite theology did explicitly connect the health of the natural order to the health of the king. The appearance of these two themes in the Kirta epic cannot be a coincidence even if the fragmentary nature of the texts allow us no conclusive proof. Coogan's interpretation accords with our own. "When Baal died, Death reigned and nothing grew; when the king was ill, the crops failed and famine resulted. Thus Kirta's sickness, the subject of the cycle's second episode, was a failure of kingship, but because of his quasidivine status the gods were also implicated in its consequences" (Stories from Ancient Canaan (Philadelphia: Westminster Press, 1978), p. 55).

la-ẓāra ʿādibū daganī
kaliya laḥmu bi-dannīhum[33]
kaliya yênu ḥimātihum
kaliya šamnu bi-qu(bʿāti)

The ploughmen lifted their heads,
upwards, the sowers of grain.
Gone was the food from their bins.
Gone was the wine from their skins.
Gone was the oil from their vats.
(CTA 16.3.12-16)

It should not be not be forgotten that Haggai's hopes for reform were
not limited simply to Temple building. He also awaited a vigorous new dynastic
house. His language concerning the newly instated king (2:21-23) is replete with
mythic fervor and hope. It should not surprise us that the lament in the Kirta
passage finds a rough parallel in Haggai. We note the passage describing the
general infertility cited above (Haggai 1:10-11) as well as the following:[34]

How were you when you went to a grain heap of 20 measures
and there were only 10?
Or when you went to the   wine vat for 50 measures from the
press and there were only 20?[35]
(Haggai 2:16)

---

[33]We understand *lẓr* as a prepositional phrase derived from the root *ẓhr*. Compare
Arabic, *ẓahrun*, "back," Hebrew, *ṣōhar*, "roof," and also Akkadian, *ina ṣēri*, "upon"). The word *ʿdb*
has been parsed as a participle to parallel *ḥrôm*. It is important to note that the text could read *ʿbd*
too. The text is mutilated here and the photograph is poor. Epigraphically the readings are very
similar. We assume a reading *bdnhm* pace Herdner (CTA) who reads: *bʿdnhm*. The text is mutilated
but the parallelism between *ḥmṯhm* and *dnhm* argues for this.

[34]As noted above, the exact source of any one curse, or as in Haggai, a description of
the curse's effects, is often difficult to pinpoint. This description also has affinities with a curse
found in the bilingual inscription of Hadad Yithi of Guzan (published by A. Abou-Assaf, P. Bordreuil
and A. Millard, *La statue de Tell Fekherye et son inscription bilingue assyro-arameenne*, (Paris:
Editions recherche sur les civilisations, 1982)). The Aramaic text (line 19) reads: *wʾlp šʿryn lzrʿ
wprys lʾḥz mnh*, "May he cultivate 1000 measures of barley, but take in only one *paris*." The
corresponding Akkadian curse is found in lines 30-31: *1,000 ḥiriš 1 sūta liṣbat.*

[35]The text has some corruptions.   *mhytm]*   The consonants are correct but the
vocalization must be *mā-hĕyîtem*.   *bʾ]*   Again there is a problem of vocalization. The infinitive
absolute is to be read here as presumed by the LXX.   The use of the infinitive absolute is much
more common in biblical times than has been previously thought (see n. 20).   *pwrh]*   A difficult term,
it occurs only twice in the Bible.   It appears to mean " wine press" in Is 63:3.   The term is
misunderstood as a measurement in the LXX.   Some suggest a reading *mpwrh* (MT loses *mem* due to
haplography after *ḥmšm*). But *pwrh* could be understood as an adverb of place: "at the winepress."
The term is absent in the Peshiṭta.   If the term appeared before *yqb*, we could say that *pwrh* is
original and *yqb* was added as a gloss of a rare word.   The reverse could not be true; *pwrh* can
hardly be a gloss on *yqb!*

YHWH, like Baal, the cloud-riding god of the storm, was a deity who provided rain and fertility. When YHWH's kingship was maligned through lack of a Temple, or through the lack of an adequate earthly counterpart, the heavens withheld their dew and the earth, its produce.

The antecedents of Haggai and Zechariah's prophetic speech can be traced in two directions. On the one hand their speech employs the idiom of covenantal curse and blessing formulae. On the other hand they also employ the archaic mythic patterns related to the Temple and king. These patterns are ultimately derivable from the Baal myth in Canaanite religion.

But how are we to interpret this prophetic idiom? Haggai and Zechariah declare quite forthrightly that fertility will ensue once the actual work of the Temple begins. At face value, this seems a rather incredible, and perhaps somewhat irrational statement. It represents a magical understanding of natural causality in a Frazerian analysis. But at this point it is important to remember Evans-Pritchard's observations about such 'irrational' statements in the context of a particular culture. Most often such language is not the language of everyday life, it does not represent the way a particular culture thinks most of the time. Instead, such statements are *only made in particular ritual settings* and so they must be understood on those terms. If Evans-Pritchard is correct, then in other circumstances we would expect to find Israelite thinkers stating the causes of fertile fields and full granaries in much more mundane and ordinary terms.

Historians face problems which are much more severe than those of the contemporary ethnographer. The biblical historian cannot ask Haggai or Zechariah how he might characterize his hopes for renewed prosperity in a non-oracular setting. But the biblical historian can look for texts which address the concerns of famine and fertility outside of the oracular or mythic genre. Up to this point we have examined a number of texts from Canaanite and biblical sources which directly correlated the state of the Temple (and its primary patron—the king) with the resultant fertility or infertility of the land. All of the texts we examined were formulaic or mythic in nature. In order to understand more fully the relationship of Temple and king to the productivity of the land it would be helpful to see how this relationship is treated in other literary genres. At this point it would be helpful to digress for a moment and investigate several means of discussing fertility in ancient Near Eastern documents.

C.   Fertility and Famine in the Ancient Near East: Mythic and Mundane Perspectives

Most often one thinks of famine as a consequence of drought and other types of natural disasters. In other words, famine is thought to be a phenomenon outside the sphere of human control. As noted above, the epic and mythological texts of Ugarit portray famine in this very manner. These texts associate various mythic constructs (the king's health, Baal's Temple, Baal's victory over Mot) with the arrival of life-giving rain. But these mythic portraits are not the only perspectives on famine and fertility that the ancient world provides. Other non-mythic texts of both Akkadian and Northwest Semitic origin treat the issue of fertility in a rather different fashion.

The Akkadian evidence is most important in this regard. Here the fertility aspects of king and Temple are very clear and well documented. In mythic texts like Atrahasis (tablet 2) drought and natural disaster are often the agents of famine. Special acts of cultic devotion are invoked as a means of alleviating it. But in the more historical, yet still somewhat formulaic world of the royal inscriptions, a different picture emerges. In the religious ideology of Akkadian royal inscriptions the fertility the king provides for the land is not simply a magical ability to alter weather patterns. Rather, it is often a system of canals and dykes for irrigation, an ability to effect social and political reforms, as well as a provisioning of storehouses for grain collection and distribution.

As to the king's role in the irrigation system, both OB letters in general as well as the Mari corpus in particular demonstrate the historical interest the king had here.   The ideological role has always been clear from the names given to the canals and their role in royal inscriptions.[36] Socio-political reform and the

---

[36]An excellent example of this is an inscription of Hammurapi (in L. King *Letters and Inscriptions of Hammurabi* (London: Luzac , 1898-1900) 95:10-26). "When (read I-nu not *ninu*) An and Enlil gave me the peoples (*KALAM* with the sense of people not 'land' in a geographical sense) of Sumer and Akkad to rule and gave me authority over them (lit.: filled my hands with their nose ropes), then I verily dug the Hammurapi canal, whose name is 'Abundance of (for) the people.' It bears the productive waters to the people of Sumer and Akkad. Both of its banks I turned to arable land. And so verily I continually piled up heaps of grain." Earlier, R. Adams had shown that before the Early Dynastic period, water courses were purely a local concern (see *The Evolution of Urban Society* (Chicago: Aldine, 1966), pp. 66-71), yet royal inscriptions like the one above assert that the king was responsible. Was the king merely trying to take credit for work still done on a local level? Rowton argues on the basis of some 50 OB letters from Larsa and Isin that this was not the case ("Watercourses and Water Rights in the Official Correspondence from Larsa and Isin," *JCS* 21 (1967), pp. 267-74). The letters from Mari also demonstrate this (e.g. *ARM* III 1-10 and VI 1-12). By the OB period, if not before, watercourses were a royal responsibility.

provisioning and distribution of grain are closely associated in the royal inscriptions. The prologue to the Code of Hammurapi is typical here. Hammurapi is the one who "seizes the enemies" (*muṭammeḫ ayyābī*, Column II, lines 47) and (so) "brings together the scattered peoples" (*mupaḫḫir nišī šapḫātim*, II:49-50).[37] Once the land is pacified the 'epithets' describing Hammurapi's role in providing agricultural abundance appear almost endless. Some of these include: *mukammer nuḫšim u ṭuḫdim*, "The one who heaps up abundance and plenty" (I:54-56); *muṭaḫḫid nuḫšim*, "The provider of abundance" (II:53-54); *bābil ḫegallim*, "Bearer of prosperity" (II:20); *šākin mê nuḫšim ana nišī*, "Supplier of abundant water for the people" (II:39-41); *mušaddil mēreštim*, "The expander of arable land" (III:18-19); *mugarrin karê*, "One who piles up grain" (III:21); *šāʾim mirītim u mašqītim*, "One who sets up pasture land and watering places" (III:38-40). The various terms used here for agricultural abundance are standard for many Akkadian royal inscriptions and find parallels, if not their origins, in earlier Sumerian texts. In a cultural tradition of some 2,000 years, scribal tradition preserved these terms as a means of expressing the king's role in providing fertility. Significantly, these formulaic statements on fertility had a grounding in socio-economic reforms and building projects. Sometimes the recipient of this abundance is the Temple (as most often in the Code), other times the people at large are understood to receive this benevolence (as in the inscription Yaḫdun-Lim dedicated to Šamaš).[38] The ideological nature of these inscriptions has long been known. What is important for us is the fact that kings like Hammurapi boasted of their 'fertile' powers in the context of their political and military victories. Hammurapi becomes the provisioner *(zanānum)* of a city or Temple once he has brought it under his control.

The picture the Code of Hammurapi provides us accords very well with the more mundane descriptions one encounters in OB letters. Here, food shortages, whatever their cause, seem to be within the control of the state. At Mari, arrangements are made for giving grain on loan to areas in need (*ARM* IV:16). In another Mari letter from Kirum to Zimri-Lim (*ARM* X 31:13-16), food provisionment is directly related to political control. In this letter Kirum complains that Zimri-Lim is not administering the land properly and that as soon as he leaves there will be a rebellion. Zimri-Lim answers, "In the midst of the

---

[37]See Oppenheim's interpretation of this process in n. 57.

[38]G. Dossin, "L'inscription de fondation de Yaḫdun-Lim roi de Mari," *Syria* 32 (1935), pp. 1-28, plates 1 and 2, especially column I:20-26.

land, the Haneans are sated with grain. How could sated ones rebel?"[39]   Another
good example is the letter of Ishbi-Erra to Ibbi-Suen which recounts   the
problems encountered in getting grain to Ur.[40]   Although the details of the
letter allow some latitude of interpretation, the overall problem is clear. Ur was a
large city dependent on substantial grain imports. As the Amorite movements
overtook the northern principalities many of the major northern cities were
isolated from each other and from Ur. Famine resulted as the fields became
unsafe to harvest and as shipments became difficult to deliver safely. Ishbi-Erra,
at this point a servant to king, Ibbi-Suen, is charged with the task of buying grain
(whose price is rapidly inflating as the supply drops) and seeing to its delivery. In
return for this service he requests jurisdiction over Nippur and Isin. The shrewd
nature of this move becomes clear when he declares himself king of Isin several
years later. The reply of Ibbi-Suen is especially notable (text A7475 at the
Oriental Institute). He is aware of his plight. He asserts that Enlil's wrath has
caused the fields to yield no more. The language is mythic yet its referrent is
most mundane. Because Ibbi-Suen is not strong enough to possess complete
power over the hinterlands his land is subject to great famine.

Omens of the OB period (which must refer to earlier times—most likely
the fall of the Ur III dynasty) speak often of Ibbi-Suen's inability to keep the
villages in line and of the general rioting which characterized the end of his
turbulent rule.[41]   It cannot be an accident that many of these same omens speak
of widespread famine during this period.[42]   Could this not have resulted from the
loss of grain acquisition mechanisms during the break-up of Ur III?   In any
event, it should now be clear why the provincial governors in the Mari kingdom
constantly reassured their kings that they were not being negligent as to their

---

[39]See *ARM* X 31:13-16. A similar phrase is used in *ARM* II 37:17-18, indicating that
this query was perhaps proverbial.

[40]For a translation and historical commentary see T. Jacobsen, "The Reign of Ibbi-
Suen," *JCS* 7 (1953) pp. 36-47. Also compare the treatment of D. Edzard, *Die Zweite Zwischenzeit
Babyloniens* (Wiesbaden: Harrassowitz, 1957), pp. 45-48.

[41]For sample omens of this type see T. Jacobsen, n. 18. Especially significant is *YOS* X
24:11: *tibût šar hammê, šanû šumšu: ḫisbu ana ekallim ul irrub,* "The rise of a usurper, its other
name is, the wealth (of taxes and tribute) shall not enter the palace." T. Jacobsen compares this
with evidence that cities within Ur's jurisdiction stop sending their *eššešu* offerings to Nanna (the
god of Ur) in Ibbi-Suen's seventh year, just after the Martu invasion.

[42]See W. Moran (in C.B. Moore ed., *Reconstructing Complex Societies* (BASOR Suppl.
20, Cambridge: ASOR, 1974), p. 14) who notes the recurrence of famine here.

grain harvests or shipments.[43]   The procuring and subsequent distribution of foodstuffs by the palace was at the very heart of the king's role as provisioner of the people and the gods.

There is some question as to the relevance of this Akkadian data for West Semitic culture. The major problem is that in the West, no centralized irrigation system exists; agriculture depends mainly on seasonal rain. The would seem to obviate any role of human intervention. Yet one should not overstate the role of irrigation in Mesopotamia. Major areas of both the Mari empire and Assyria fell within the bounds of rain agriculture. One should note that West Semitic kings could fend off unnecessary famine in much the same way that their East Semitic counterparts did. By establishing well stocked storehouses and providing a means of keeping them filled, the king could provide for a population through periods of climatic fluctuation. The Joseph story in particular shows how a king could actually increase his power in times of natural food shortages by keeping central storehouses in good supply.[44]   Although this story has an Egyptian setting, its genre is clearly folkloristic in scope, and the type of grain collection and distribution it describs is not incompatible with that of Syria-Palestine.[45]

When, for whatever reason, the king could not keep peace and various enemies were allowed to besiege the land, the danger of famine was great.[46] Because cities depended on a stable countryside to provide basic foodstuffs, any disruption in the welfare or internal security of the countryside could lead to famine. In II Kg 6 we read of Ben Hadad's siege of Samaria. As the armies approach and cut off the village food supply, famine (rā'āb) results (6:25). Due to the shortage, food prices inflate dramatically and the food stores are depleted (6:27). A similar episode is recorded during the Babylonian siege of Jerusalem (II

[43]In the letters of Kibri Dagan, governor of Terqa, to Zimri-Lim, king of Mari, this is well represented (ARM III 3:30-32, 34). ARM III 17:29-31 is typical: "As to the grain collecting in Terqa due to the palace, I am not negligent (aḥam ul nadēku)." Also compare the correspondence of Baḥdi-Lim, another provincial governor (ARM VI 4,37,47,65).

[44]See the study of F. Crüsemann, Der Widerstand gegen das Königtums (Neukirchen-Vluyn: Neukirchener Verlag, 1978), pp. 143-55. He argues that the Joseph story was used to legitimate the newly evolved royal house in Jerusalem. It did so by depicting a strong king as one who could provision the people in times of want.

[45]At least two biblical stories come to mind in this connection. In Gen 26 a famine begins in the area of southern Judah. Earlier, Abraham had gone to Egypt (12:10) to find food under similar circumstances, but now Isaac is commanded to seek help in the city of Gerar. The story presumes that the city, being a place of grain storage and distribution, could aide semi-autonomous tribespeople through periods of crop failure or loss of pasturage. The same motif gives occasion for Elimelekh and Naomi to flee Judah in the book of Ruth.

[46]This is exactly the reason for the great famine in Samaria (II Kg 7:4) and for a famine which occurred during Gibeon's time due to the Midianite raids (Jg 6:3-4).

Kg 25:3). As the King's power over the countryside subsides so does his ability to provide abundance for the people.

As a counterpoint to this, Northwest Semitic royal inscriptions emphasize the close linkage between a king's royal reforms and a new availability of foodstuffs. The royal inscription of Bir Rākib is a case in point. In this text Bir Rākib attributes his ability to feed the people to his political power. The inscription begins with a description of the land before his rule. The drastically inflated food prices imply that supply was not meeting demand (lines 5-6).[47] It was only when the legitimate dynasty of Bir-Rākib was set up (line 2)[48] and political reforms were enacted (lines 7-8, 10) [49] that the food supply returned to adequate levels.

> wa-haytibih min qadmatih
> wa-kabarat hittāh wa-švʿārāh wa-θaʾāh wa-θaw(rāh)
> bi-yawmih wa-ʾað ʾakalat wa-šata(yat).....
> zvlat mwkrw....

> He made it better than its predecessor,
>   wheat, barley, ewes,[50] and cows[51] were abundant in his

---

[47]The text reads: *wa-qām pars bi-θiql wa-štrbt...bi-θiql wa-ʾsnb.* The terminology is difficult but there can be no doubt that a period of rapid inflation is being described. The context demands this, as do the first two monetary terms. J. Friedrich has shown (*Wiener Zeitschrift für die Kunde des Morgenlandes* 49 (1942), p.174, No. 1) that in the texts from Boghazkoi a *parīsu* was a fraction of a shekel. Here the shekel has been devalued to the point of equaling a *parīsu*. For a similar situation see II Kg 7:1. The inclusion of low prices as political propaganda in Akkadian royal inscriptions has been noted by Grayson, *Assyrian Royal Inscriptions* 1 (Weisbaden: Harrassowitz, 1972) p. 21. The usage begins early with the inscriptions of Sin-Kashid (D. Edzard, *Die Zweite Zwischenheit Babyloniens*, p. 154) and Sin-iddinam (E. Sollberger, *Ur Excavation Texts* 8 (London: British Museum), No. 72:61-68) and continues down to the period of Nabonidus (L. King *Babylonian Boundary-Stones and Memorial-Tablets in the British Museum* (London: British Museum, 1912), No. 37).

[48]"My father, Pana(mmu), by the legi(timate) rule of his father....The god Hadad stood with him (*abī Pana(mmū) bi-(sid)q ʾabuh...qām ʾilâ Hadad immih*, lines 1-2)." There is no need to reconstruct an exact history of this dynastic house for this study. In brief, it appears that Bir-Rākib's father, Panammu, had difficulty establishing his kingship against familial contestants (2-4). Bir-Rākib sees his father's success as proof of his divine election and of the legitimacy of his dynastic line.

[49]Again it is difficult to determine the details with any sort of precision, but there was a conspiracy in the royal house. The winning faction represented by Bir-Rākib overcame these troubles by appealing to Assyria (7). Thereupon the destructive forces were rid from the land and the captives were freed (8). Peace and prosperity were more abundant than before the conspiracy (9).

[50]θaʾāh, "ewes." This could be derived from Akkadian*šeʾûm,* "barley."

[51]θawrāh, "cows." This term and the previous term are taken as collectives. Gibson says this reading is impossible (*Textbook of Syrian Semitic Inscriptions,* 2 (London: Oxford University Press, 1975), p. 83), but he gives no explanation. He prefers reading *šawrat,* a type of grain (see Is 28:25 for Hebrew *śurâ.*). This reading is accepted by *KAI* as well.

days and so (the land) ate and drank[52] ......
cheapness of price[53] ...
(*KAI* 215:9-10)

Although this inscription is badly preserved at least two things are
evident. During the reign of a weak king the land languishes, but through the just
actions and proper administration of a legitimate king, one by whom Hadad
stands, the land flourishes. This ideology has close associations with Canaanite
myth, but here it is replete with socio-economic referents.

The inscription Panammu dedicated to Hadad (*KAI* 214) offers a
similar picture. Unfortunately this inscription is fragmentary too, but the general
structure is clear. It begins with an account of his divine call to kingship (lines 1-
4)[54] and then recounts the fertility of the land (5-7). [55] He too notes that in his
days the land ate and drank (9).[56] Significantly, this description of agricultural
abundance is accompanied by a description of his building program. Building
programs are a common feature in royal inscriptions whether West or East
Semitic. They represent the ability of the king both to requisition labor (*ṣābum*
in Akkadian) and to settle new areas of the country or bring them under royal

---

[52]Note that this exact idiom "(Israel and Judah) ate and drank" occurs after Solomon
has proclaimed his kingship and begun his reorganization of the nation (I Kg 4:10).

[53]The text is fragmentary, but significant. The point is that prices have come down
under a stable rule. The dynamics of this politically fueled inflationary cycle are paralleled quite
nicely in the biblical account of the Aramean siege of Samaria (II Kg 6-7).

[54]The idiom is similar to that of Bir-Rākib: "In my youth, the gods Hadad, El, Rešep,
Rākib-El and Šemeš stood with me and Hadad, El, Rākib-El, Šemeš and Rešep gave the sceptre of
ḥlbbh into my hand." The word *ḥlbbh* has no accepted etymology but it generally is assumed to
connote some royal sense.

[55]Lines 5-7 are very fragmentary. They are immediately preceded by the assertion
that the gods gave Panammu whatever he asked for (line 4). This is a common motif in Akkadian
royal inscriptions where the god is said either to hear (*šemû*) or grant (*magāru*) the prayers (*ikribū*,
tesītu) of the king. The text is complete again in lines 8-10, wherein Panammu again recounts his
election (8-9), the prosperity which accompanied his rule (9), and the divine commissioning of public
works(10). Lines 5-7 can hardly be anything but further emphasis on the splendor of his reign. The
words which are readable are a description of agricultural produce: *ʾarḍ švʿrl...ʾarḍ ḥiṭṭi wa-ʾarḍ
θûml...wa-ʾarḍ ....yaʿbidû ʾarḍ wa-karm,* "a land of barley...a land of wheat and a land of garlic...a
land... and they tilled the land and vineyard."

[56]see n. 52.

control.[57]   Panammu speaks of the cities *(qyrt)* and villages *(kpyry)* he establishes (line 10).

Finally we should mention the inscription of Azitawadda. Although this is not precisely a royal inscription—Azitawadda seems to be ruling on another's behalf, not on his own [58]—it does use similar vocabulary and ideas and seems to fit the form quite nicely. The connections between his internal domestic policies and the abundant harvests and food stores could not be more apparent.

yaḥwi[59] ʾanōk ʾiyyot danuñīyīm
yarḥib ʾanōk ʾarṣ ʿimq ʾadana[60]
la-mimmôṣōʾ šamš wa-ʿad mabōʾiya
wa-kōn bi-yōmōtiya kull nuʿm la-danuñīyīm
wa-šubʿ wa-manʿam
wa-malliʾ ʾanōk ʿqrt pʿr

I restored the *Dnnym*
I widened the land of the plain of *'dn*
from the East unto the West
In my days there all good things existed for the *Dnnym*

---

[57]For an example, see the Karatepe inscription discussed below (esp. Aiii:1-6) and the inscription of Yaḥdun-Lim (F. Thureau-Dangin, "Iaḥunlim, roi de Hana," *RA* 33 (1936), pp. 49-54), which reads: *ina sawê qaqqar naṣmī, ša ištu um ṣiatim šarrum šumšu ālam lā ipušu, anāku lālâm arṣī-ma, ālam ēpuš....māti urappiš, išdê Mari u māttya ukinma (ukimma),* " In the arid land in which no king had ever built a city in times past, I got the urge and so I built one....(and so) I settled the countryside and the foundations of Mari and my peoples (in the countryside) I made firm." (II:9-26). Also note that Solomon's building projects (I Kg 3-11) accompanied his reform and redistricting of the country. In this connection we find the observations of Oppenheim most illuminating (*Ancient Mesopotamia* (Chicago: University of Chicago Press, 1977), p. 83): "The most effective remedy against these potentially dangerous elements were projects of internal and frontier colonization which only a powerful king could set afoot. The inscriptions of such kings speak triumphantly of the ingathering *(puḫḫuru)* of the scattered, the resettling *(šūšubu)* of the shiftless on new land, where the king forced them to dig or re-dig new canals, build or resettle cities, and till the soil, pay taxes, do corvée work to maintain the irrigation system, and —last but not least—perform military service."

[58]Line two reads: "*wrk* made me powerful," indicating the subordination of Azitawadda to *ʾwrk*. On the problems of the identification and vocalization of *ʾwrk* and the relationship of *ʾwrk* to Azitawadda see F. Bron, *Recherches sur les inscriptions phéniciennes de Karatepe* (Paris: Librarie Droz, 1979), pp. 159-163.

[59]This vocalization assumes a *yipʿil* stem in the infinitive absolute. The vocalization is uncertain due to the difficulty of reconstructing infinitive forms in Semitic.

[60]For the problems of vocalizing *dnnym* and *ʾdn* see F. Bron, pp. 169-171.

both satiety and savory things.[61]
I filled granaries of *p^cr*. [62]
(*KAI* 26: Ai 3-6)

Elsewhere he speaks of his building projects (Ai:14-17) which followed
from his ability to pacify all of his land. He speaks of settling the *Dnnym* in
places where formerly there was unrest (Aii 1-6). As a result of these successes
he asserts:

wa-kōn bi-kull yōmōtiya šub^c wa-man^cam
wa-šabt / šibōt na^cīmat wa-nuḥt libb la-danunīyīm
wa-la-kull ^cimq ʾadana

And there existed in all my days satiety and savory things
a pleasant dwelling and peaceful heart for the *Dnnym*
and for all the valley of ʾ*dn*. (Aii:7)

At this point it would be helpful to reconsider the data provided by
Northwest Semitic blessing and curse formulae. As noted above, famine was a
favorite theme within this genre.   Many times the blessing of agricultural
prosperity or the curse of famine would have been directly attributable to a
divine control of the heavens. Consider, for example, the blessing formula of Lev
26:4 and its parallel curse formula in vv. 19-20. The blessing formula begins with
the condition, "if you walk in my statues..." The result clause follows:

wěnātattī gišmêkem bě^cittām

---

[61]The term *šb^c* can mean wheat or grain in Phoenician. See Dahood, *Psalms III* (AB
17a, Garden City: Doubleday, 1970), p. 348, where he says: "abstract *šb^c* assumes a concrete
meaning "wheat" by reason of being coupled with the concrete substantive *trš*, "wine" (the pairing
occurs in Karatepe C IV:7,9 which equals A III:7,9)." He cites Pr 3:10, where the two terms appear
in parallel verse, as further evidence. Ginsberg concurs with this analysis in reference to Karatepe
(*ANET*, p. 654). Tomback goes further and says that *šb^c* means "wheat" even when not paired with
trš (*Comparative Semitic Lexicon of the Phoenician and Punic Languages* (Missoula: Scholars
Press, 1978), p. 311). We have been cautious and given the term a more standard translation of
"satiety." The fact that it is paired with *mn^cm* ("savory things" cf. Psalm 141:4) could argue for the
meaning "wheat." A metaphoric inclusiveness might be intended, "(common) grain and savory
delicacies." Surprisingly Bron (p. 44) discusses none of this and offers an unsatisfactory translation
of "abondance et bien-être."

[62]The term *^cqrt* has no satisfactory etymology. The proposed solutions are presented
by Bron, pp. 45-46. Fortunately the hieroglyphic text is clear; the writing *ga-ru-na-i* indicates some
sort of agricultural building. This is what one would expect from the context. The term *p^cr* is
definitely geographic. The hieroglyphic text reads *pa-ḫa + r-wa-na-i*, which has been compared to
URU. *Pa-aḫ-ri* in Akkadian texts. See Bron, pp. 176-177 for an explanation of the data.

wĕnātĕnâ hāāreṣ yĕbûlâ
wĕ^cēṣ haśśādeh yittēn piryô

I will give you your rains in their time,
and the earth will yield its produce,
and the trees of the field its fruit.
(26:4)

As would be expected, just the reverse occurred when Israel
disobeyed God and fell under the curse. Thereupon God declares:

I will set the heavens as iron,
and the earth as bronze...
your earth will not yield its produce,
nor the trees of the field give its fruit.
(26:19-20)

Elsewhere this formula is attached more directly to the Temple itself,
as one would expect from the role of Temple building in the cosmogonic myth. In
Solomon's prayer it is said that proper prayer toward the Temple will yield rain (I
Kg 8:35), and that proper prayer can stop famine, pestilence, or enemy
besiegement (8:37). The latter trio *(rā^cāb, deber, ḥereb)* is found over thirty
times in the Bible[63] and is clearly traditional.

Not all curse formulae, though, attributed famine to divine intervention
in the heavens. Like the royal inscriptions cited above, these curses could
employ a very mundane and non-mythic idiom. Compare these two texts from
Jeremiah and Ezekiel:

If I go out to the field, then there are those slain by the sword.

---

[63]This trio is not expressed exactly in this fashion in Solomon's prayer. There,
enemies is substituted for sword, a minor change. Sometimes only sword and famine are paired. The
formulaic quality of these has been argued above. Also note that in the Atrahasis narrative,
pestilence and famine are paired. The text is fragmentary and evidence for a third element is
absent, but not impossible. The trio is also found in tablet XI of Gilgamesh, lines 182-185: "Instead
of your establishing a flood, would that a (1a)*lion* had arisen and diminished the people. Instead of
your establishing a flood, would that a (1b) *wolf* had arisen and diminished the people. Instead of
your establishing a flood, would that a (2) *famine* had been set and had slain the country. Instead of
your establishing a flood, would that a (3) *pestilence* (^dErra) had arisen and slain the people." In this
mythic portrait, the wild animals fill in the slot of war. This is a perfectly acceptable substitution in
light of the importance of the ritual hunt in Assyria. In some Assyrian royal inscriptions the
language describing the king as hunter and warrior are very similar. As for the biblical use of the
formulaic trio, it is found most often (about 90% of the time) in Jeremiah and Ezekiel.

If I enter the city, then there is the disease of famine.
(Jer. 7:18)

The sword is without, pestilence, and famine within.
He who is in the field, by the sword dies,
he who is in the city, famine and pestilence consume him."
(Ezek. 7:15)

Both of these texts interpret the curse of "sword, famine, and pestilence," in a non-mythic fashion. The historical event presumed by such a curse seems clear. As the approaching enemy gutted the countryside, those who took refuge in the city, weakened by lack of food, die from starvation or rampant disease.

In connection with this, Jeremiah's description of an enemy advance is revealing.

(The enemy) shall eat your harvest and bread,
they shall eat your sons and daughters,
they will eat your flocks and herds,
they will eat your vines and fig trees.
(5:17)

Jeremiah's description closely parallels a familiar curse in the Bible: to sow grain and have enemies eat it.[64]   This curse is none other than a description of vassalage. The counterpoint to such a curse is obvious, the blessing of being able to eat what one produces.[65]   Kilamuwa, the king of *Y*ᵓ*dy*, recognized the importance of this dynamic. In speaking of his own accomplishments, in contrast to former (and weaker) kings, he says:

kōn bêt ᵓabiya bimō-tôkt milakīm ᵓadīrim
wa-kull šalōḥ yadō la-laḥm
wa-kattī bi-yod milakīm kamō ᵓiš ᵓōkilt zaqan
wa-kamō-ᵓiš ᵓōkilt yod

My father's house was amid powerful kings.

---

[64]Expressions of this can be found in the curse lists of Deuteronomy (28:30-33) and of Leviticus (26:16, 23-26).
[65]See Lev 26:5.

> Though each one sent forth his hand for food,[66]
> I was like a consuming fire[67] of the beard or hand
> in the hand of the kings.
> (KAI 24:5-7)

Kingship, in the language of royal inscriptions, entailed the proper provisioning of the people. This could be unduly hindered by foreign razzias or full-scale invasions. Famine was kept at bay not by careful adherence to the ritual prescriptions of a 'fertility cult'. Rather a strong king—by whom the proper divine patron stood—could provide proper provisions for his people by ensuring autonomy and secure borders for the state.

D. Famine in the Post-Exilic Period

This study has uncovered two different types of speech which address the issue of fertility. In mythic literature, the fate of the land resides in the hands of the god(s). It is the storm god who assures for the land a healthy produce. When this god's kingship is contested or Temple under duress, the land languishes; when this god is honored as king and receives a Temple, the land flourishes. In royal inscriptions, the issue of fertility is *equally important*, but the language is much less mythological. In these texts the strong king enables the land to become fertile by pacifying the borders and executing building projects.

The curse formulae of covenantal texts represent a mixture of these two types. Sometimes the curse of famine is described in mythic terms, but often the reference is quite mundane. As to the latter, the invasion of foreign armies and the consequent unsettling of the rural countryside are depicted as major sources of food shortage and famine.

What then can be concluded from the texts of Haggai and Zechariah? They steadfastly declare that a rebuilding of the Temple will result in a new age of prosperity and fertility. Is this language simply symbolic speech about the

---

[66]This translation of *la-laḥm* follows M. Lidzbarski, *ESE* III, p. 228. S. Herrman has suggested reading a *nipʿal* infinitive "to fight" in his article, "Bermerkungen zur Inschrift des Königs Kilamuwa von Sengirli," *OLZ* 48 (1953), pp. 295-97. The problem with this reading is that is must assume the loss of *heh* from an original *lḥlḥm*. It could be an intervocalic syncope, or a scribal error. The reading *la-laḥm* is easier.

[67]This translation is problematic because the text has no word-divider between *km* and *ʾš*. Thus, some prefer to read the word *kmʾš* (prep. *km* + rel. *ʾš*). But this makes no sense. The image of fire on the other hand is appealing. See in particular the article of P. Miller, "Fire in the Mythology of Canaan and Israel," *CBQ* 27 (1965), pp. 256-61. He notes the common use of fire as a war image.

religious significance of the Temple? If so, then the real point of the prophetic message is to focus the hearer's mind on the *spiritual* importance of the Temple in the religious life of the community and not on the supernatural power of a particular stone and wood structure. The images of supernatural fertility, in this view, would simply be *literary metaphors* which emphasize the profound role the Temple plays in the *symbolic world* of Israelite religion. An opposite approach to this prophetic speech would be to understand it as instrumental in function. If this is the case, then the reconstituted Temple, in the minds of these prophets, really would have an effect on the agricultural life of the community.

In order to address this important issue of interpretation, it would be helpful to see if there are other texts in the restoration period which describe the impoverishment of Judah. Perhaps these texts could provide a different perspective from the descriptions found in Haggai and Zechariah. Unfortunately there are no texts which explicitly describe the plight of the returning exiles outside of the prophets themselves.[68]   What is available are descriptions of Israel at the beginning of the exile and at the time of Nehemiah as well as the Chronicler's own description of the hoped for restoration obliquely (but not unclearly) seen through his re-telling of Israel's history.

It would be helpful to trace briefly the theme of covenantal curse in the exilic era before turning to these texts. The use of this theme in the prophetic corpus of Jeremiah was mentioned above. The second redactor of the Deuteronomistic history also used these curse formulae. In one text (Dt 28:47-68) the advance of the Babylonian armies is described as the agent of YHWH's wrath. In this text, it is the physical destruction of war that brings a curse upon the land. Significantly Ezekiel and Lamentations use this curse pattern as a means of describing exilic Judah. The physical devastation of the Babylonian invasion had been extensive.[69]

Food shortages were extensive in this period, but they were not simply the result of military devastation. With the exiling of Judah's leadership, the land of Judah experienced social unrest. Gedaliah was appointed governor by the Babylonians and installed at Mitzpah, a short distance from the destroyed

---

[68]To be sure there is a pertinent section in Ezra (1-6) but it is not relevant to our purpose.

[69]See, in this regard, the discussion of M. Greenberg, *Ezekiel 1-20* (AB 22, Garden City: Doubleday, 1983), pp. 124-125, in which a close relationship is drawn between Ezek 4-5 and Lev 26. Zimmerli, *Ezekiel I* (Hermenia, Philadelphia: Fortress Press, 1979), pp. 51-52, includes a number of parallels as well as a discussion of their significance.

Jerusalem. But Gedaliah's ability to rule greatly suffered when the Neo-Babylonian empire labored under its own internal problems after the death of Nebuchadnezzar. In a short time, Gedaliah was murdered by a group of zealous patriots led by the Davidid Ishmael. In this bloody coup many other Babylonians were killed along with the Judeans who had collaborated with their captors. The power of the state had reached its nadir; the rural countryside was no longer within its control. Grain collection and distribution became troublesome. As Jeremiah tells the story of his death, the social unrest of the countryside unfolds before us.

> (after the murder)...Men came from Shechem, Shiloh and Samaria, 80 in number with shaven beards, torn clothes and gashed bodies, bringing grain *(minḥâ)* and frankincense to the house of YHWH. Ishmael came out to meet them from Mitzpah, weeping as he came. When he met them he said, "Come to Gedaliah." When they came to the middle of the city he slew them and cast them into a cistern. But 10 men were found among them who said to Ishmael, *"Don't kill us, for we have hidden stores of wheat, barely, oil and honey in the fields."* So he refrained and did not kill them with their companions.[70]   (Jer 41:5-8)

From this we see the difficulties of grain deliveries as well as the high value put on stored food. *Without the proper internal controls the ability of centralized structures such as the Temple and palace to procure provisions is extremely*

---

[70]The MT in Jeremiah is full of expansions as is clearly shown now in the Qumran fragments. These Qumran texts indicate that the LXX was not abbreviating a proto-Rabbinic text but instead represented a pre-Rabbinic text type considerably different from the *textus receptus* (see J. Janzen, *Studies in the Text of Jeremiah* (Cambridge: Harvard University Press, 1975)). One of the most common expansions in the MT is the filling out of names and titles. In these verses three such pluses are found: *bn ntnyh* (v. 6); *bn ᵓḥyqm* (v. 6) and *yšmᶜᵓl bn ntnyh....hᵓ whᵓnšym ᵓšr ᵓtw* (v. 7). Also, in verse 6, BH³ suggests that the LXX reading *hēmmâ hōlēk* be adopted over the Hebrew *hōlēk hālōk*. We would suggest that the second *hlk* is a dittography and that the infinitive absolute be retained so as to preserve the common idiomatic expression, *yēṣēᵓ.....hālōk ûbākōh* (against MT *bōkēh*). Verse 7, *ᵓl tkl* This expression occurs twice in this verse and its second occurrence is very awkward. We suggest that it is a dittograph, as it is not in the LXX. If we excise both this dittograph and the expansion of the subject by the inclusion of a proper name (see above) we are left with *wayyišḥātēm habbōr*. This sentence does not make sense. The Peshitta has *yašlîkem* which is also present in verse 9. The Peshitta may be supplying it here from verse 9 and not represent a different text, but this seems unlikely. If it is assumed to be original, a number of problems are solved. One can see how the *Vorlage* became corrupt. The verbal sequence *wyšḥtm . .. wyšlykm* led to the loss of *wyšlykm* by haplography. Moreover this is the very type of error we would expect in the LXX as Janzen notes (p. 120): "G is marked by a high incidence of haplography, which in many instances can be shown to have occurred in the Hebrew *Vorlage*. This together with the general absence of correction toward MT pluses (especially the larger ones) suggests two conclusions: First the *Vorlage* was the product of a quite narrow transmission so that when haplography occurred, there was little pressure to correct from sister manuscripts, and the different readings endured. Second, the *Vorlage* probably represented a pre-recensional text."

limited. What we have here are the social difficulties strong kings like Bir Rākib, Panammu or Kilamuwa boasted of overcoming.

The situation is not that much different a century later. Although the political configuration has changed a great deal, Nehemiah cannot keep even the precincts of Jerusalem safe let alone the province of Judah. His workers must be accompanied by armed guards wherever they go (4:15-23). Although the initial building activity of Zerubbabel had been greeted with much fanfare, the surrounding city of Jerusalem was in disarray until the arrival of Nehemiah. It is difficult to imagine that the countryside fared any better. If the borders were not secure, how could grain collection proceed properly?[71]

At the end of the book of Nehemiah, the period of the restoration draws to a close. Jerusalem is rebuilt, the proper duties *(mišmĕrôt)* of the priest are enacted and the regular offerings are contributed. Whereas in the earlier period of social upheaval, the Levites had to flee to the countryside while the Temple languished (13:10-11), now Nehemiah has gathered them up again and put them at their posts. Now all of Judah can bring the tithe of her grain, new wine, and oil into the storehouse (13:12). Nehemiah explicitly states that now the house of God is not forsaken because the store-chambers *(lĕšākôt)* are filled (10:39).[72] Israel is bringing her offerings.

The reforms of Nehemiah enable the province of Judah to repair the damage done to her political structure during the Babylonian invasion. Whereas earlier the power of the central authorities was weak, now in Nehemiah's time it is strong. Whereas earlier gifts and offerings were brought only sporadically to the proper authorities and even then, only in an environment of extreme danger, now a system of regular contributions is again in place. In the book of Nehemiah,

---

[71]The social conditions of post-exilic Judea have been the subject of several studies in the recent. Although these studies have areas of disagreement, they agree as to the profound social changes taking place in Judea and the consequent disruptions this produced in the economic environment. See, in particular, H. Kreissig, *Die sozialökonomische Situation in Juda zur Achämenidenzeit;* J. Weinberg, "Das Beit 'Abot im 6-4 Jh. v.u. Z.", *VT* 23 (1973), pp. 400-14; *idem,* "Demographische Notizen zur Geschichte der nachexilischen Gemeinde in Juda," *Beiträge zur Alten Geschichte* 54 (1972), pp. 45-58, *idem,* "Die Agrarverhältnisse in der Bürger-Tempel-Gemeinde der Achämenidenzeit," in J. Harmatta and G. Komcrocza (eds.) *Wirtschaft und Gesellschaft im alten Vorderasien,* (Budapest, 1976), pp. 473-86; H. Kippenberg, *Religion und Klassenbildung im antiken Judäa* (Göttingen: Vandenhoeck und Ruprecht, 1978) W. Schottroff, "Zur Sozialgeschichte Israels in der Perserzeit," *Verkündigung und Forschung* 27 (1982), pp. 46-68 and "Arbeit und sozialer Konflikt im nachexilischen Juda," in W. and L. Schottroff (eds.) *Mitarbeiter der Schöpfung* (München: Chr. Kaiser, 1983), pp. 104-148.

[72]The proper administration of these storehouses is explained in great detail in Ezek 40-42. As we shall develop further in section IV this is another link between the theological programs of Ezekiel and the Chronicler. The difference is only one of emphasis; the former is concerned with proper handling of goods once they reach the *lĕšākôt* while the latter is concerned with the goods' initial delivery to the *lĕšākôt.*

Israel's restoration is achieved when the priestly *mišmĕrôt* are properly observed
and the storehouses are filled. The needs of the hungry find a solution through
religious and political reform.[73]

But what about the earlier part of the restoration? What did it hope to
accomplish? It would seem logical to posit that its goals were little different than
those of Nehemiah. After all, the time span involved here is rather narrow, from
ca. 580 to 450 B.C.E. Apart from Haggai and Zechariah we have only one other
source to examine, the earliest edition of the Chronicler's history. As D.N.
Freedman has suggested, this earliest edition should be separated from the later
addition of Ezra and Nehemiah. In Freedman's view, the first edition of Chronicles
was a royalist work composed ca. 520 B.C.E. in support of Zerubbabel and his
Temple project.

> The author is above all a legitimist, and he is concerned with the divinely
> appointed institutions and duly authorized personnel which administer them
> on behalf of the people of Israel. Thus his interest focuses on the Kingdom
> of Judah, its capital city Jerusalem, and at the very center the Temple.[74]

As a legitimist, the Chronicler reads back many of his later ideals into
the reigns of David and Solomon. One idea of primary importance is the priestly
hierarchy and responsibilities. Like the author of the memoirs of Ezra and
Nehemiah, the proper keeping of the priestly *mišmĕrôt* is of paramount
significance. These chapters (I Chr 23-27) have few parallels in the material of
Samuel-Kings, and though some of the material is archaic (e.g. I Chr 27:25-31)
much reflects the post-exilic situation.

The Chronicler does not only advance his viewpoints in the reigns of
David and Solomon. Often times when he is speaking of reforming rulers, the
Chronicler can be expansive. The rule of Asa (II Chr 14-16) has a good deal of
new material as does the account of Jehoshapat (II Chr 17-20). For our purposes

---

[73]Another good example of Nehemiah's ability to relieve hunger due to famine (*rāʿāb*, v.
3) through political reform is found in Neh. 5:1-13. This text is treated extensively in several of the
sources mentioned in note 71.

[74]"The Chronicler's Purpose," *CBQ* 23 (1961), pp. 436-37. This view has been
supported by subsequent work. Several of the more important recent studies are those of F. Cross,
"A Reconstruction of the Judean Restoration," *JBL* 94 (1975), pp. 4-18, J.D. Newsome, "Toward New
Understanding of the Chronicler and his Purposes," *JBL* 94 (1975), pp. 201-17 and D. Petersen, *Late
Israelite Prophecy* (SBLMS 23, Missoula: Scholars Press, 1977), pp. 57-60. For, us the decisive
argument is the royalist interest found in the book of Chronicles proper. This cannot be a fifth
century literary construct. For a contrasting, older, view see W. Rudolf, *Chronikbucher* (HAT 21,
Tübingen: J.C.B. Mohr, 1955).

the Chronicler's treatment of Hezekiah is especially significant. In II Chr 32: 27-31 the richness of the land during Hezekiah's reign is described. It is a rather bland description with few embellishments. His treasuries are described and his stores are said to be full. The passage roughly parallels II Kg 20:12-19 and is tied to a similar narrative format; this is what the Babylonian envoy saw when visiting Jerusalem. Out of this brief description of economic prosperity a whole story is fashioned in 31:2-19 to account for it. The story is filled with late features. Its priestly terminology includes the division of priests into priests and Levites (32:2). The apportionment of priestly responsibilities is replete with late technical terms such as *hityāḥēṣ*, *maḥlĕqôt*,[75] and *mišmĕrôt*.[76] The sacrificial schedule includes the priestly idea of a morning and evening *ʿōlâ*.[77] In Kings only a morning *ʿōlâ* was known, the evening sacrifice was a *minḥâ* (II Kg 16:13). The formula *hāʿōlôt laššabbātôt wĕleḥŏdāšîm wĕlammôʿădîm* is late.[78] The use of *mĕnāt* as a sacrificial portion and *tĕrûmâ* as a generic offering are characteristic of P and the Chronicler.[79]

The Chronicler's account of Hezekiah's reform and the return of prosperity to Judah is most instructive. Once the king has made his contribution (31:3) he issues a command to the people to turn over their offering portion to the priests and Levites.

> When the word was spread, the Israelites produced grain, wine, oil, honey, and all the produce of the field in abundance. As for the tithe of it all, they brought it in also in abundance. . . they laid it in heaps. . . Hezekiah questioned the priests and Levites about the heaps and the high priest Azariah of the house of Zadok said: As soon as the contributions *(tĕrûmôt)* came to the house of YHWH there was eating, satisfaction and a great deal left over.[80]   For YHWH has blessed his people so that even this great amount remains." (II Chr 31:5-6,9-10)

---

[75]*Hityāḥēṣ* occurs 20 times, always in the Chronicler. *Maḥlĕqôt* occurs 40 times of which 36 are in the Chronicler.

[76]*Mišmĕrôt* occurs 78 times in the Bible, 37 times in P, 8 in Ezek 40-48, 19 in the Chronicler, 8 in the Deuteronomistic history and 4 in the prophets.

[77]Cf. Num 28:1-8.

[78]It is found mainly in the Chronicler (4 times). Elsewhere it is in Ezek 40-48 (twice).

[79]See G.R. Driver, "Three Technical Terms in the Pentateuch," *JSS* 1 (1956), pp. 99-105.

[80]One might wish to compare this to the phrase "the land ate and drank" found in West Semitic royal inscriptions (see notes 52 and 56).

With the amount left over the storehouses were filled and various priests were given charge of them (31:11-19). This section concludes with a precis of the theological program. If the work pertinent to the Divine Temple (ʿăbôdat bêt hāʾĕlôhîm) is done properly YHWH will bring prosperity (31:21). Our exegesis should make us wary of viewing the process as pure religious reform; the overflowing grain heaps required an ability to procure the offerings. Religious strictures required effective socio-economic structures.[81]

Post-exilic prophecy was cognizant of this too. Although Haggai is never quite so clear in this regard, Malachi is explicit. In a book that is concerned with proper religious practice, we read the following accusation:

> Can man rob God?   Yet certainly you are robbing me! You say, "How do we rob you?"[82]   (It is through) the tithe and offering (tĕrûmâ). With a curse you are cursed, for it is me you are robbing the whole nation of you. Bring the whole tithe to my storehouse, then there will be food in my house. "Test me in this" says the Lord of Hosts. "I will surely open for you the sluice gates of heaven and pour out a boundless blessing for you. I will rebuke for you the 'eaters', they will not destroy the fruit of your land. Your vines in the field will not miscarry," said the Lord.
> (Mal 3:8-11)

Malachi chooses to describe the cause of the curse in very mundane historical terms. The land of Israel suffers because the tithes and offerings were not forthcoming and the storehouse was empty. Yet, when Malachi looks forward to a return to an era of blessing his language becomes mythic; God shall open the sluice gates of heaven. But these assurances of YHWH's blessing, his mythic 'fertile rain from above', do not presume a magical stance toward the Temple itself. This is not simply the rising vegetation god bringing new rains. Material abundance was predicated on proper religious observance, but in that observance there were sown the grains of social and political reform. To test YHWH's faithfulness in this regard required not simply faith but works as well.

---

[81]In this connection we might want to consider again that Zechariah does not describe the land's barrenness as due to natural factors (see n. 27). Social chaos is what precedes Temple building, while fertility and social order are what follows it. We can now see that Haggai is isolated in his use of natural factors to describe the land before Temple building. If we combine this evidence with the fact that Haggai's actual descriptions are formulaic, we have good reason to understand them as less than fully objective descriptions.

[82]The LXX reflects a reading hyʿqb. The MT reading is found in Aquila, Symmachus, and Theodotion, which must reflect a correction to the Hebrew. But which was correct in the first place, the LXX or the MT? This is difficult; both make good sense and a corruption could have gone in either direction. We take the MT as correct on the basis of lectio difficilior, and because the LXX could very well be creating a word play here on Jacob (cf. Hos 12:4).

E. The Rhetoric of Post-Exilic Prophecy

The aim of our study has been to examine the dynamics of the Temple rebuilding hopes of Haggai, Zechariah and Ezekiel 40-48. In particular we have sought to identify more precisely the economic and political *Sitz im Leben* out of which the rhetoric of reform and restoration developed. In order to accomplish this we have wandered in several tangential directions in hope of opening up new insights into our era.

Two language systems, or 'games' to use Wittgenstein's term, have appeared which concern themselves with fertility. On the one hand we have the language of mythology. This language is ultimately traceable to the storm god Baal, the one who majestically appears in the skies, the one who supernaturally provides food for the masses. His fecund powers are not unpredictable, they follow upon his accession to kingship through victory over divine enemies (chaos) and the building of his Temple. Like the divine king Baal, the human king also has power over the forces of fertility. In the stories of Aqhat and Kirta, the king's health and ability to rule properly directly affect the agricultural yield.

On the other hand there is the more mundane (and so more historiographic) language of the royal inscriptions and chronicles. To be sure the language here is often formulaic and ideological, yet the *bruta facta* of human history receive some mention. There is a strong interest in the fertility of the land, and as should be expected, this fertility is attributed to royal capabilities. But the language of fertility we meet here is not that of the storm god theophany; rather it is that of royal reform. Just as in Hezekiah's reform so also in the reigns of Kilamuwa, Panammu and Bir-Rākib, the land "ate and drank" because the borders were safe and grain collection mechanisms were in place.

The language of the treaty curses is mixed in metaphor. Sometimes its reference to famine or plenty seems directly derivative from the social climate; other times its more mythic component is prominent. These formulaic compositions bridge the gap between the symbolic world of myth and the real world of human history.

Our thesis has been that the low agricultural yields faced by Haggai and Zechariah were not without political cause. The texts we examined from the whole temporal scope of the restoration (Jer 41 ca. 580; II Chr 31 ca. 515; Mal ca. 500-475, and Neh ca. 450) indicated a rather uniform description and solution to the problem. The inability to collect and distribute grain was preventing the land from prospering. In sum, our point has been to show how the prophetic rhetoric of Haggai and Zechariah, while drawing on the patterns of ancient myth, was at the same time firmly grounded in historical fact. A renewed Temple cultus and offering system accompanied by a strong leader could inaugurate an era of prosperity (at least for some), not simply because these were magical or supernatural institutions, but because the social realities they represented had historical referents.

The rhetoric of these prophets does have an instrumental quality. A renewed Temple cult would be of considerable importance in returning the land to prosperity. But it is important to note that this belief in role of the Temple as a purveyor of fertility is not simply irrational magic. The anthropologist R. Horton has argued that non-Western religious myth and ritual has a strong instrumental component; its practitioners really expect their rites to produce physical change in the environment. He also asserts that not all of these beliefs are irrational and, in some cases, Western thinkers could learn from them.[83] In particular he mentions the insights many tribal religions possess as to the psychosomatic causes of physical illness.[84] Many tribal healing rites, when approached in a sympathetic fashion, show a strong connection between emotional well-being and physical healing. Horton, in arguing against the symbolist school of anthropology, states that these instrumental effects must be taken seriously in any interpretation of a non-Western culture.[85]

But this is not to argue that Haggai, Zechariah, and Ezekiel took a simply instrumental stand toward the Temple reconstruction process. There were also some very important symbolic referents attached to Temple building.[86] In particular one should note the symbolism involved in the rite of laying the

---

[83]In this fashion he refutes the claim of some anthropologists who would compare Horton's beliefs with those of Frazer. That is, they claim that Horton, by comparing primitive religion with modern science, necessarily underestimates the mental capacities of primitive peoples. For his response to his critics see his article, "Tradition and Modernity Revisited," in *Rationality and Relativism*, pp. 201-260.

[84]Horton, "African Thought and Western Science," pp. 138-140.

[85]Horton argues that another strength of his approach is that it takes the participants' view seriously ("Tradition and Modernity Revisited, pp. 208-09). These participants always, in Horton's view, claim that the instrumental nature of their rituals and myths is of primary importance. On the other hand there is the perspective of E. Leach, a symbolist, who argues that the participant's explanation of a ritual action is of little utility. See his essay "Virgin Birth" reprinted in his *Genesis as Myth and Other Essays* (London: Jonathon Cape, 1969).

[86]The symbolic role of the Temple in Israelite and Canaanite thought has been well described in R. Clifford, *The Cosmic Mountain in Canaan and the Old Testament* (HSM 4, Cambridge: Harvard University, 1972) and J. Levenson, *Sinai and Zion*. Also see Ackroyd's perceptive treatment of this material in his *Exile and Restoration*, pp. 138-217.

cornerstone of a newly (re-)built Temple.[87] This rite is explicitly mentioned in Zech 4:6b-10a, Ezra 3:10-11 and certainly implied in Haggai 2:15-19.[88] It is important to note that it is in the context of this particular ritual activity that the prophets composed their mythological idiom concerning the return of fertility to the land. Outside of the ritual *Sitz im Leben*, the hopes for renewed fertility are composed in a wholly different idiom.[89]

As we argued in our introduction, it is probably best to understand the rhetoric of primitive and archaic myth as having both an instrumental and a symbolic component. What we as Westerners would neatly separate, the ancients saw as an integral unit. The Temple was both an economic and a spiritual center. The metaphorical images of myth combined both these elements. Frazer chose to take these metaphors literally and argued that primitive and archaic peoples had vastly different ideas of natural causality from our own. He labeled this thought 'magic'. Biblical scholars, to the degree to which they have subscribed to this system, have been uncomfortable with many mythic images in the Bible because they implied a more magical, and hence (in Frazer's system) less ethical means of conceptualizing the deity. Our contention has been that if we put aside the often unacknowledged Frazerian assumptions about myth and ritual, a rather different interpretation of mythic thought in prophetic rhetoric might emerge. Studies in the recent past which have attempted to portray these prophets in a positive light have attempted to emphasize the symbolic meanings behind the Temple rebuilding rhetoric.[90] Because of the legacy of Frazer the instrumental nature of their speech was not treated in any detail.

It has not been the purpose of this study to examine the symbolic meaning found in the prophetic rhetoric of Ezekiel, Haggai, and Zechariah. This is not because the symbolism is unimportant. On the contrary, its importance has

[87]See A. Kapelrud, "Temple Building, A Task for Gods and Men, *Or* 32 (1962), pp. 56-62; R. Ellis, *Foundation Deposits in Ancient Mesopotamia* (1968); D. Petersen, "Zerubbabel and Jerusalem Temple Reconstruction," *CBQ* 36 (1974), pp. 366-72; B. Halpern, "The Ritual Background of Zechariah's Temple Song," *CBQ* 40 (1978), pp. 167-80.

[88]For the Haggai text, see the discussion of D. Petersen, *Haggai and Zechariah 1-8*, pp. 87-96.

[89]It should be noted that this observation supports the conclusions of Evans-Pritchard (see the introduction, pp. 10-12). Statements which imply a magical or mystical orientation to natural phenomena are not the everyday vocabulary of primitive or ancient peoples. They represent a special type of vocabulary which is limited to certain ritual or oracular moments. Parallels exist in modern religious communities as well. Most modern believers are perfectly able to use one type of vocabulary in a worship or prayer setting and another in their daily non-religious life. Neither use of language, when taken on its own, represents the manner in which the believer apprehends the world.

[90]For example, the excellent works of P. Ackroyd, *Exile and Restoration*, and D. Petersen, *Haggai and Zechariah 1-8*.

been well documented in recent research. Rather, it has been the concern of this study to examine the social function of their oracles. It has been our contention that a closer examination of the social function of Temple rebuilding provides new insights into the Temple's role in agricultural fertility. It allows us to describe the instrumental aspects of this prophetic rhetoric without diminishing the spiritual or religious value of their message. By clarifying the social role of a rebuilt Temple the rhetoric of post-exilic prophecy can be appreciated in a new fashion.

APPENDICES

Appendix A: *Maś'ēt*

The word is a *mem* preformative noun from the root *nś'*, "to bear, carry." This historical development is unusual: *manśi't* > *maśśi't* > *maśśē(')t* > *maś'ēt*. The loss of *'alep* and the change in vowel quality from *i* to *e* are quite common *(bi'r* > *bēr)*, as is the preservation of the *'alep* in the orthography even after it was lost in common speech (cf. *bēr* > *bĕ'ēr*). The pronunciation *bĕ'ēr* is an example of Massoretic hypercorrection to account for the preserved consonantal *'alep* in the preserved text. Perhaps *maś'ēt* shows a comparable--and historically incorrect--restoration of the *'alep*. The loss of doubling is difficult to explain, but an analogy exists. The word *kissē'*, "throne," has a plural *kis'ōt*. Perhaps the form *maś'ēt* is the result of a backformation from an original (and still attested) plural *maśō't*.

In Punic, the term *mś't* is used many times in temple tariff texts. Almost all of the occurrences are in the famous Marseilles text (*KAI* 69). It is also found in two Carthage tariff texts (*KAI* 74 and 75). The term is used in a very precise technical fashion to denote the fee due the priest in the course of offering sacrifices. It represents that part of the offering which the priest may keep.

The Bible also makes provisions for a priestly share but it never uses the *maś'ēt* to denote it. The earliest record of it in the Bible is found in II Sam 11:8. In this text it simply refers to a gift Uriah receives from king David. A similar meaning is found in Jer 40:5 and Est 2:18. On the other hand, two texts in the Bible use *maś'ēt* as a technical term for a religious offering. In II Chr 24:6 and 9 it is used to refer to a temple tax which is given Mosaic precedent. In Ezek 20:40 it is said that in a restored Jerusalem people will bring the *tĕrûmâ*, "gifts," the *rēšīt maś'ēt*, "first offerings," and the *qŏdāšīm*, "holy things." We are left with one last text, Amos 5:11: "You have trampled on the poor; a *maś'ēt* of grain you have taken from them." In this instance the referent, be it secular or religious, is ambiguous. Perhaps in this very ambiguity we see that making harsh contrasts between the secular and sacred economies is somewhat artificial. As we shall see below, the artificial quality of this contrast is apparent in poetic texts like this prophetic oracle. Could not the Amos text refer to any type of onerous extraction of revenue from the poor, whatever its ultimate purpose within the urban center?

Appendix B: *Maṭniʾu

In Phoenician the verb *ṭnʾ* can have both a secular and a sacred meaning. Its basic sense is "to set up, erect," mostly referring to building or statues. This basic meaning is found in Old South Arabic as well. It has a derived meaning "to appoint." It can also be used in religious texts with the meaning "to donate (a gift)." From this meaning we get the Phoenician noun *mṭn*, "offering," and perhaps the Hebrew noun *ṭeneʾ*, "(offering) basket."

In a recent article W. Moran solved an important crux in the Amarna correspondence with a new reading involving this root.[1] The text in question is *EA* 337, where we read: "The king, my lord, has written to me, *šūšir-me IGI.KÁR.MEŠ ma-aD-ni-a ana pāni ÉRIN.MEŠ GAL MEŠ,* prepare.....before the great army arrives" (lines 7-10). The problem is *ma-aD-ni-a*. The previous solution was to read *malānia* ("a place to stay the night" cf. Hebrew *mālōn*).[2] There were many problems with this proposal. For one, it still left unexplained the Sumerian equivalent *IGI.KÁR*. Secondly, the writing *ma-la-ni-a* is not the expected rendering of the proposed Canaanite cognate. If it is a Canaanite word (and so it appears, as a gloss of *IGI.KÁR*), the writing does not reflect the Canaanite shift (*malān > mālōn,* thus we expect a *lu* writing *(lō)* instead of *la*). Also *ni-a* is anomalous. We expect either *na* (masc. sing.), *nīma* (masc. pl.) or *nūti* (fem. pl.) for the oblique accusative.

Moran draws on a recent lexicographical distinction proposed by Steinkeller.[3] The latter argues that *IGI.KÁR* and *GÙRUM* are different words in Sumerian, not graphic variants. In the Ur III period and earlier, *IGI.KÁR* meant "provisions, supplies." Later the term was equated with Akkadian *aširtu*, an offering to a temple. Its earlier, more general meaning was taken over by *GÙRUM* and equated with Akkadian *piqittu*, "provisions."

This meaning, "provision, supplies," is perfect for *EA* 337 because this is exactly what a vassal king was to provide for the troops of his sovereign. Moran provides numerous examples. One problem for this translation is the meaning of *IGI.KÁR* in Mesopotamia in the LB period. There the word was now

---

[1]"A Note on *igi-kár*, 'provisions, supplies," *Acta Sumerologica* 5 (1983), pp. 75-77.

[2]O. Shroeder, "Kanaanäisch *malania* = 'Quartier, Lager," *OLZ* 18 (1915), p. 105-106.

[3]"On the Reading and Meaning of *igi-kár* and *gùrum (IGI.GÀR),* " *Acta Sumerologica* 4 (1982), pp. 149-51.

associated with *aširtu*, "offering." But the preservation of the more archaic value, "supplies," is not insoluble, because occasionally archaic values for Sumerian words survive in the geographical periphery long after they have disappeared in the mainland.

The meaning "provisions," if correct, also suggests a solution to *ma-aD-ni-a*. We should read *maṭniʾa*. Moran argues that the *maqtil* formation suggests a "means of standing, a support or what one erects." Whatever the semantic development, it is difficult to separate this LB Canaanite word from its later use in Phoenician. Moreover, we see the parallel development of sacred and cultic use. *Ṭanaʾ* can mean both "to set up, support" and "to donate, give" and *mṭnʾ* can mean both "sacred offerings" and "provisions or supplies."

The evolution of *mṭnʾ* is instructive for the development of cultic vocabulary which Levine proposed. Cultic vocabulary often has secular origins. In many respects, the lexical development of the Canaanite word *mṭnʾ*, parallels the lexical development of *IGI.KÁR* in Mesopotamia. Both terms have early meanings "provisions, supplies" which were later lost in favor of a more specifically cultic sense of "offerings."

Appendix C: *Tĕnûpâ*

The term *tĕnûpâ* has been the subject of considerable discussion in recent years. No true consensus has been reached. Previously, the meaning "wave-offering" (from *hēnîp*, "to wave") was assumed. This meaning is first attested in the Mishnah and Talmud.[1] G. R. Driver was one of the first to question this Rabbinic etymology and definition.[2] He noted several problems. First, the earlier evidence of the Versions offers no hint that the *tĕnûpâ* offering was a special rite characterized by waving or any other movement. Often the terms used to translate *hēnîp* and *tĕnûpâ* are freely interchanged with those for *hērîm* and *tĕrûmâ*. There seems to be no specific technical usage known to either of these terms at the time the Versions took shape.

The meaning "wave offering" is often simply impossible in context. For instance, the whole body of Levitical priests at their ordination are called a *tĕnûpâ* (Num 8:11, 15,21). Or in Ex 35:22 and 38:29 each Israelite is said to bring a *tĕnûpâ* before the altar. As Driver notes, it would be highly unlikely that each Israelite performed his own cultic act of waving a gift toward the altar in the liturgy. More likely, the *tĕnûpōt* are simply gifts each Israelite turned over to the priest who, in turn, brought them to the altar during the liturgy. Finally the mention of whole animals being waved before YHWH is very implausible (Lev 23:17,20).

Driver then compares the constituent elements of the *tĕnûpâ* and *tĕrûmâ* offerings and finds a remarkable similarity. They are both capable of including a diverse range of items. Jewelry and other precious goods are mentioned,[3] along with individual parts of a victim's body,[4] but both can be simply a *tĕrûmâ* (Lev 9:18-21) while occasionally the thigh can be a *tĕnûpâ* (Ex 29:23-24 and Lev 8:26-27)). Moreover, Driver notes that the purpose of the offerings is

---

[1]For the specific texts, see J. Milgrom, "The Alleged Wave-Offering in Israel and in the Ancient Near East," *IEJ* 22 (1972), pp. 33-38.

[2]"Three Technical Terms in the Pentateuch," *JSS* 1 (1956), pp. 100-105.

[3]Compare Ex 35:22 with its parallel texts Ex 25:1-9, Ex 35:5-9 and 36:2-6. Both sets of texts enumerate similar offerings, yet the former is called *tĕnûpâ*, while the latter, *tĕrûmâ*.

[4]The breast of the *šĕlāmîm* is often called the *tĕnûpâ* and the thigh, the *tĕrûmā* (Lev 7:29-31 and 11:32-34).

always the same, they are offerings made to YHWH but are received for use by the priest.

Driver concluded that both of these terms, which are found mainly in P, are late loan words from Neo-Babylonian. His Babylonian evidence for tĕrûmâ is impossible.[5] In the case of tĕnûpâ he suggests as a cognate, the Akkadian word nūptu (nāpu) meaning 'additional payment.'

While Driver's solution has not received acceptance, the problems he raised for the traditional meaning 'wave-offering' have been discussed. Milgrom argued that the basic meaning of the root n-w-p was not 'to wave' but 'to elevate.'[6] He compared the Arabic nāfa / yanūfu and noted the retention of this meaning in two Hebrew nouns: nôp, 'elevation' and nāpâ, 'height.' In addition he examined several passages in Isaiah where hēnîp is parallel to hērîm. He argues that the meaning 'to wave' in each of these passages is far more difficult than 'to raise.' Finally Milgrom noted the Egyptian formula for an offering presentation; 'Come, O King, elevate offerings before the face (of the god).' In the illustration accompanying this text there is a supplicant raising a plate full of a variety of items, not unlike the varied materials of the tĕnûpâ. Milgrom concludes that it is this elevation of the offerings which effects their change from profane to sacred.

There are several problematic points in this analysis. First concerns the comparative evidence. It is true that Arabic has a root n-w-f which connotes the idea of 'tallness.' But the root can also yield nouns meaning 'excess' or 'surplus.' Von Soden noted the connection of this to Hebrew tĕnûpâ.[7] He suggested the Arabic noun nawf, 'surplus,' was the best cognate to the Hebrew term. Unfortunately, he did not comment on Driver's proposal of nūptu, 'additional payment.' This Akkadian noun is often found in conjunction with the verb nâpu: 'to make (nāpu) a nūptu (additional) payment.'[8] This nicely parallels the Hebrew idiom hēnîp tĕnûpâ: 'to make (henîp) a tĕnûpâ offering.' Moreover this etymology fits in quite nicely with many of Milgrom's insightful observations as to why a tĕnûpâ offering is required in the first place. The tĕnûpâ offering is not an independent type of offering. Most often it constitutes a special treatment of an already existent offering. As Milgrom notes, the 'specialness' or 'additional'

---

[5] He suggested the root tarāmu, 'to levy,' an unknown Akkadian verb! See Appendix D for a comprehensive treatment of tĕrûmâ.

[6] 'The Alleged Wave-Offering.'

[7] 'Miryam—Maria '(Gottes—)Geschenk,' ' UF 2 (1970, p. 271.

[8] One should also note the Old South Arabic verb hnf which appears to mean 'to give, grant.' See J. Biella, Dictionary of Old South Arabic (Chico: Scholars Press, 1982) p. 298.

quality of this rite confers a sanctity or holiness on the item being offered which was not there in the first place.[9]

Milgrom states that several texts in Isaiah also suggest that the basic verbal sense of *nāpâ* is "to raise, elevate."[10] Besides Is 10:15, he cites 11:15, 13:2 and 19:16. The latter three texts refer to the lifting of a hand while the first refers to the lifting of a rod. Again, the comparative evidence suggests the more traditional rendering, "to wave or wield." In Jewish Aramaic, Syriac and Mishnaic Hebrew, the verbal sense of this stem is "to wave," often referring to the hand. In Mishnaic Hebrew and Jewish Aramaic it can refer to the waving action of winnowing or fanning. Syriac preserves a number of idioms pertaining to the waving of the hand. This waving can be either friendly or aggressive in nature, reflecting the usage of Is 13:2 (waving as an invitation) and 11:15, 19:16 (waving in a menacing manner). The Gt usage, "to brandish," recalls the usage of Is 10:15.

In conclusion one can say that the Hebrew offering type *tĕnûpâ* is related to the Akkadian term *nūptu* as well as the Arabic noun *nawf*. Not only does the Akkadian verbal usage closely parallel that of the Hebrew, but also the meaning of the Akkadian and Arabic terms (something done in addition, or excess) accords quite nicely with the purpose and function of the Isrealite sacrificial rite.[11] Again these cognate terms show one important manner in which cultic terms develop. The terms of the cult are derivative of other, often secular spheres of life. In the context of the cult they take on highly specialized and idiosyncratic meanings.

---

[9]See his article "Hattĕnûpâ," in *Studies in Culitc Theology and Terminology* (Leiden: Brill, 1983), pp. 139-158.

[10]"The Alleged Wave-Offering," p. 34.

[11]For the sake of completeness one should mention the proposal of D. Hillers ("Ugaritic *Šnpt* 'wave-offering,'" *BASOR* 198 (1970), p. 142 and *BASOR* 200 (1970), p. 18. He analyzes the Ugaritic noun *šnpt* (*Ugaritica* V 13:24) as a *shin* preformative noun, from the causative inflection *šnp*, "to wave." He argues that this noun is related to Hebrew *tĕnûpâ*. He supports his hypothesis by stating that in Hebrew *taqtūl* nouns are associated with the C stem. Thus *tĕnûpâ* is to *hēnîp* what *šnpt* is to *šnp*. Hillers' statement, though true at a synchronic level for the Hebrew lexicon, has serious problems elsewhere. See Appendix D for the problems attendant here.

Appendix D: *Těrúmã*

On the basis of an inner-biblical study and an inaccurate Akkadian cognate, G.R. Driver concluded that *těrúmã* was a late loan word in Hebrew from Neo-Babylonian.[1] The occurrence of the term at Ugarit plus an Akkadian cognate from the OB period argue against this. The biblical term occurs almost always in P, which might suggest a late date, but at least two other possibilities exist. It could be an example of the archaizing tendency of P, who takes great interest in the technical terms and offices which had fallen into desuetude during the monarchy.[2] Or more likely, the term, which also occurs in Dt 12:6,17, may have been much more prevalent in the pre-exilic period than our biblical text indicates.

The term has both religious and secular uses. In P it is a very inclusive, almost generic, term for sacred offerings and gifts. Such is its use at Ugarit as well.[3] At Mari it refers to some sort of payment due to the palace (*ARM* I 80:5-14).[4] In Proverbs (29:4) the term refers, very cynically, to forced imposts: *melek běmišpāṭ yaʿămōd ʾāreṣ // wěʾîš těrûmôt yehersennāh*, " The king upholds the earth with justice, while the man of (forced) imposts destroys it." In this passage a just king is contrasted with an individual who takes too much in the way of revenue. The term, thus, demonstrates a non-cultic nuance.

The etymology of *těrûmã* remains highly problematic. Since the publication of von Soden's provocative article, "Mirjam--Maria '(Gottes--) Geschenk," a good deal of scholarly attention has been focused on its etymology

[1]"Three Technical Terms."

[2]See F. Cross, *CMHE*, pp. 321-23 for other examples of P's use of archaic terms.

[3]The term now appears in *KTU* 1.43.3, thanks to a new collation. Gordon (*UT* 5) had read the word as *ðrmt*. The first sign is unusual in the drawing (See C. Virolleaud, "Les inscriptions cunéiformes de Ras Shamra," *Syria* 10 (1929), pl. LXV for the drawings; the troublesome sign is *ð*. Gordon argued that this was a rare writing of *ð*. But the writing of *ð* in this line is unlike the frequent writings of *ð* in other lines of this text. Herdner (*CTA* 33) did not try to read the sign but simply left a bracket. The new collations made in *KTU* evaluate these unusual wedges as an erasure.

In a recent article, Dietrich, Loretz and Sanmartin ("Das Ritual *RS* 1.5 = *CTA* 33," *UF* 7 (1975), pp. 525-528) showed how a *trmt* reading fit the context as well. It opens a section which lists various cultic gifts. The structure appears chiastic: *trmt*: items of *trmt* (clothes and gold) // items of *šlmm* (faunal): *šlmm*. The next section follows the chiasm as well: Items of offering (a) : divine recipient (b) // divine recipient (b) : offerings (a). Both sections are opened by the liturgical line *k (or ʿlm) tʿrbn DN bt mlk*, "When the goddess enters the royal house."

[4]It also occurs in NB. Note also the PNs *Tarîmtu* (OB) and *Tarîndu* (NB).

and function. Von Soden, in his article, suggested that the Hebrew PN was a *kurzname* of a longer Mirjam—DN (" Gottes—Geschenk"), where Mirjam was analyzed as a *mem* preformative noun formed on an old Amorite root *r-y-m.* [5]

His major piece of evidence is from Akkadian sources. In Akkadian, von Soden argues, there is an independent root *r-y-m* (*râmu* III in *AHw* " schenken"). This root, von Soden feels, is distinct from *râmu* I (" lieben"; cf. Arabic *ra²ima)* and *rêmu* (" sich erbärmen," from common Semitic *rḥm*). Von Soden believes the root is not originally Akkadian because the verbal use of the root only begins about 1400. Until then one only finds the verbs *qâšu* and *šarāku* meaning " to give." The verbal root is first used in *kudurru* texts, but previously the nominal form *rīmu* had been found in Old Akkadian and OB names such a *rīmuš* (" His gift," i.e. the god's) and Rim-Sin (" gift of Sin"). Even the noun, in this period, did not seem to have a free use, for it is limited to personal names. The same holds true in Assyrian. There the nominal form *rīmūtu* only appears in the MA period, and the verb is never used.

Other evidence for the peripheral or perhaps non-Akkadian origin of the root is the fact that the noun *tarīmtu,* " gift," only appears in the periphery in the OB period.[6] More support for von Soden derives from the nominal form. This is a *taprīsu / taprīstu* form. It is typically formed from the D stem;[7] but in Akkadian *râmu* has no D form which would account for this nominal formation! The noun-verb combination *tarīmtu / râmu* does not fit the expected Akkadian pattern. An Amorite borrowing would be supported by the presence of a very similar *t* preformative noun in Hebrew and Ugaritic.

If von Soden is correct that there is an Akkadian root *r-y-m* which means " to give" and this root is of peripheral or even Amorite origin, then the etymology of Hebrew *těrûmâ* must be reconsidered. In the past the etymology of Hebrew *těrûmâ* seemed clear; it was from the C inflection of the root *r-w-m,* " to raise, or lift high." From this came the sense " to lift up (and take away)" or perhaps " to bear up (and carry as a gift)." Such a development would be parallel to the Hebrew and Phoenician term *mś²t,* " tax, levy," from a verb *nś²*, "to lift up."

---

[5]For similar nominal formations cf. *ma ʿyān,* "spring" and *midyān,* "strife, contention" a bi-form of *mādôn.*

[6]*ARM* 80:7.

[7]Cf. the Arabic D *maṣdar tafʿīl.*

But there is one flaw in such an etymology. The form *taqtul* in Hebrew is often formed from the G stem.[8] This statement requires some explanation because recently Hillers and Levine have asserted that they are associated with the C stem.[9] The nouns and their associated verbal stems are outlined below:

Verbal Root	Nominal form	Associated inflection (G or C)
bwʾ	tĕbûʾâ	G (see Lev 25:22)
bws	tĕbûsâ	G
byn	tĕbûnâ	G or C
yšᶜ	tĕšûᶜâ (as though from šwᶜ)	C (but see note 13 below)
kwn	tĕkûnâ	C
lwn	tĕlunnâ	C
mwr	tĕmûrâ	C
verb not used	tĕmûnâ	–
mwt	tĕmûtâ	G (usage is related to G)
nwʾ	tĕnûʾâ	C (Num 32:7, read with *Qĕrē*)
nwb	tĕnûbâ	G
nwm	tĕnûmâ	G
nwp	tĕnûpâ	C
nqp	tĕqûpâ (as though from qwp)	G or C
ʔᶜ hd?[10]	tĕᶜûdâ	–
qwm	tĕqûmâ	G
rwᶜ	tĕrûᶜâ	C
rwm	tĕrûmâ	C
śwm	tĕśûmet	G
verb not used	tĕšûʾâ	–
šwb	tĕsûbâ	G (C?)[11]
verb not used	tĕšûqâ	–

---

[8]See J. Barth, *Die Nomenalbildung in den semitischen Sprachen* (Leipzig: Hinrichs, 1894), § 188b.

[9]B. Levine, "Assyriology and Hebrew Philology: A Methodological Re-Examination," in *Mesopotamien und Seine Nachbarn* (XXV Rencontre Assyriologique Internationale II, Berlin: Dietrich Reimer, 1982), p. 527; D. Hillers, *BASOR* 198 (1970), p. 142.

[10]The complicated development of this root was shown by Albright, *YGC,* p. 104, n. 28, and p. 106, n. 136.

[11]We include *tĕšûbâ* as though from the G. Its G derivative ('return') is the most common meaning in biblical Hebrew. Only two usages, both found in Job, derive from the C ('answer').

Out of 22 examples, 8 are related to the G stem, 8 to the C, 4 can be eliminated due to the absence of a verb, or uncertain root, while two are G or C. The numerous examples of nominal forms associated with the C stem would appear to be quite problematic for the proposition that this nominal type is related to the G stem. A closer look at 7 of nouns associated with the C stem, though, is revealing. These would be: *těšûʿâ, těkûnâ, tělunnâ, těmûrâ, těnûʾâ, těrûʿâ, and těnûpâ*. Of these 7 forms, 4 exist only in the C and N inflections *(těšûʿâ, těkûnâ, tělunnâ, těmûrâ)*, 2 have only C inflections *(těnûʾâ, těrûʿâ)* while another has all inflections in the C except for 1 G and 1 Polel *(těnûpâ)*. This is important for the lexicographer to note. Several of these verbs are not problems because they did not originally have C inflections. In roots where all that is attested are C and N forms, the lexicographer must be quite suspicious. In many, if not most, of these forms, an original G--N distinction in proto-Hebrew became the somewhat idiosyncratic biblical Hebrew C--N distinction, where the causative inflection is active and the N is passive.   This C--N distinction is a late development in Hebrew that does not represent the original situation in Northwest Semitic.[12] The reason for this occurrence is not difficult to trace. It is well-known that in Hebrew, the common Semitic active-transitive *a-i* vowel class *(*qatala /yaqtilu)* left the G stem and was absorbed by the C. In triliteral roots only *nātan /yittēn* survived. Once these original G verbs of the *a-i* class became C forms, the *taqtul* nouns—which had derived from the G stem—became secondarily associated with the C stem.

The original G inflection of one verb may be retained in the Septuagintal rendering of the name for one of the pillars in the Solomonic Temple (I Kgs 7:21). The Massoretes vocalized this name *yākîn*. The LXX has *Yachoum*. This reading must be accepted *lectio difficilior*. But its "difficultness" is not unexplainable. This vocalization probably preserves the original G inflection of the root which is attested in Ugaritic, Arabic and Phoenican. Another possibility is that this LXX vocalization reflects an archaic N form *yakkōn*. In any event, the Massoretes, or their predecessors—no longer knowing of such a verbal inflection—corrected the text to its subsequent Hebrew equivalent.

---

[12]The development of a C--N distinction (active—passive) in Hebrew from an original G--N distinction was noticed by T. Lambdin, but is as yet unpublished. Previous scholars had noted that the C inflection was secondary in a number of Hebrew verbs (including Barth, see n. 13 below) but had not traced this development in any detail.

With this observation in mind, several of problem forms are clearly not problems at all. The roots *yš*ʾ, *kwn*, *lwn*, *mwr*, *nw*ʿ, and *rw*ʿ which occur only in the C or in the N and C, probably had an original G base.[13]   We are left then with *tĕnûpâ* , *tĕšûbâ* , and *tĕrûmâ*. As was observed in appendix C, the etymology of *tĕnûpâ* is problematic. *Tĕšûbâ* is not good evidence because three of its uses are derived from the G stem.[14] Only in Job do we find the C derived noun "answer." By the time of the writing of Job there would have been a sufficient number of interfering forms such as *tĕmûrâ* and *tĕrûʿâ* to allow a noun to form from the C by analogy. But this could not as easily explain the development of *tĕrûmâ*. The *t* form of a *r-w/y-m* root is very old as shown by the forms from Ugarit and Mari (Amorite?) derivation in the cognate material. We could hardly explain these forms by an inner-Hebrew development. Barth, without these data from archaic cognate sources, arrived at essentially the same conclusion about these few problematic *taqtul* forms.[15] He conjectured that even these forms were from an old G-base.

An examination of *taqtul* nouns outside of the hollow roots is also instructive. There are some 15 examples. One can be eliminated from discussion due to the lack of a corresponding verb.[16] Of the other 14, 8 seem to be related to the D or Dt.[17] This fits the Aramaic usage of *taqtul* nouns and also fits a well known pattern in Semitic to associate *t* nouns with the D stem. Some of these Hebrew examples are probably loans from Aramaic, or nouns formed under the influence of Aramaic. The other 6 include 2 which must be based on the G since this is the only inflection of the verbal root, [18] and 3 others which most likely are G.[19] Only one is *possibly* from the C stem.[20] This sampling shows that an association of *taqtul* nouns to the C stem is not very likely.

The Hebrew evidence, then, could be the conclusive data von Soden needed for his thesis of an old Amorite root *r-y-m* meaning " to give." If this

---

[13]See also Barth, *Nomenalbildung*, § 188b. Additional support for an original G inflection for *yš*ʿ is the PN *yĕsa*ʿ-DN, "God has delivered."

[14]See note 11.

[15]*Nomenalbildung*, § 188b.

[16]*talʾûbôt*.

[17]*tahlûkâ* (see the D usage, "to walk in a throng"), *tahnûnîm*, *tamrûq* (Prv 20:30 has textual problems), *tanhûmîm*, *taʿlûmîm*, *taʿlûmâ*, *taʿnûg*, and *taʿrûbôt*.

[18]*tagmûl* and *tahlûʾîm*

[19]*tahpûkâ*, *tahbûlâ* and *taʿṣûmôt*.

[20]*tamrûr* (could also be G or D).

were the case, *těrûmâ* would not be a problematic form at all. It could have been formed from an original *rāma, yarīmu* root in proto-Northwest Semitic which meant "to give," and then later subsumed under the C stem when the Hebrew language took shape and the original *a-i* vowel class was lost. Moreover, an original G stem meaning "to give" would explain the free use of *hērîm*, " to present, offer." Earlier we mentioned that scholars said the semantic development of *nś*ʾ › *mśʾt* was similar to *rwm* › *trmh.* But the similarities are not complete. The verb *nśʾ* is never freely used with the sense "to contribute, give" as *rwm* is. Moreover, the semantic development is limited to Israel and Phoenicia. In *trmt,* we have a geographically widespread noun.

Unfortunately, the etymology of *těrûmâ* will remain somewhat ambiguous because von Soden's Akkadian data is not as strong as he would have it. Von Soden equivocates in *AHw* and suggests a possible etymology of *rāmu,* "beschenken," as *rîmu.* In his article he allows no such possibility. His case would seem quite solidly based on the Assyrian form *riāmu* he cites in *AHw* but unfortunately, no such form has been found! The Assyrian form is reconstructed on the basis of von Soden's etymology and should have been marked with an asterisk to show its hypothetical quality. Von Soden' s proposal for a *riāmu* root thus has no concrete evidence. All of the arguments are elusive and can only be said to have a semblance of credibility when taken as a whole. His evidence in sum includes 1) the Hebrew name Miryam, 2) Amorite names like Yarim-Lim, 3) the supposed peripheral quality of the use of the *riāmu* root, and 4) Hebrew *těrûmâ* . We greatly strengthened his case for 4, but 1 is still difficult because its use as evidence depends on the overall argument. The Amorite PN Yarim-Lim is susceptible to other interpretations ("Lim has exalted"). Finally we note that 3 is only valid if 1 and 2 are true!

Von Soden argues that it is a peripheral root because of the lack of verbal uses of the root until the MB period and the Amorite names. The names are ambiguous evidence as we noted above. The lack of verbal usage could point to peripheral origins (cf. the discussion of *tarīmtu* above), but it could also point to a late semantic development in Akkadian from (a) *rêmu,* " to show mercy," to (b) "to bestow mercy through a gift." Von Soden distinguishes the two graphically (*irīm* vs. *irēm* in the preterite) and semantically ("to give," "to show mercy"), though he admits that the two are *often* indistinguishable in actual spelling. In fact, according to the dictionary listings, there are *no* graphically distinct forms;

i-ri-im could be read *i-re-em*. A present form *i-ra-am*, or an Assyrian form *i-ri-am*, which would separate *rêmu* and *râmu*, is non-existent.

The semantic distinction is not as clear as von Soden would have it either. In a brilliant work, Y. Muffs[21] analyzed the use of *rḥm* in Aramaic legal grants. In a formal gift document—which emphasizes the spontaneous volition of the donor, as opposed to a sale document which emphasizes full payment, receipt of payment and satisfaction in the transaction—the giver is said to give a gift *b-rḥmn*, literally, "in mercy" but more idiomatically, "by free volition." The legal function of this idiom is to emphasize the spontaneous volition of the donor. This is in contrast to the sale document which is concerned with full payment, receipt of payment and satisfaction with the transaction.

For Muffs, the bestowing of a gift was conceived as an extension of the concept "to show kindness to someone, to be beneficent"; a gift was simply conceived of as a "kindness." Thus, Akkadian *irīm* "he gave" represents a simple semantic development from *irēm* "he showed kindness." Support for Muffs exists in the very use of the putative *râmu* III root in Akkadian. It is first used in royal grants, precisely the type of text which would emphasize the spontaneous volition of the donor in bestowing a gift. The term *rḥmt* in Aramaic is so close in form and usage to the Akkadian noun *rēmūt*, "gift" that Muffs suggests that the Aramaic term is calqued from the Akkadian. In other words, Aramaic speakers in Elephantine used their own root *rḥm* to create a new legal term based on the legal usage of the Akkadian term *rēmūt*.

For Levine, the presence this calque conclusively proves that *râmu* III "to give as a gift" is ultimately derivable from *rḥm* not *rym*.[22] But there are still problems. In Aramaic one word is used in situations where Akkadian uses at least two different roots, *ra'āmu* and *rêmu* (and possibly *riāmu!*). Aramaic *yhb brḥmn* = Akkadian *ina nar'amatīšu iddin*, "he gave willingly" and Aramaic *mn zy rḥmt* = Akkadian *ana ša irammu*, "to whomever he wishes (he shall give)." The Aramaic calque *rḥmt*, though it evinces the close relationship between mercy and gift, proves nothing about the use of root in earlier times. A calque, far from clarifying things, only makes the issue more complicated. We now know how Aramaic speakers in the fifth century etymologized a Neo-Babylonian legal term, but we do not know the terms earliest etymology in Semitic.

---

[21]*Studies in the Aramaic Papyri from Elephantine* (Leiden: Brill, 1969), pp. 128-37.
[22]"Assyriology and Hebrew Philology."

In sum, the data is confusing. If there is a *r-y-m* root meaning "to give" in Old Amorite, two other roots have provided much interference and linguistic "noise" in the subsequent development of the root in Hebrew and Akkadian, that is, *rwm* ("to be high") and *rḥm* ("to show kindness"). For us the association of *taqtul* nouns to the G and the archaic quality of a *t* preformative noun in West Semitic gives slight favor to von Soden's proposal. The inner-Hebrew phenomenon of moving *a-i* verbs to the C, and the resultant development of some backformed *t* -nouns on the newly developed stem, could account for the Hebrew form *tĕrûmâ* . But the West Semitic evidence as a whole (Ugaritic *trmt* and the possible Amorite form *tarīmtu*) cannot be analyzed by means of an inner-Hebrew development.

BIBLIOGRAPHY

Abou-Assaf, A., P. Bordreuil, and A. Millard. *La statue de Tell Fekherye et son inscription bilingue assyro-arameenne.* Paris: Editions recherche sur les civilisations, 1982.

Ackroyd, P. *Exile and Restoration.* Philadelphia: Westminster, 1975.

Adams, R. *The Evolution of Urban Society.* Chicago: Aldine, 1966.

Aharoni, Y. *Arad Inscriptions.* Jerusalem: Bialik Institute, 1981.

———. *Beer-Sheba I.* Tel Aviv: Tel Aviv University, 1973.

Albright, W. F. "Specimens of Late Ugaritic Prose," *BASOR* 150 (1958), pp. 36-38.

———. "The Early Alphabetic Inscriptions from Sinai and their Decipherment," *BASOR* 110 (1948), pp. 6-22.

———. *Vocalization of the Egyptian Syllabic Orthography.* New Haven: American Oriental Society, 1934.

———. *Yahweh and the Gods of Canaan.* 1968. Reprint. Winona Lake: Eisenbrauns, 1978.

Alonso-Schökel, L. "Erzählkunst im Buche der Richter," *Biblica* 42 (1961) pp. 148-58.

Alter, R. *The Art of Biblical Narrative.* New York: Basic Books, 1981.

Artzi, P. "The First Stage in the Rise of the Middle-Assyrian Empire, *EA* 15," *Eretz Israel,* 9 (1969), pp. 26-27.

Astour, M. "Political and Cosmic Symbolism in Gen 14 and in its Babylonian Sources." In *Biblical Motifs.* Edited by A. Altmann. Cambridge: Harvard, 1966 pp. 65-112.

Avigad, N. "Two Phoenician Votive Seals," *IEJ* 16 (1966), pp. 243-51.

Barr, J. "Some Semantic Notes on the Covenant." In *Beiträge zur Alttestamentlichen Theologie: Festschrift für W. Zimmerli.*. Edited by H. Donner et. al. Göttingen: Vandenhoeck und Ruprecht, 1977.

Barth, J. *Die Nomenalbildung in den semitischen Sprachen.* Leipzig: Hinrichs, 1894.

Barthelemy D. *Les devanciers d'Aquila.* Leiden: Brill, 1963.

———, and J. Milik. *Qumran Cave I. Discoveries in the Judean Desert* I. Oxford: Clarendon Press, 1955.

Beattie, J. *Other Cultures.* London: Cohen and West, 1964.

Beidelman, T. W. *Robertson Smith and the Sociological Study of Religion.* Chicago: University of Chicago Press, 1974.

Biella, J. *Dictionary of Old South Arabic.* Chico: Scholars Press, 1982.

Blau, J. and J. Greenfield. "Ugaritic Glosses," *BASOR* 200 (1970), pp. 11-17.

Bloch, M. "The Past and the Present in the Present," *Man* 12 (1977), pp. 278-92.

Bodine, W. *The Greek Text of Judges.* HSM 23. Missoula: Scholars Press, 1980.

Bowker, J. "Psalm CX," *VT* 17 (1967), pp. 31-41.

Bron, F. *Recherches sur les inscriptions phéniciennes de Karatepe.* Paris: Librarie Droz, 1979.

Burkert, W. *Homo Necans: The Anthropology of Ancient Greek Sacrificial Ritual and Myth..* Berkeley: University of California, 1983.

——. *The Structure and History of Greek Mythology and Ritual..* Berkeley: University of California Press, 1979.

Burney, C. *The Book of Judges.* 1918. Reprint. New York: KTAV, 1970.

Caquot, A., M. Sznycer, and A. Herdner. *Textes ougaritiques, I. Mythes et légendes.* Littératures anciennes du Proche-Orient 7. Paris: Les Éditions du Cerf, 1974.

Cassirer, E. *An Essay on Man.* Oxford: Oxford University Press, 1944.

Cassuto, U. "Baal and Mot in the Ugaritic Texts," *IEJ* 12 (1962), p. 79.

——. *Biblical and Oriental Studies,* vol. II. Jerusalem: Magnes, 1975.

Charbel, A. *Zebaḥ Šělāmîm: Il sacrificio pacifico.* Jerusalem: Commercial Press, 1967.

Clifford, R. *The Cosmic Mountain in Canaan and the Old Testament.* HSM 4. Cambridge: Harvard, 1972.

Coogan, M. *Stories from Ancient Canaan.* Philadelphia: Westminster Press, 1978.

Cooper, J. *The Curse of Agade.* Baltimore: Johns Hopkins University Press, 1982.

Cross, F. M. *Canaanite Myth and Hebrew Epic.* Cambridge: Harvard University Press, 1973.

——. "The Epic Traditions of Early Israel." In *The Poet and the Historian.* Edited by R. Friedman. HSS 26. Chico: Scholars Press, 1983, pp. 13-39.

———. "The Evolution of the Proto-Canaanite Alphabet," *BASOR* 134 (1954), pp. 15-24.

———. "Notes on the Ammonite Inscription from Tell Siran," *BASOR* 212 (1973), pp. 12-15.

———. "Prose and Poetry in the Mythic and Epic Texts from Ugarit," *HTR* (1974), pp. 1-15.

———. "A Reconstruction of the Judean Restoration," *JBL* 94 (1975), pp. 4-18.

———. "The Song of the Sea and Canaanite Myth," *Journal for Theology and the Church* 5 (1968), pp. 1-25.

———. "Studies in the Structure of Hebrew Verse." In *The Word of the Lord Shall Go Forth.* Edited by C. Meyers and P. O'Connor. Winona Lake: Eisenbrauns, 1983, pp. 129-55.

Crüsemann, F. *Der Widerstand gegen das Königtum.* WMANT 19. Neukirchen-Vluyn: Neukirchener Verlag, 1978,

Dahood, M. *Psalms III.* AB 17a. Garden City: Doubleday, 1970.

Daniel, S. *Recherches sur le vocabulaire du cult dans las Septante.* Paris, 1966.

Dietrich, M. and O. Loretz. "Neue Studien zu den Ritualtexten aus Ugarit (I). Ein Forschungsbericht," *UF* 13 (1981), pp. 63-100.

———. "Eine Abrechnung aus Ras Hani (782)," *UF* 12 (1980), pp. 401-02.

———. "Das Ritual *RS* 1.5 = *CTA* 33," *UF* 7 (1975), pp. 525-528.

Diodorus of Sicily. Translated by R. Geer. Loeb Classical Library, 1954.

Duhm, B. *Die Psalmen.* 2nd edition. Tübingen: Mohr, 1922.

G. Dossin, "L'inscription de fondation de Yaḫdun-Lim roi de Mari," *Syria* 32 (1935), pp. 1-28.

Douglas, M. *Purity and Danger.* New York: Praeger, 1966.

Driver, G.R. *Canaanite Myths and Legends.* Edinburgh, T. & T. Clark, 1956.

———. "Three Technical Terms in the Pentateuch," *JSS* 1 (1956), pp. 100-105.

Dussaud, R. *L'art phénicien du IIe millénaire.* Paris: Geuthner, 1949.

———. *Les origines Cananéenes du sacrifice Israéalite.* Paris: Leroux, 1941.

Edzard, D. *Die Zweite Zwischenzeit Babyloniens.* Wiesbaden: Harrassowitz, 1957.

Eichrodt, W. *Theology of the Old Testament*, 2 vols. London: SCM Press, 1961.

Eisenbeis, W. *Die Wurzel ŠLM im Alten Testament*. BZAW 113. Berlin: de Gruyter, 1969.

Eissfeldt, O. *Erstlinge und Zehnte im alten Testament*. BWANT 22. Leipzig: J. C. Hinrichs, 1917.

Emerton, J. "The Riddle of Genesis XIV," *VT* 21 (1971), pp. 403-37.

Engnell, I. *A Rigid Scrutiny*. Translated by J. Willis. Nashville: Vanderbilt University Press, 1969.

Evans-Pritchard, E. *A History of Anthropological Thought*. New York: Basic Books, 1981.

——. *Witchcraft, Oracles and Magic among the Azande*. Oxford: Clarendon, 1937.

——. "Lévy-Bruhl's Theory of Primitive Mentality," *Bulletin of the Faculty of the Arts* (Egyptian University, Cairo) II,1 (1934).

——. *Theories of Primitive Religion.*. Oxford: Oxford University Press, 1965.

Fensham, F. "Notes on Treaty Terminology in Ugaritic Epics," *UF* 11 (1979), pp. 265-74.

Finkelstein, J. "The Middle-Assyrian Šulmānu Texts," *JAOS* 72 (1952), pp. 77-80.

Finley, M. *The World of Odysseus*. 3rd ed. New York: Penguin Books, 1982.

Firth, R. *Primitive Polynesian Economics*. London: Routledge and Kegan Paul, 1965.

Fisher, L. "Abraham and his Priest-King," *JBL* 86 (1962), pp. 246-70.

——, and S. Rummel, eds. *Ras Shamra Parallels*. 3 Vols. Analecta Orientalia 49-50. Rome: Pontifical Biblical Institute, 1972-81.

Fitzmyer, J. *The Aramaic Inscriptions of Sefire*. Rome: Pontifical Biblical Institute, 1967.

Forde, C.D. and M. Douglas. "Primitive Economics." In *Man, Culture and Society*. Edited by H. Shapiro. New York: Oxford University Press, 1960, pp. 330-44.

Frazer, J.G. *The Golden Bough: A Study in Magic and Religion*, 13 vols. 1913. Reprint. London: Macmillan, 1980.

Freedman, D. "The Chronicler's Purpose," *CBQ* 23 (1961), pp. 436-42.

——. *Poetry, Pottery and Prophecy*. Winona Lake: Eisenbrauns, 1980.

Fried, M. *The Evolution of Political Society.* New York: Harper and Row, 1967.

Friedrich, J. "Hethitisch ZU = GIN 'sekel," *Wiener Zeitschrift für die Kunde des Morgenlandes* 49 (1942), pp. 172-179.

Gaster, T. *Thespis.* New York: Schuman, 1950.

——. "The Service of the Sanctuary." In *Mélanges syriens offerts á Monsieur René Dussaud,* vol II. Paris: P. Geuthner, 1939, pp. 577-82.

Geller, S. *Parallelism in Early Hebrew Poetry.* HSM 20. Cambridge: Harvard, 1979.

De Geus, C.H.J. *The Tribes of Israel.* Amsterdam: Van Garcum, 1976.

Gevirtz, S. *Patterns in the Early Poetry of Israel.* Chicago: University of Chicago Press 1963.

Gibson, J.C. *Canaanite Myth and Legends.* Edinburgh: T & T Clark, 1977.

——. *Textbook of Syrian Semitic Inscriptions,* 3 vols. London: Oxford University Press, 1975.

Gill, D. "*Thysia* and *Šĕlāmîm:* Questions to R. Schmid's *Das Bundesopfer in Israel.,*" *Biblica* 47 (1966), pp. 255-62.

Ginsberg, H. "*Nwšpwt lclylt ʾlʾyn—Bcl*", *Tarbiz* 4 (1934), p. 384.

Goody, J. *The Domestication of the Savage Mind.* New York: Cambridge, 1977.

Gottwald, N. *The Tribes of Yahweh.* Maryknoll: Orbis Books, 1979.

——. "Were the Early Israelites Pastoral Nomads?" In *Rhetorical Criticism: Essays in Honor of James Muilenburg.* Edited by J.J. Jackson and M. Kessler. Pittsburgh Theological Monographs Series 1. Pittsburgh: Pickwick, 1974, pp. 223-255.

Gray, G.B. *Sacrifice in the Old Testament.* 1925. Reprint. New York: KTAV, 1971.

Gray, J. *Joshua, Judges and Ruth.* London: Nelson, 1967.

——. *The Biblical Doctrine of the Reign of God.* Edinburgh: T & T Clark, 1979.

——. *The Legacy of Canaan.* SVT 5. Leiden: Brill, 1965.

A. K. Grayson, *Assyrian Royal Inscriptions.* 2 vols. Weisbaden: Harrassowitz, 1972.

Greenberg, M. *Ezekiel 1-20.* AB 22. Garden City: Doubleday, 1983.

——. "On the Refinement of the Conception of Prayer in the Hebrew Scriptures," *AJSR* 1 (1976), pp. 64-70.

Greenfield, J. "Našû—nadānu and its Congeners." In *Essays on the Ancient Near East in Memory of Jacob Joel Finkelstein.* Edited by M. Ellis. Memoirs of the Connecticut Academy of Arts and Sciences 19. Hamden: Archon Books, 1977, pp. 87–91.

Gruber, M. *Aspects of Nonverbal Communication in the Ancient Near East.* Studia Pohl 12. Rome: Biblical Institute Press, 1980.

Güterbock, H. *Siegel aus Bogazköy* 1. AfO Beiheft 5. Osnabrück: Biblio Verlag,1942.

De Gugielmo, A. "Sacrifice in the Ugaritic Texts," *CBQ* 17 (1955), pp. 76–96.

Halpern, B. "The Ritual Background of Zechariah's Temple Song," *CBQ* 40 (1978), pp. 167–80.

Hammershaimb, H. *Some Aspects of Old Testament Prophecy.* Cophenhagen, 1966.

Hanson, P. *Dawn of Apocalyptic.* Philadelphia: Fortress Press, 1975.

———. "Zechariah." In the *IDBS,* pp. 982–83.

Harris, M. *The Rise of Anthropological Theory.* New York: Harper and Row, 1968.

Hayes, J. and J. Miller, eds. *Israelite and Judean History.* Philadelphia: Westminster, 1977.

Herrman, S. "Bermerkungen zur Inschrift des Königs Kilamuwa von Sengirli," *OLZ* 48 (1953), pp. 295–97.

Hertzberg, A. *Die Bücher Joshua, Richter, Ruth.* ATD 9. Gottingen: Vandenhoef und Ruprecht, 1953.

Hesse, F. "Haggai," In *Verbannung und Heimkehr.* Edited by A. Kuschkek. Tübingen, 1961, pp. 109–34.

Hillers, D. *Micah.* Hermenia. Philadelphia: Fortress Press, 1984.

———. *Treaty Curses and the Old Testament Prophets.* Rome: Pontifical Biblical Institute, 1964.

———. "Ugaritic ŠNPT 'wave-offering," *BASOR* 198 (1970), p. 42.

———. *BASOR* 200 (1970), p. 18.

Hollis, M. and S. Lukes, eds. *Rationality and Relativism..* Oxford: Blackwell, 1982.

Horton, R. "African Traditional Thought and Western Science," *Africa* 37 (1967), pp. 50–187.

Horton, R, and R. Finnegan, eds. *Modes of Thought.* London: Faber and Faber, 1973.

Jacobsen, T. "The Reign of Ibbi-Suen," *JCS* 7 (1953), pp. 36-47.

Jagersma, H. "The Tithes in the Old Testament." In *Remembering All the Way . . .* OTS XXI. Leiden: Brill, 1981, pp. 116-28.

Jakobson, R. "Grammatical Parallelism and its Russian Facet," *Language* 42 (1966), pp. 399-429.

Janowski, B. "Erwängungen zur Vorgeschichte des Israelitischen Šĕlāmîm-Opfers," *UF* 12 (1980), pp. 231-259.

Janzen, J. *Studies in the Text of Jeremiah.* HSM 6. Cambridge: Harvard University Press, 1975.

Josephus, F. *Jewish Antiquities,* vols 1-4. Translated by J. Thackeray. Loeb Classical Library, 1930.

Kapelrud, A. "Temple Building, A Task for Gods and Kings," *Or* 32 (1962), pp. 56-72.

Kaufman, Y. *The Religion of Israel.* Chicago: University of Chicago Press, 1960.

L. King. *Letters and Inscriptions of Hammurabi.* London: Luzac, 1898-1900.

———. *Babylonian Boundary-Stones and Memorial-Tablets in the British Museum.* London: British Museum, 1912.

Kippenberg, H. *Religion und Klassenbildung im antiken Judäa.* Göttingen: Vandenhoeck und Ruprecht, 1978.

Kirk, G.S. "The Homeric Poems as History." In *CAH* 2, pp. 820-50.

Köhler, L. *Old Testament Theology.* Translated by A.S. Todd. London: Cutterworth Press, 1957.

König, F.E. *Lehrgebäude der hebräischen Sprache II: Syntax.* Leipzig: Hinrichs, 1897.

Kraus, H.J. *Worship in Israel.* Richmond: John Knox Press, 1965.

Kreissig, H. *Die sozialökonomische Situation in Juda zur Achämenidenzeit.* Berlin: Akademie Verlag, 1973.

Labuschagne, C.J. "The Formula *našû—nadānu* and Its Biblical Equivalent." In *Travels in the World of the Old Testament, Studies Presented to Prof. M.A. Beeks at the Occasion of his 65th Birthday.* Assen: van Gorcum, 1975, pp. 176-80.

Leach, E. *Genesis as Myth and Other Essays.* London: Jonathon Cape, 1969.

——. "On the Founding Fathers," *Current Anthropology* 7 (1966), pp. 560-67.

——. *Political Systems of Highland Burma.* London: London School of Economics, 1954.

Lemaire, A. *Inscriptions Hébraïques I.* Paris: Éditions du Cerf, 1977.

Leslau, W. "Observations on Semitic Cognates in Ugaritic," *Or* 37 (1968), pp. 347-66.

Levenson, J. "I Sam 25 as Literature and History," *CBQ* 40 (1978), pp. 11-28.

——. *Sinai and Zion.* Chicago: Seabury Press, 1985.

——. *Theology of the Program of Restoration of Ezekiel 40-48.* HSM 10. Missoula: Scholars Press, 1976.

Levine, B. "Assyriology and Hebrew Philology: A Methodological Re-Examination." In *Mesopotamien und Seine Nachbarn.* XXV Rencontre Assyriologique Internationale II. Berlin: Dietrich Reimer, 1982, pp. 176-80.

——. "The Descriptive Ritual Texts from Ugarit." In *The Word of the Lord Shall Go Forth.* Edited by C. Meyers and M. O'Connor pp. 467-85.

——. " The Descriptive Tabernacle Texts of the Pentateuch," *JAOS* 85 (1965), pp. 307-18.

——. *In the Presence of the Lord.* Leiden: Brill, 1974.

——, and W. Hallo "Offerings to the Temple Gates at Ur," *HUCA* 38 (1967), pp. 17-58.

——. "Priestly Writers." In *IDBS,* pp. 683-687.

——. "Ugaritic Descriptive Rituals," *JCS* 17 (1963), pp. 105-11.

Lienhardt, G. *Divinity and Experience.* Oxford: Clarendon Press, 1961.

Liverani, M. "Element innovativi nell-ugaritico non letterario," *Rendiconti Lincei* 19 (1964), pp. 173-91.

——. "Elementi 'irrazionali' nel commercio amarniano," *OA* 12 (1972), pp. 297-317.

Loewenstamm, S. "The Ugaritic Fertility Myth—the Result of a Mistranslation," *IEJ* 12 (1962), pp. 87-88.

Lord, A. *The Singer of Tales.* Cambridge: Harvard University Press, 1964.

Malinowski, B. *Argonauts of the Western Pacific.* London: Routledge and Kegan Paul, 1965.

Marshall, L. "N!OW," *Africa* 27 (1957), pp. 232-40.

Mayer, G. "Debher." In *Theological Dictionary of the Old Testament.* Edited by G. Botterweck and H. Ringgren. Grand Rapids: Eerdmanns, 1975, pp. 125-27.

Mayer, W. *Untersuchungen zur Formensprache der babylonischen 'Gebetsbeschwörungen.'* Studia Pohl, series maior 5. Rome: Pontifical Biblical Institute, 1976.

McCarter, P.K. *I Samuel.* AB 8. Garden City: Doubleday, 1980.

Mendelsohn, I. "Samuel's Denunciation of Kingship in the Light of Akkadian Documents from Ugarit," *BASOR* 143 (1956), pp. 17-22.

Mendenhall, G. *The Tenth Generation..* Baltimore: The Johns Hopkins University Press, 1973.

Milgrom,J. "The Alleged Wave-Offering in Israel and in the Ancient Near East," *IEJ* 22 (1972), pp. 33-38.

——. *Cult and Conscience.* Leiden: Brill, 1976.

——. *Studies in Cultic Theology and Terminology.* Studies in Judaism in Late Antiquity, vol. 36. Leiden: Brill, 1983.

Miller, P.D. "Animal Names as Designations in Ugaritic and Hebrew," *UF* 2 (1971), pp. 177-86.

——. "Fire in the Mythology of Canaan and Israel," *CBQ* 27 (1965), pp. 256-61.

De Moor, J.C. "The Peace-offering in Ugarit and Israel." In *Schrift en Uitleg.* Kampfen: J.H. Kok, 1970, pp. 112-117.

Moore, C.B., ed. *Reconstructing Complex Societies.* BASOR Suppl. 20. Cambridge: ASOR, 1974

Moore, G.F. *Judges.* ICC vol 7. Edinburgh: T & T Clark, 1895.

Moran, W. "The Ancient Near Eastern Background of the Love of God in Deuteronomy," *CBQ* 25 (1963), pp. 77-87.

——. "Gen 49,10 and its Use in Ez 21,32," *Biblica* 39 (1958), pp. 405-25.

——. "A Note on igi-kár, 'provisions, supplies," *Acta Sumerlogica* 5 (1983), pp. 75-77.

——. "A Note on the Treaty Terminology of the Sefire Stelas," *JNES* 22 (1961), pp. 173-76.

——. "The Use of the Canaanite Infinitive Absolute as a Finite Verb in the Amarna Letters from Byblos," *JCS* 4 (1950), pp. 169-172.

Muffs, Y. *Studies in the Aramaic Papyrii from Elephantine.* Leiden: Brill, 1969.

156   Sacrifices and Offerings

Müller, K. *Texte zum Königsritual.* MVAG 41/3. Leipzig: Hinrichs, 1937.

——. "Divine Freedom and Cultic Manipulation in Israel and Mesopotamia." In *Unity and Diversity.* Edited by H. Goedicke and J. Roberts. Baltimore: The Johns Hopkins University Press, 1975, pp. 112-117.

——. "Myth *versus* History: Relaying the Comparative Foundations," *CBQ* 38 (1976), pp. 1-13.

——. and P. Miller. *The Hand of the Lord.* Baltimore: Johns Hopkins, 1977.

Rowley, H. "Zadok and Nehustan," *JBL* 58 (1939), pp. 113-41.

——. "Melchizedek and Zadok. (Gen 14 and Ps 110)," in *Festschrift für Alfred Bertholet.* (Tübingen: Mohr, 1950), pp. 461-72.

Rowton, M. "Autonomy and Nomadism in Western Asia," *Or* 42 (1973), pp. 247-58.

——. "Urban Autonomy in a Nomadic Environment," *JNES* 32 (1973), pp. 201-215.

——. "Enclosed Nomadism," *JESHO* 17 (1974), pp. 1-30.

——. "Dimorphic Structure and the Tribal Elite," *Studia Instituti Anthropos* 30 (1976), pp. 219-58.

——. "The *Abu Amurrim., Iraq* 31 (1969), pp. 68-73.

——. "Dimorphic Structure and Topology," *OA* 15 (1976), pp. 17-31.

——. "The Physical Environment and the Problem of the Nomads," *RAI* 15 (1967), pp. 109-21.

——. "The Woodlands of Ancient Western Asia," *JNES* (1967), pp. 261-67.

——. "The Role of Watercourses in the Growth of Mesopotamian Civilization," *Alter Orient und Altes Testament* 1 1969), pp. 301-316.

——. "Watercourses and Water Rights in the Official Correspondence from Larsa and Isin," *JCS* 21 (1967), pp. 267-74.

——. "The Topological Factor in the *Ḥapiru* Problem," *AS* 16 (1965), pp. 375-87.

——. "Dimorphic Structure and the Problem of the ʿApirû-ʿIbrîm.," *JNES* 35 (1976), pp. 13-20.

——. "Dimorphic Structure and the Parasocial Element," *JNES* 36 (1977), pp. 181-98.

Rudolf, W. *Chronikbucher.* HAT 21. Tubingen: J.C.B. Mohr, 1955.

Sahlins, M. "Political Power and the Economy in Primitive Society." In *Essays in the Science of Culture in Honor of Leslie White.* Edited by G. Dole and R. Carneiro. New York: T.Y. Crowell, 1960, pp. 390-415.

——. "Economic Anthropology and Anthropological Economics." In *Explorations in Anthropology*. Edited by M. Fried. New York: T.Y. Crowell, 1973, pp. 390-415.

Schmid, H. "Yahwe und die Kult Traditionen von Jerusalem," *ZAW* 67 (1965), pp. 168-97.

Schmid, R. *Das Bundesopfer in Israel*. Studien zum Alten und Neuen Testament 9. München: Kosel, 1964.

Schottroff, W. "Arbeit und sozialer Konflikt im nachexilischen Juda." In *Mitarbeiter der Schöpfung* Edited by W. and L. Schottroff. München: Chr. Kaiser, 1983, pp. 104-48.

——. "Zur Sozialgeschichte I, pp. 46-68.

Sellin, E. "Melchizedek," *Neue Kirchliche Zeitschrift* 16 (1905), pp. 929-51.

Sharpe, E.J. *Comparative Religion*. New York: Scribners, 1975.

Shroeder, O. "Kanaanäisch *malānia* = 'Quartier, Lager,'" *OLZ* 18 (1915), pp. 105-106.

Smart, J.D. *History and Theology in Second Isaiah*. Philadelphia: Westminster, 1965.

Smith, J.Z. "When the Bough Breaks," *History of Religions* 12 (1973), pp. 342-71.

Smith, M. "Divine Travel as a Token of Divine Rank," *UF* 16 (1984), p. 359.

Smith, W.R. *Lectures on the Religion of the Semites*. 1889. Reprint. Jerusalem: KTAV, 1969.

Snaith, N. "Sacrifices in the Old Testament," *VT* 7 (1957), pp. 308-17.

Von Soden, W. "'Als die Götter (auch noch) Mensch waren': Einige Grundgedanken des altbabylonischen Atramhasis-Mythus," *Or* 38 (1969), pp. 415-532.

——. "Aramäische Wörter in neuassyrischen und neu und spätbabylonischen Texten," *Or* 37 (1968), pp. 261-71.

——. "Die erste Tafel des altbabylonischen Atramhasis-Mythus. 'Haupttext' und parallel Version," *ZA* 68 (1978), pp. 50-94.

——. "Mirjam—Maria '(Gottes—)Geschenk,' " *UF* 2 (1970), p. 269-72.

Soggin, A. *Judges*. London: SCM Press, 1981.

E. Sollberger, *Ur Excavation Texts* 8. London: British Museum.

Speiser, E. "Akkadian Documents from Ras Shamra," *JAOS* 75 (1955), pp. 154-65.

Sperber, D. "Drought, Famine and Pestilence in Amoraic Palestine," *JESHO* 17 (1974), pp. 272–98.

Stager, L. "Agriculture." In the *IDBS*, pp. 11-13.

———. "The Archaeology of the Family in Ancient Israel," *BASOR* 260 (1985), pp. 1-36.

Steinkeller, P. "On the Reading and Meaning of *igi-kár* and *gúrum (IGI.GAR)*, " *ASJ* 4 (1982), pp.149-51.

Tadmor, H. and M. Cogan. "Ahaz and Tiglath-Pileser in the Book of Kings," *Biblica* 60 (1979), pp. 481-508.

De Tarragon, J.M. *Le cult à Ugarit d'apres les textes de la pratique en cunéiformes alphabétiques.* Cahiers de la Revue Biblique, 19. Paris: J. Gabalda, 1980.

Thomas, E. Marshall. *The Harmless People.* New York: Knopf, 1959.

Thompson, R.J. *Penitence and Sacrifice in Early Israel outside the Levitical Law.* Leiden: Brill, 1963.

Thureau-Dangin, F. "Iaḫdunlim, roi de Ḫana," *RA* 33 (1936), pp. 49-54.

Tigay, J. *The Evolution of the Gilgamesh Epic.* Philadelphia: University of Pennsylvania, 1982.

———. "Some Aspects of Prayer in the Bible," *AJSR* 1 (1976), pp. 363-72.

Tomback, R. *Comparative Semitic Lexicon of the Phoenician and Punic Languages.* Missoula: Scholars Press, 1978.

De Vaux, R. *Ancient Israel,* 2 volumes. New York: McGraw-Hill, 1961. Originally published as *Les institutions de l'Ancien Testament* (Paris: Les editions du Cerf, 1961).

———. *Studies in Old Testament Sacrifice.* Cardiff: University of Wales Press, 1964.

Virolleaud, C. "Les inscriptions cunéiformes de Ras Shamra," *Syria* 10 (1929) pp. 304-310.

Weber, M. *From Max Weber: Essays in Sociology.* Edited by H. Gerth and C. Mills. New York: Oxford, 1946.

Wellhausen, J. *Prolegomena to the History of Ancient Israel.* 1885. Reprint. Translated by Menzies and Black. Gloucester: Peter Smith, 1973. Originally published as *Prolegomena zur Geschichte Israels* (Berlin: Rimer, 1883).

Weinberg, J. "Das Beit 'Abot im 6-4 Jh. v.u. Z," *VT* 23 (1973), pp. 400-14.

———. "Demographische Notizen zur Geschichte der nachexilischen Gemeinde in Juda," *Beiträge zur Alten Geschichte* 54 (1972), pp. 45-58.

———. "Die Agrarverhältnisse in der Bürger-Tempel-Gemeinde der Achämenidenzeit," In *Wirtschaft und Gesellschaft im alten Vorderasien.* Edited by J. Harmatta and G. Komcrocza. Budapest, 1976, pp. 473-86.

Weinfeld, M. "Tithe," *EJ,* pp. 1156-1162.

———. "The Royal and Sacred Aspects of the Tithe in the Old Testament," *Beer-Sheva* I (1973), pp. 122-31 (Heb.)

Weippert, M. " Heiliger Krieg' in Israel und Assyrien: Kritische Anmerkungen zu G. von Rads Konzept des 'Heiligen Krieges im alten Israel,'" *ZAW* 84 (1972), pp. 460-93.

Westermann, C. *Genesis.* BKAT I/2. Neukirchen-Vluyn: Neukirchener Verlag, 1981.

Wevers, J. "The Infinitive Absolute in the Phoenician Inscription of Azitawadd," *ZAW* 62 (1949), pp. 316-317.

Whitaker, R. "A Formulaic Analysis of Ugaritic Poetry." Unpublished Ph.D dissertation.   Harvard University, 1970.

Wilson, B. *Rationality.* Oxford: Blackwell, 1970.

Wilson, R. *Genealogy and History in the Biblical World.* New Haven: Yale University Press, 1977.

Winckler, H. *Die Keilschrifttexte Sargons,* volulme 1. Leipzig: Pfeiffer, 1889.

Wiseman, D. *The Alalakh Tablets.* London: British Institute of Archaeology in Ankara: Occasional Publications, 1953.

Zaccagnini, C. *Lo scambio dei doni nel Vicino Oriente durante i secoli XV-XIII.* Orientis antiqui collectio 11. Rome: Centro per le antichita e la storia dell 'arte del Vicino Oriente, 1973.

Zimmerli, W. *Ezekiel 1.* Hermenia. Philadelphia: Fortress Press, 1979.